AN ESSENTIAL SAFEGUARD

For Marcia [illegible],
with appreciation
[illegible signature]
May 12, 1991

Recent Titles in
Contributions in Legal Studies

Lawyers, Courts, and Professionalism: The Agenda for Reform
Rudolph J. Gerber

John Marshall's Achievement: Law, Politics, and Constitutional Interpretations
Thomas C. Shevory, editor

Affirmative Action and Principles of Justice
Kathanne W. Greene

Unfounded Fears: Myths and Realities of a Constitutional Convention
Paul J. Weber and Barbara Perry

Protecting Constitutional Freedoms: A Role for Federal Courts
Daan Braveman

The Employment Relationship in Anglo-American Law: A Historical Perspective
Marc Linder

The Aristocracy of the Long Robe
J. M. Sosin

Equal Separation: Understanding the Religion Clauses of the First Amendment
Paul J. Weber, editor

Common Law in Southern Africa: Conflict of Laws and Torts Precedents
Peter B. Kutner

A History of the Anglo-American Common Law of Contract
Kevin M. Teeven

"We Have a Duty": The Supreme Court and the Watergate Tapes Litigation
Howard Ball

The Shaping of Nineteenth-Century Law: John Appleton and Responsible Individualism
David M. Gold

Comparative Constitutional Federalism: Europe and America
Mark Tushnet, editor

Church-State Constitutional Issues: Making Sense of the Establishment Clause
Donald L. Drakeman

The Politics of Obscenity: Group Litigation in a Time of Legal Change
Joseph F. Kobylka

An Essential Safeguard

ESSAYS ON THE UNITED STATES SUPREME COURT AND ITS JUSTICES

Edited by D. Grier Stephenson, Jr.

CONTRIBUTIONS IN LEGAL STUDIES, NUMBER 63
Paul L. Murphy, *Series Editor*

GREENWOOD PRESS
New York • Westport, Connecticut • London

Library of Congress Cataloging-in-Publication Data

An Essential safeguard : essays on the United States Supreme Court and its justices / edited by D. Grier Stephenson, Jr.
p. cm. — (Contributions in legal studies, ISSN 0147-1074 : no. 63)
Based on rev. essays that grew out of a series of lectures designated "The John Marshall lectures on the Constitution, the Supreme Court, and the justices," delivered 1985–1989 at Franklin and Marshall College.
Includes bibliographical references and index.
ISBN 0-313-27438-X (alk. paper)
1. United States. Supreme Court. 2. Judges—United States. 3. Judicial review—United States. I. Stephenson, D. Grier. II. Title: John Marshall lectures on the Constitution, the Supreme Court, and the justices. III. Series.
KF8742.A5E87 1991
347.73'26—dc20
[347.30735] 90-46699

British Library Cataloguing in Publication Data is available.

Library of Congress Catalog Card Number: 90-46699
ISBN: 0-313-27438-X
ISSN: 0147-1074

First published in 1991

Greenwood Press, 88 Post Road West, Westport, CT 06881
An imprint of Greenwood Publishing Group, Inc.

Printed in the United States of America

The paper used in this book complies with the Permanent Paper Standard issued by the National Information Standards Organization (Z39.48-1984).

10 9 8 7 6 5 4 3 2 1

For
Richard F. Schier, John Vanderzell, and Sidney Wise
—retired, but not forgotten

Contents

Preface

In recent years, there has been no shortage of national observances in the United States. Beginning with those commemorating the first shots fired in the Revolutionary War and the signing of the Declaration of Independence, numerous occasions have celebrated the Articles of Confederation, the calling and convening of the Philadelphia Convention, the writing and signing of the Constitution, the debates over ratification, and the first elections and organization of the new government. In 1991, Americans mark not merely the ratification of the Bill of Rights but the successful completion of the nation's first experiment in constitutional change under the new charter.

These events in turn have given rise not just to flags and fireworks but to rethinking one of the most remarkable fifteen-year periods in the history of any nation. This look backward has sparked debates over national beginnings and "first principles" in classrooms, informal study sessions, books, journals, newspapers, television and radio programs, legislative halls, and the councils of the executive. It is surely not coincidence that this period of commemoration witnessed a renewed and heated exchange over "the intent of the framers," the significance of whatever of their views we can uncover, and the relevance of their ideas to contemporary issues.

The years that we have commemorated formed a crucial stage in the development of constitutionalism and limited government. Contributing to both was a written Constitution shortly joined to an institution—the Supreme Court of the United States—which assumed the dual roles of guardian and shaper of the nation's fundamental law.

This book is a collection of chapters that grew out of lectures at Franklin and Marshall College. The lectures were part of what Chief Justice Warren Burger called "a national seminar . . . to stimulate reexamination of the ideas upon which the Constitution rests." Designated "The John Marshall Lectures on the Constitution, the Supreme Court, and the Justices," and with primary funding from the National Endowment for the Humanities and additional funding from Armstrong World Industries, the series commemorated three special 200th anniversaries: first (and obviously), the writing and signing of the Constitution of the United States; second, the founding of Franklin College in 1787; and third, the first session of the U.S. Supreme Court in 1790. Rex E. Lee opened the series of lectures on October 24, 1985. Martin M. Shapiro delivered the last lecture on February 23, 1989. In between were presentations by Henry J. Abraham, James F. Simon, Harold J. Spaeth, Jesse H. Choper, Walter F. Murphy, and William M. Beaney.

It was entirely appropriate for Franklin and Marshall College to sponsor these lectures. In celebrating the College's 200th birthday, we honored two of the nation's founders. Benjamin Franklin, one of the first benefactors of the College, was the senior delegate at the Constitutional Convention. John Marshall was a delegate at the Virginia ratifying convention and later was the fourth Chief Justice of the United States. He learned shortly before his death in 1835 that a college in Pennsylvania was to be named after him. Both men were convinced of the importance of education to free government and to a nation of free people. We like to think that the linking of Marshall and Franklin Colleges in Lancaster, Pennsylvania, nearly 140 years ago created a college that, inspired by their precepts and examples, has met their expectations.

These chapters are more than a celebration of our national beginnings. They are a contribution to an understanding of constitutional government. To this end the chapters do not focus on the framers and their accomplishments. Rather, as an acknowledgment of the role of the Constitution in the life of the nation today, the collection examines the record of both current and recent Justices in fashioning the Constitution as well as the larger political context in which their work occurs.

A word should be added about citations. Endnotes accompany each chapter in this volume. Where appropriate, citations in the notes adhere to the standard legal style. This means that the citations for books are abbreviated. Full bibliographic data for all books cited in the notes as well as for most other sources appear in the selected bibliography that follows the last chapter.

Finally, a warning is in order for those uninitiated in guiding a lecture series from start to finish. The business is hard work. No project of this magnitude can be the product of a single pair of hands. Especially in the early stages of planning the lecture series and writing the grant application for the National Endowment for the Humanities, the advice and instruction of my mentor and colleague John Vanderzell were invaluable. I remember with gratitude as well the support I received from Bradley R. Dewey. During most of the time the series of lectures was under way, Brad was Dean of the College and Vice-President for Academic Affairs at Franklin and Marshall. At the time of his premature death in early 1989, he was Professor of Religious Studies. He did more than offer "deanly" encouragement for the project; he and his wife Marcia attended the lectures, thus helping by their presence to give the series the visibility it deserved, as it competed with other worthy events for the attention of the campus and the wider community of Lancaster.

I have been fortunate to have had the cooperation of each lecturer/author at crucial steps along the way. At times, however, it seemed as if the lecturers had the easier task; their assignment, after all, was "merely" to make a complex subject understandable to novices and interesting to experts. By contrast, my assignment encompassed other roles including, but not limited to, scheduler, dispatcher, publicity agent, travel agent, accountant, caterer, and stage hand. To paraphrase Harlan Fiske Stone's comment about the chief justiceship, the coordinator of a lecture series does the things the janitor won't do.

These "things" once involved an additional chore. The occasion was the second lecture: Henry J. Abraham's presentation on "Can Presidents Really Pack the Supreme Court?" on April 10, 1986. Professor Abraham had lectured for about ten minutes in Stahr Auditorium of the just-renovated Stager Hall when the building's fire alarm sounded. President of the College James L. Powell quickly left the room to investigate. (The new alarm system was known to have a mind of its own.) He returned shortly to announce that the fire department had arrived and that we should evacuate the building at once. It was a cool Thursday evening in the springtime. The hundred or so in attendance stood outside as firefighters searched for the source of the alarm. The culprit proved to be a particularly smoky cigar in a washroom. When the chief sounded the "all clear," we reclaimed our seats in the auditorium and Professor Abraham resumed. But we had acquired an additional guest. A cat, it seems, had wandered in during the excitement. At this point I learned that coordinating a lecture series included yet one more duty.

Throughout the series, Joan R. Henderson made all the other aspects of my job far less taxing than they otherwise would have been. At the time, Mrs. Henderson was Director of the Bicentennial at Franklin and

Marshall College. She brought to her work not only a wealth of ideas and skills but also the perfect disposition and an eagerness to help. Without her guidance and good cheer, I would have come even closer than I did to the caricature of the harried professor.

1

Introduction: The Supreme Court in American Government

D. Grier Stephenson, Jr.

In April 1788, when Alexander Hamilton imagined the Supreme Court and a national judicial power in *The Federalist*, No. 78, he defended the "independence of the judges" as "an essential safeguard against the effects of occasional ill-humors in the society." Of primary concern to Hamilton were "infractions of the constitution," which the anticipated power of judicial review would not only check once they had occurred but perhaps even discourage at their outset. Thus, the separate institutions mandated by the Constitution have made judicial independence possible; its shared powers have made occasional breaches of that independence probable and have allowed the federal judiciary to become a partner in governing the nation.

This constitutional dimension of the business of the Supreme Court has contributed mightily to the institution's prominence in American government. Even though the Court performs an important conflict-resolution function—essential in any political system—and even though the great majority of its decisions have not raised constitutional questions, the Court achieved the stature it enjoys through its role as chief expositor of the nation's fundamental charter. As Attorney General Robert Jackson addressed the Justices in 1939 on the 150th anniversary of the establishment of the Supreme Court, "Few tribunals have had greater opportunity for original and constructive work, and none ever seized opportunity with more daring and wisdom."[1] Issues that legislative bodies and executive agencies settle in other nations have become judicial ones here. Judicial review has made the Court a force in the plan of union the framers devised. The Court has contributed to the design James Madison envisioned to overcome the twin difficulties of statecraft: those of "enabl[ing] the government to control the governed" and "oblig[ing] the government to control itself."[2] Attempting to resolve issues that divide and perplex the nation, the Court has contributed both symbolically and substantively to the strength and vitality of constitutional government—but at times has sapped that strength in cases, fortunately infrequent, such as *Dred Scott*.[3]

The Court occupies a key place in the American scheme of constitutional democracy in spite of professed weakness. "Courts are mere instruments of the law, and can will nothing," Chief Justice Marshall contended in 1824,[4] although hardly, one suspects, without arousing incredulity. In answering charges during the debates over ratification of the Constitution that the Court would be too powerful, Hamilton maintained that "the judiciary, from the nature of its functions, will always be the least dangerous to the political rights of the constitution; because it will be least in a capacity to annoy or injure them."[5] Lacking the "sword" of the executive branch and the "purse" of the legislature, the Court was to possess "merely judgment." As if to bolster Hamilton's argument, the practicalities of starting up a new government made the court appear as the most dependent branch. Because the judiciary's establishment required the consent of both the President and Congress, there could be no Court until the other two branches came into being and acted. Accordingly, the new House and Senate transacted their first business on April 2 and April 5, respectively, with George Washington's inauguration following on April 30. On September 24, Washington signed legislation creating the Supreme Court and setting February 1, 1790, as the day of its first session. Confirmation by the Senate of the first nominees followed on September 26, one day shy of Congress's adjournment. The Supreme Court as a functioning branch of the national government thus followed the other two by nine months.[6]

From practical and constitutional dependency came strength. From the outset the Justices claimed the duty to interpret the Constitution, taking on the burden of settling disputes the framers had not anticipated or had been unwilling or unable to resolve. Because of the widespread, if not uniform, acceptance throughout most of American national history of constitutional interpretation as a judicial function, the Court has converted Hamilton's characterization of the judicial power as "merely judgment" into one of the greatest misstatements of all time.

Since the Supreme Court matters politically, it has understandably been subject to continuing scholarly and journalistic oversight. Such scrutiny has partially substituted for the direct political accountability provided for the executive and legislative branches, but absent for the federal judiciary. The Court's visibility has consequently been a source of the institution's legitimacy as a check on popular power. As William Howard Taft observed nearly a century ago,

> Nothing tends more to render judges careful in their decisions and anxiously solicitous to do exact justice than the consciousness that every act of theirs is to be subject to the intelligent scrutiny of their fellow men, and to their candid criticism.... In the case of judges having a life tenure, indeed, their very independence makes the right freely to comment on their decisions of greater importance, because it is the only practical and available instrument in the hands of a free people to keep such judges alive to the reasonable demands of those they serve.[7]

Moreover, circumstances conducive to study and analysis make it easier for scholars of the Court to do their work. The scale of the institution invites and facilitates scrutiny. After 200 years, the entire succession of Justices numbers only slightly more than the present number of U.S. Senators. While there have been forty-one Presidents, there have been only sixteen Chief Justices. Second, the work of the Court is relatively open. In the churning sea of government today, the Court institutionally seems an island of calm. Previous rulings, briefs, arguments, and opinions are public and readily available. Only the conference and the actual shaping of opinions remain hidden from view. Even the veil shrouding this stage of the process partly lifts after a time, as some Justices take steps to preserve their papers. Third, the scope of the Court's business is intellectually manageable. One can begin to grasp the substance and significance of the decisions of one term in a way that cannot be matched in a survey of the voluminous output of a session of Congress or the rulings of executive agencies.

STUDY OF THE COURT

Serious study of any political institution requires a framework of analysis. Helpful in understanding the Supreme Court are five key elements: the political and intellectual environment, personalities, the past, processes, and product. The first stands for prevailing political theories as well as the governmental system and social context in which the Court operates. The second denotes the individual Justices who decide cases. The third encompasses not only the history of the nation, but more particularly the body of decisions rendered by former Justices. The fourth represents the manner in which the Court arrives at its decisions, including the role of advocacy and the institution's internal dynamics. Product, the fifth and last element, consists of the Court's current rulings—the end result of the decision-making process—and their acceptance and implementation. Each element is reflected in varying degrees in the chapters chosen for this volume. This introductory chapter will briefly discuss each element.

POLITICAL AND INTELLECTUAL ENVIRONMENT

The political and intellectual environment influences the selection of Justices (personalities) who come to the bench with various values and approaches to constitutional interpretation. The environment also largely determines the kinds of issues at stake in cases presented to the Court for decision. Moreover, the political acceptability of decisions and the degree to which the Court's decisions accomplish their objectives determine the impact of the Supreme Court.

For example, one of George Washington's first concerns as President was the selection of Justices for the Supreme Court. Uncertainties about the future of the new government under the Constitution and, indeed, about the possibility of union itself lay behind a letter to his future Attorney General, Edmund Randolph, in 1789. "Impressed with a conviction that the true administration of justice is the firmest pillar of good government, I have considered the first arrangement of the judicial department as essential to the happiness of our country and the stability of its political system." Even though the Court's place in this new system was unclear, Washington apparently realized the impact the Court might have in the young republic. This possibility required, he instructed Randolph, "the selection of the fittest characters to expound the laws and dispense justice. . . ."[8] As he selected the six Justices Congress had authorized, Washington made sure that each section of the nation was represented and that the six were strong supporters of the new Constitution.

The political and intellectual environment also meant that the kinds of constitutional questions the Court confronted in the nineteenth century, for example, differed significantly from the questions the Court faced later. If the Marshall (1801–35) and Taney (1836–64) Courts are remembered for decisions on federalism, the Waite (1874–88) and Fuller (1888–1910) Courts were marked by decisions developing the limits of governmental power chiefly as it confronted rights in property. Such matters began to give way to others after 1937, so that from the time of the Stone Court (1941–46), non-property aspects of civil liberties and civil rights have been prominent on the docket.

Environment affects the Court through a host of external checks on judicial power. Of course, Supreme Court Justices and other federal judges enjoy substantial independence from outside political control. Thanks to the Constitution, they never face the voters in an election and may not have their salaries decreased by Congress. Yet, while the Court is a potent institution in U.S. government, it does not enjoy unlimited power.

Most obviously, the Constitution entrusts the composition of the Supreme Court to both the President and the Senate. The choices of the former require the approval of the latter. New Justices may bring new values and hence a new direction to constitutional jurisprudence. This constitutionally prescribed duty of the President and the Senate, however, may threaten the same judicial independence the Constitution presumes. Both senators and Presidents properly have an interest in the views of the nominees. To the degree that this interest becomes overweening by creating an expectation that nominees should, or perhaps even must, publicly lay bare before the Senate their positions on current constitutional controversies, their independence as justices may be severely constrained.

Ironically, Charles Evans Hughes—the only Associate Justice ever to resign from the Supreme Court to run for President (in 1916)—partly anticipated this problem and proposed a solution two years before the battle over his confirmation as Chief Justice in 1930.

> If conscientious, able, and independent men are put on the bench, you cannot predict their course as judges by reference either to partisan motives or to personal or party loyalties. If you could get further down to the bedrock of convictions as to what are conceived to be fundamental principles of government and social relations, you might be able to get closer to accurate prophecy. But you cannot expect to have judges worthy of the office who are without convictions. . . .[9]

Hughes's statement was made eleven years before Felix Frankfurter became the first Supreme Court nominee to appear before the Senate Judiciary Committee. If Hughes was correct, senators may learn more about nominees and still preserve judicial independence by probing "fundamental principles" than by enticing them to commit themselves publicly on current constitutional issues.

The Court is subject to other checks as well. In inflationary times, Congress may—and has—decreased judicial salaries by inaction. Through constitutional amendment, Congress and the states may "correct" the Supreme Court's construction of the Constitution. Admittedly, amending the Constitution is not easy, but the Justices have been reversed by amendment four times. Similarly, Congress may correct the Court's interpretation of a statute by statutory amendment. Less difficult than amending the Constitution, passage of a bill is still no easy task.

Impeachment of Justices by Congress may be "scarcely a scarecrow," as President Thomas Jefferson once said, but it is a weapon available in extraordinary situations. On grounds of misconduct, Congress has removed six judges of lower federal courts, but never a Supreme Court Justice. In fact, the Senate has not held an impeachment trial for a Justice since the Jefferson administration attempted to have Justice Samuel Chase removed in 1805. The House of Representatives might have begun impeachment proceedings against Justice Abe Fortas after improprieties came to light in 1969, but he resigned.[10] Moreover, the House took action against Justice William O. Douglas the following year, but the special investigating subcommittee declined to recommend impeachment. Five other federal judges (but no Justices) have either been acquitted by the Senate or have had charges against them dismissed before a Senate trial began.

Congress may restrain the Court by withdrawing jurisdiction to review certain types of cases. This is an extreme measure, sometimes threatened but rarely carried out. Congress may also change the size of the Court, but only prospectively. Between 1789 and 1869, Congress changed the number of Justices from six to five, five to six, six to seven, seven to nine, nine to ten, ten to seven, and seven to nine—each time with an eye to influencing the Court's constitutional jurisprudence. This authority was the heart of President Franklin Roosevelt's "Court-packing" proposal in 1937, which would have enlarged the bench to a maximum of fifteen. Congress never adopted the plan, but the Court changed its interpretation of the Constitution to uphold the President's New Deal program.

To be effective, Supreme Court decisions require acceptance and compliance. "[W]hile the Judges' decision makes law, it is often the people's view of the decision which makes history."[11] Leading cases of the Marshall era lending a strong nationalist cast to the nature of the union hardly settled the question later contested on the battlefields of the Civil War. Similarly, some of the landmark rulings of the Warren Court (1953–69) on civil rights and criminal justice met resistance for years, testing the limits of judicial power. Judicial decisions are not self-enforcing. Hostile reaction to the 1954 school integration decision in particular highlighted an additional check on the courts: litigation. Black families were sometimes afraid to initiate legal action against local officials who continued to disregard the Supreme Court's decision. Without a case, no court could act. Unlike legislators, who may introduce bills, judges do not initiate the cases they decide.

The political and intellectual environment may influence the Court's product as well—that is, the decisions and the judicial opinions justifying them. Justice John Paul Stevens asserted that "it is the business of judges to be indifferent to unpopularity,"[12] but Judge (later Justice) Benjamin Cardozo advised that "[t]he great tides and currents which engulf the rest of men do not turn aside in their course and pass the judges by."[13]

With capital punishment, for example, most states reenacted death penalty laws after the Supreme Court set rigorous new standards in 1972.[14] State legislatures were in effect telling the Court that they did not think capital punishment was "cruel and unusual," but instead considered it a form of punishment that Americans accepted. When the Court reexamined capital punishment on its merits four years later,[15] these new laws may have made it easier for some Justices to conclude that the death penalty was not inherently at odds with the Eighth Amendment.

In *Patterson v. McLean Credit Union*, when the Court declined to reconsider *Runyon v. McCrary*,[16] Justice Anthony Kennedy also acknowledged the influence of public opinion on his vote. *McCrary* had construed the Civil Rights Act of 1866 to allow black parents to challenge racially segregated nonsectarian private schools. Suggesting that this decision might have been based on a mistaken interpretation of the Civil Rights Act of 1866, he nonetheless explained that the existing interpretation was "not inconsistent with the prevailing sense of justice in this country."[17] So the Court left *Runyon* in place, although a majority declined to extend the law's coverage.

PERSONALITIES

The interest that accompanies each appointment to the Supreme Court exemplifies the force of individuals on the bench. Since Washington's day, Presidents, senators, and others have recognized that Justices do not decide cases in a vacuum, that "judicial decisions are not babies brought by constitutional storks."[18]

This chapter and those that follow speak frequently of "the Constitution." The Justices, commentators say, interpret the Constitution. This short sentence presumes a consensus on what it is that the Justices interpret. Yet when Justices engage in constitutional interpretation, it may not be clear at the outset what they include within the word "Constitution." One might suppose that "the Constitution" includes at least the text of the document of 1787, as amended. But even such a seemingly conventional declaration needs qualification. There are, after all, parts of the text (the privileges and immunities clause of the Fourteenth Amendment comes to mind) that the Court has largely neglected. Moreover, tensions exist between some provisions of the text. For example, how does one satisfy fully the demands of both free exercise (freedom *for* religion) and non-establishment (freedom *from* religion)?

The Constitution may also encompass more than the document because its meaning must be sought apart from the text itself. One may turn to the intent of those who drafted and ratified its provisions. Similarly, a Justice might look to other documents that describe the kind of system the framers established. In speaking of "liberty" and the "consent of the governed," the Declaration of Independence, for instance, anticipated constitutional government to cure the evils of unchecked power.

Does custom count as part of the Constitution? As the Supreme Court noted in 1919, "Long settled and established practice is a consideration of great weight in a proper interpretation of constitutional provisions. . . ."[19] Similarly, in the Steel Seizure Case, Justice Felix Frankfurter argued that

> a systematic, unbroken, executive practice, long pursued in the knowledge of Congress and never before questioned, engaged in by Presidents who have also sworn to uphold the Constitution, making as it were such exercise of power part of the structure of our government, may be treated as a gloss on the 'executive power' vested in the President. . . .[20]

Even interpretations of the text of the Constitution have sometimes become part of the Constitution. One thinks of judicial review itself, nowhere (even in amendments) expressly authorized for the U.S. Supreme Court, although implied in Article VI for the state courts.

Political values may also shape the Court's decisions. A jurist firmly convinced of the necessity of remedial policies to reduce racial inequality, for instance, may be more inclined than one who is not to place affirmative action programs within the strictures set by the Constitution and federal statutes. One who does not place high value on the free exchange of views will probably not be a strong defender of the First Amendment's guarantee of free speech.

Akin to, but different from, political values is perception of role. What does being a Justice mean to an individual named to the Supreme Court? "[D]oes a man cease to be himself when he becomes a Justice?" Felix Frankfurter asked nearly four decades ago.

> Does he change his character by putting on a gown? No, he does not change his character. He brings his whole experience, his training, his outlook, his social, intellectual, and moral environment with him when he takes a seat on the supreme bench. But a judge worth his salt is in the grip of his function. The intellectual habits of self-discipline which govern his mind are as much a part of him as the influence of the interest he may have represented at the bar, often more so. . . . To assume that a lawyer who becomes a judge takes on the bench merely his views on social or economic questions leaves out of account his rooted notions regarding the scope and limits of a judge's authority.[21]

One does not have to accept all of Frankfurter's belief in the disinterestedness of judges to recognize that perception of role is likely to be important in shaping a jurisprudence.

Some Justices, for instance, have been result oriented. They have conceived American government as a system designed to protect certain rights through a series of constitutional restraints on the majority. Accordingly, their task is one of writing their political values into decisions to assure the correct results. In the 1930s, George Sutherland was one of several members of the Court who thought not only that the Constitution protected property from many forms of government regulation but that his task as a judge was to protect property from government. Later, Hugo Black was one of several Justices who believed just as fervently that their duty required them to protect not property but other liberties enshrined in the Bill of Rights.

Other Justices have been process oriented, appearing most concerned with the Court's place in a political system designed to foster democratic, or popular, government. For them, judicial review is antidemocratic. Because the Court's invalidation of a statute is an impediment to majority rule, they are less inclined to apply the judicial brakes to legislatures than their result-oriented colleagues. Instead, they believe that because the meaning of the Constitution is often difficult to discern, they should respect interpretations that disagree with their own. Accordingly, judges should strike down legislation only in "clear" or "extreme" cases.[22] In the 1930s, for example, Justice Harlan Stone personally disapproved of much of President Franklin Roosevelt's New Deal measures. Stone nonetheless disagreed with Sutherland and argued that the Court had only a modest role. "Courts are not the only agency of government that must be assumed to have the capacity to govern," he maintained.[23] Frankfurter later made the same point against Black's enthusiastic defense of the Bill of Rights.

THE PAST

Whether process or result oriented, no Justice today writes on a blank slate. The past is a factor in judicial decisions. The past includes the nation's history and traditions, to be sure, but also the Court's own past decisions: the legacy of jurists, themselves part of history. "Our jurisprudence is distinctive in that every great movement in American history has produced a leading case in this Court."[24] The past contains the gloss that the Justices have spread over the Constitution.

Robert Jackson contrasted the Court in its earliest days with the Court of the twentieth century.

> When it first convened, . . . [a]ll questions were open ones, and neither the statesmanship of the Justices nor the imagination of the advocate was confined by the ruling case. . . . During its early days it had the aid of counsel who expounded the Constitution from intimate and personal experience in its making. They knew that to get acceptance of its fundamental design for government many controversial details were left to be filled in from time to time by the wisdom of

> those who were to follow. This knowledge made them bold. The passing of John Marshall marked the passing of that phase of the Court's experience. Thereafter the Constitution became less a living and contemporary thing—more and more a tradition. The work of the Court became less an exposition of its text and setting and purposes and became more largely a study of what later men had said about it. The Constitution was less resorted to for deciding cases, and cases were more resorted to for deciding about the Constitution. This was the inevitable consequence of accumulating a body of judicial experience and opinion which the legal profession would regard as precedents.[25]

Charles Warren once asked Americans not to forget that "however the Court may interpret the provisions of the Constitution, it is still the Constitution which is law and not the decision of the Court."[26] While running for the governorship of New York, Charles Evans Hughes bluntly asserted in contrast that "the Constitution is what the Judges say it is."[27] It is little wonder, then, that the Constitution comprises less than 2 percent of most textbooks on constitutional law. Much of the remaining 98 percent consists of what the Court has said about the Constitution.

So any case almost assuredly implicates the past and also implicates the doctrine of stare decisis—the rule that resolutions of former controversies should govern current ones. It is, in Cardozo's words, "the everyday work rule of our law."[28] In Justice Byron White's words, "The rule of stare decisis is essential if case-by-case judicial decisionmaking is to be reconciled with the principle of the rule of law, for when governing legal standards are open to revision in every case, deciding cases becomes a mere exercise of judicial will, with arbitrary and unpredictable results."[29] In constitutional adjudication, however, stare decisis has been less confining. According to White,

> [D]ecisions that find in the Constitution principles or values that cannot fairly be read into that document usurp the people's authority, for such decisions represent choices that the people have never made and that they cannot disavow through corrective legislation. For this reason, it is essential that this Court maintain the power to restore authority to its proper possessors by correcting constitutional decisions that, on reconsideration, are found to be mistaken.[30]

This old fiction of the Constitution as an act of "the people" remains useful even if not persuasive as a fact.

Richmond v. J. A. Croson Co.[31] provides a useful illustration of the imprint of the recent constitutional past on the present. In 1989, *Croson* invalidated on equal protection grounds a municipality's 30 percent set-aside for minority business enterprises in the subcontracting of a city's construction projects. Similar laws were in force in 36 states and in at least 190 cities. The decision took some civil rights activists by surprise.

Croson was controversial not only because of the policy it invalidated but because of the restrictions it supposedly placed on the reach of another decision, *Fullilove v. Klutznick*,[32] which the Supreme Court decided in 1980. In this case, the Court upheld a congressionally mandated 10 percent set-aside for minority businesses in local public works projects under the Public Works Employment Act of 1977. Considered together, *Fullilove* and *Croson* lead to some interesting, perhaps even surprising, conclusions. First, the federal program only barely passed constitutional scrutiny in 1980. Second, despite the outcome of the 1989 case, federally mandated set-asides are more firmly grounded in the Constitution after *Croson* than before. Third, *Croson* does not mean that state and local governments are powerless to enact their own set-aside programs.

In *Fullilove*, six Justices concluded that the 10 percent set-aside did not violate the equal protection component of the Fifth Amendment. However, not so many as five Justices could agree on a single statement as to why no constitutional violation existed. Instead, Justices White and Powell joined an opinion by Chief Justice Burger, and Justices Brennan and Blackmun joined an opinion by Justice Marshall. These two groups of three Justices each comprised the majority vote upholding the congressional set-aside. The remaining three members of the Court—Justices Stewart, Rehnquist, and Stevens—concluded that even this limited set-aside crossed the line of constitutionality.

Of the six Justices voting to uphold the law, only three—Marshall, Brennan, and Blackmun—gave it approval without significant qualification. The remaining three Justices in the affirmative went out of their way to demonstrate a very qualified approval. Their first qualification consisted of the particular significance of findings by Congress and the Civil Rights Commission that continuing effects of discrimination in the construction industry had kept minority participation to a minimum. Their second qualification was the limited nature of the set-aside itself. The figure of 10 percent fell roughly halfway between the percentage of minority contractors and the percentage of minority group members in the nation. The Public Works Act of 1977 appropriated $4 billion, meaning that approximately $400 million would go to minority contractors. The set-aside would thus reserve only about .25 percent of all the funds expended yearly on construction work in the United States for the 4 percent of the nation's contracting businesses that were minority owned. The remaining 96 percent of the contractors could freely compete for the remaining 99.75 percent of the funds, public and private. The third major qualification rested on Congress's authority under the enforcement clause in Section 5 of the Fourteenth Amendment. No fewer than ten times did Chief Justice Burger refer specifically to Congress's unique role under the Fourteenth Amendment. "Here we deal," he wrote, "with the broad remedial powers of Congress. It is fundamental that in no organ of government, state or federal, does there repose a more comprehensive remedial power than in the Congress."[33] Yet even with this unique role, the Burger three hinted that the set-aside came close to the line, in a recognition that the "program press[ed] the outer limits of congressional authority. . . ."[34] In other words, the 1977 congressional set-aside survived its 1980 review by a whisker.

The vote in *Croson* nine years later was also 6 to 3, but this time it was against the constitutionality of Richmond's 30 percent set-aside. Consistent with their position in *Fullilove*, Justices Marshall, Brennan, and Blackmun would have approved the municipal set-aside with no significant qualifications. Two holdovers from *Fullilove*—Chief Justice Rehnquist and Justice Stevens—were also consistent in their view that Richmond had stepped over the line. Justice White plus the recent arrivals—Justices O'Connor, Scalia, and Kennedy—voted against the plan.

Within this division, eight Justices accepted the constitutional underpinnings of *Fullilove*: that Congress had special powers under the Fourteenth Amendment, including a limited distribution of federal funds on the basis of race even under circumstances where the federal government had not been guilty of discrimination in the awarding of contracts. The eight Justices included everyone except Justice Kennedy, who reserved judgment on the question. Even Justice Scalia, who took the most restrictive position, recognized Congress's powers in *Fullilove*. From this perspective, the victory of non-minority contractors in *Croson* may have been Pyrrhic. The *Fullilove* position picked up two votes it lacked in 1980—the votes of Stevens and Rehnquist.[35]

The final point to be made is that the 6 to 3 defeat for the Richmond program does not mean that states and their subdivisions are necessarily powerless to adopt set-asides. What must be understood, however, is that the Court will apply high standards when they do.

First, six Justices agree that race-based policies, including those designed to help minorities, must be judged by the demanding test of strict scrutiny. There were at most four votes for that position in *Fullilove*. Marshall, Brennan, and Blackmun, by contrast, prefer a lesser standard for racial classifications that do not stigmatize.

Second, because the standard of acceptability is high, states and localities must do what Richmond did not—they must demonstrate a pattern of discrimination, the effects of which are to be overcome. Individual localities may not extrapolate a pattern of discrimination from findings made by Congress for the nation as a whole. Neither are findings about discrimination fungible from one jurisdiction to the next. And if one assumes an absence at the state level of the deference normally extended to Congress, the level of proof will probably be higher than that expected of Congress. One detects in *Croson* a strong suspicion that localities are more susceptible to falling prey to those whose interests lie more in taking advantage of government largesse than in overcoming effects of past discrimination. What remains to be seen is the level of proof the Court will find sufficient. Litigation will have to flesh out this crucial detail.

Third, a local set-aside must be, as the Court says, narrowly tailored. The Richmond program included Spanish-speaking persons, Orientals, Indians, Eskimos, and Aleuts as well as blacks, without reference to any prior discrimination against any but the last group. Similar questions were raised about the 30 percent figure. In *Fullilove*, the Court deferred to Congress in its choice of 10 percent—the explanation was plausible and the number was low. *Croson* suggests that no such deference is due the states.

Fourth, given the deference paid to Congress in *Fullilove* and acknowledged in *Croson*, Congress may wish to give serious attention under its Fourteenth Amendment powers to legislation authorizing the states to act. Congress could establish standards for both findings and the implementation of set-asides. National action would offer uniformity and would assure suspicious Justices that local policies are truly remedial.

Nonetheless, even without congressional action, there is a firm majority in *Croson* for the position that cities are not limited to correcting official discrimination, but that they may eradicate the effects of private discrimination as well. Furthermore, in proving discrimination, almost the entire Court agrees that a clear statistical disparity between eligible minority businesses and minority business membership in trade organizations could support an inference of discriminatory exclusion. In short, *Croson*, properly understood in the light of *Fullilove*, should not end racial set-asides. It has instead flashed a bright light of caution that racial classifications today are suspect and will be found compatible with the Constitution only when local governments make a convincing case for a closely tailored remedy to rectify the effects that flow from a proven history of discrimination.

PROCESS

The Court's decision-making process also shapes its decisions. Briefs and oral argument inform the Justices and usually define the issues the case presents. They often supply the reasoning the Court uses in justifying its decisions. Moreover, because all Justices normally participate in each case, collegial interaction becomes a factor. Discussion in conference and comment by one Justice on an opinion drafted by another contribute to the form an opinion eventually takes. Such comments can be so persuasive that Justices may change their votes in a case.

The leading reapportionment cases of the 1960s illustrate the difference collegiality makes. The Court's subtle rules of process implicate the political and intellectual environment. *Baker v. Carr*[36] in 1962 addressed a major "threshold question"—the availability of the Court as a forum to resolve a political conflict. As students of the Court know, *Baker* stands for the proposition that the Supreme Court has jurisdiction over the apportionment of state legislatures. Yet the decision did not lay down particular standards the district courts were supposed to apply in entertaining suits challenging apportionment. *Baker* established the justiciability of the question. The standards later appeared in cases such as *Wesberry v. Sanders*[37] and *Reynolds v. Sims*[38] when a majority imposed the one-person/one-vote rule on congressional districts and on both houses of state legislatures. According to Bernard Schwartz's biography of Chief Justice Warren,[39] *Baker* came close to being a different decision. Moreover, had this alternate course of events occurred, the rule that followed in *Wesberry* and *Reynolds* would probably have been more flexible.

When *Baker* came down on March 26, 1962, Justice Brennan's majority opinion spoke for six members of the Court. Concurring opinions by Justices Douglas and Clark indicated that they would reach the merits of the case if the allegations of inequality in the suit could be sustained. Justice Stewart also concurred, stating that the merits of the case were not before the Court for review. Justices Frankfurter and Harlan dissented, and Justice Whittaker did not take part. When the case was initially argued during the 1960 term, however, Schwartz explains that the conference vote was 4 to 4, with Clark and Whittaker joining Frankfurter and Harlan.

Stewart, it seems, was undecided on the issue of jurisdiction, and at his urging the case was carried over for reargument in October 1961. At the conference on October 13, Warren explained, "This is a violation of equal protection. I don't think we have to decide the merits. . . . All we have to decide is that there is jurisdiction. We don't have to say that the state must give complete equality."[40] By this time, Stewart had come around to the view that the Court should take jurisdiction, thus giving a 5 to 4 vote in favor of the Tennessee plaintiffs. But Stewart emphasized two points: "I can't say whether we can or can't frame appropriate relief. On the merits, I couldn't say that equal protection requires representation approximately commensurate with voting strength. So the state doesn't have to justify every departure from a one-man vote basis." He then added that "the greatest burden of proof [was] on a plaintiff to show an arbitrary and capricious system."[41]

Chief Justice Warren and Justices Black, Douglas, and Brennan wanted to do more than simply to announce jurisdiction. Going to the merits, they would hold that the Fourteenth Amendment required Tennessee to provide "approximately fair distribution or weight in votes." This was not the equality rule the Court later imposed in 1964. Moreover, the four Justices favoring "approximately fair weight" were prepared to impose that standard only on one house of a state legislature. To keep

Stewart's vote, however, Brennan (to whom Warren had assigned the opinion) would have to stick to jurisdiction and leave standards alone.

After Frankfurter circulated his dissent in February, Clark quickly indicated agreement. Frankfurter then suggested to Clark that he write separately "on failure to exhaust other remedies." Presumably, Frankfurter wanted to make sure that Clark's vote held firm by getting him to convince himself that Tennessee voters had other channels for relief. But the plan backfired. As Clark wrote to Frankfurter on March 7,

> Preparatory to writing my dissent in this case, along the line you suggested of pointing out the avenues that were open for the voters of Tennessee to bring about reapportionment despite its Assembly, I have carefully checked into the record. I am sorry to say that I cannot find any practical course that the people could take in bringing this about except through the Federal courts.... I am sorry to say that I should have to ask you to permit me to withdraw from your dissent.[42]

Attached to the letter was a copy of Clark's concurring opinion. This meant that Stewart's vote was no longer necessary to give Brennan's opinion majority status and that *Baker* could reach beyond the jurisdictional point. But because of Stewart's insistence on going no further (a broadened opinion might have led Stewart to press for reargument), Brennan notified Warren, Black, and Douglas on March 10 that he would not press Stewart on changes. So the opinion Brennan announced in Court on March 26 was basically the opinion he had written before Clark switched his vote. Had Clark sided with Brennan initially, or shortly after reargument in October 1961, *Baker* probably would have set forth a standard as well as settled the question of jurisdiction. The standard would have been the one of "approximately fair weight" for only one house of a state legislature. Had the case worked out this way, it seems improbable that the same Justices would have changed their minds to adopt the nearly inflexible equality rule imposed shortly afterwards.

This view receives support, Schwartz shows, from the Court's deliberations in late 1963 and early 1964 on *Reynolds v. Sims*. As late as the discussions at conference on the case, the majority had agreed to a standard of population equality for a single house of each state's legislature. Apparently, neither Warren nor the other Justices were prepared to go so far as to make that rule applicable to both chambers. Once beginning work on the opinion, however, Warren changed his mind. He then persuaded Brennan, and before circulating a draft he convinced Black, Douglas, and Goldberg of the correctness of the one-person/one-vote standard for both houses.[43]

The saga of the process by which a majority of the Court came to the one-person/one-vote rule bears out the observation J. Woodford Howard made of the Supreme Court in the years 1940–49: "[H]ardly any major decision in this decade was free from significant alteration of vote and language before announcement to be public."[44]

PRODUCT

The Court's process is of interest because of its impact on product: the decisions. At one level, a decision is a resolution of a particular conflict. Normally the Court accepts all or some of the claims of one side and rejects all or some of the claims of the other side. At this level, the Supreme Court is like every other court in the United States. A court's judgment is said to prevail if the parties agree to abide by the outcome. At a different level, the Supreme Court is unlike most courts in the United States because it is an appellate court: Its decisions are supposed to govern the decisions of other courts within its jurisdiction. Indeed, as far as federal questions are concerned—those that involve the interpretation of the national Constitution, a national statute, or a treaty of the United States—decisions of the Supreme Court are binding on all other courts in the land, both state and federal. Here lies the primary political significance of the Supreme Court. A decision attempts to resolve a single dispute. The opinion and its reasoning, which are attached to that decision, become authority for thousands of lower courts in similar cases. Were this not so, much less excitement would attend the Court's pronouncements on many issues. True, some cases in the Supreme Court are noteworthy precisely because of the individual controversies they involve. *United States v. Nixon*,[45] after all, effectively ended the political career of a President, whatever else can be said about the ruling's applicability to other situations. But the outpouring of amici briefs in dozens of cases each term testifies to the Court's impact beyond any single case. The opinion in an abortion decision, for example, is awaited because of the policies Congress as well as state and local governments, not parties themselves to the case at bar, will be permitted to adopt.

Of course, the Supreme Court's authority to hold other courts to its interpretation of the Constitution is not expressly acknowledged in the Constitution. Article VI explicitly declares "This Constitution" to "be the supreme Law of the Land," binding "the Judges in every State . . . , any Thing in the Constitution or Laws of any State to the Contrary notwithstanding." Article VI, however, says nothing about the source of the authoritative construction of the Constitution that is supposed to be supreme. By 1803, when Chief Justice Marshall announced that "it is, emphatically, the province and duty of the judicial department to say what the law is,"[46] the Supreme Court in several decisions had already implied that the judicial power included the authority to construe the Constitution.

Thomas Jefferson later demurred, believing that "the constitution, in keeping three departments distinct and independent, restrains the authority of the judges to judiciary organs, as it does the executive and legislative to executive and legislative organs."[47] Andrew Jackson as president agreed: "The opinion of the judges has no more authority over Congress than the opinion of Congress has over the judges, and on that point the President is independent of both."[48] Yet Marshall's view persisted. As the Court explained in a 1958 case pitting a state governor against the federal courts, *Marbury v. Madison* "declared the basic principle that the federal judiciary is supreme in the exposition of the law of the Constitution. . . ."[49]

Judicial opinions, however, frequently do not end debate over the wisdom of the policy they contain. The fact that public officials might consider the Court's decision binding does not necessarily mean they consider it final. In the extreme conditions following *Dred Scott,* Abraham Lincoln in his first inaugural address let it be known that he did not regard Chief Justice Taney's opinion in that case as forever settling the question of Congress's authority over slavery in the territories. After acknowledging that Supreme Court decisions "must be binding in any case, upon the parties to a suit, as to the object of that suit . . . ," he added: "[T]he candid citizen must confess that if the policy of the government, upon vital questions, affecting the whole people, is to be irrevocably fixed by decisions of the Supreme Court, . . . the people will have ceased to be their own rulers, having to that extent, practically resigned their government, into the hands of that eminent tribunal."[50] In our own time, the Supreme Court's constitutional nationalization of state criminal justice as well as the abortion controversy has hardly settled those divisive issues. If anything, *Roe v. Wade* and *Webster v. Reproductive Health Services* stoked the fires of a blaze that shows few signs of subsiding.[51] Moreover, announcement of each of President Reagan's nominations to the Supreme Court was unabashedly accompanied by the hope that the new Justice would not regard the 1973 decision as controlling. Even Judge David Souter, President Bush's first nominee to the Supreme Court, pointedly acknowledged the continuing and pervasive effect of *Roe* as "the one case which has been on everyone's mind and everyone's lips since the moment of my nomination."[52]

Likewise, the Court's extension of an exclusionary rule in 1961 to put "teeth" into the Fourth Amendment went a long way toward reinvigorating debate over the wisdom of the rule as a means of enforcing Fourth Amendment rights.[53] Indeed, reaction to Supreme Court opinions involving the exclusionary rule points out another way in which the Justices sometimes have less than the final word on constitutional matters. Judicial federalism concerns the relations between state and federal courts. One dimension of judicial federalism exists when the Supreme Court reviews state court decisions that arguably rest on a state's constitution, not the national Constitution.

For example, in 1984 the U.S. Supreme Court modified its holding in 1961 that made the exclusionary rule applicable to the states.[54] For both state and federal courts, a majority of the bench recognized a "good-faith exception" to the existing policy that suppressed evidence obtained in violation of the Fourth Amendment. The supreme courts of a few states, however, have refused to accept the U.S. Supreme Court's position as controlling in matters of state constitutional law. The result is that the constitutional law of these states offers greater protection against searches and arrests than is available under the Fourth Amendment.

Of course, a provision in the Constitution applicable to the states may not mean "less" in a state court than it does in a federal court. But because the national Constitution sets a floor beneath which a citizen's rights may not fall, judicial federalism permits a state court to construe its state constitution to require a greater degree of protection for individual liberties than does the national Constitution. The only proscription is that, in doing so, the state court must be careful not to appear to enlarge the meaning of the nationally protected right but rather to rest its ruling on an adequate and independent state ground. In other words, once a federal question is present, the Supreme Court becomes the ultimate arbiter of its resolution. This rule encourages uniformity among the states. In contrast, the absence of a federal question encourages diversity because final resolution of an issue rests with individual states.

So the Supreme Court's decisions do not fully comprise the "American Constitution." To know what this Constitution fully includes, one must examine not only the federal decisions and reactions to them, but also the constitutional law of the fifty states.

THE CHAPTERS

Henry Abraham's "Can Presidents Really Pack the Supreme Court?" combines emphasis on both the political and intellectual environment within which the Court functions and the personalities chosen by Presidents to sit on the high bench. As the title of the chapter suggests, these elements are noteworthy because of their impact on the Court's product. Indeed, it is in staffing the federal courts that the Constitution creates the clearest opportunity for the so-called political branches to influence the Court.

By dictating selection of judges by an executive chosen by electors themselves selected in a manner directed by elected state legislators, the

Constitution sharply diminished whatever immunity the Court might otherwise have enjoyed from clashing political values. This was especially so once the political dimension of constitutional adjudication became clear. Moreover, with the advent of political parties, election of the President by the electoral college evolved within a half-century for all practical purposes into popular election by states, allowing Presidents and presidential candidates the opportunity to build, and retain, partisan constituencies.

Nor was executive designation all there was to an arrangement that bound the Court to the political process. Executive designation would take effect only if the Senate approved. And by rejecting Washington's choice of John Rutledge to be the second Chief Justice,[55] the Senate assumed a role that has since alerted Presidents that the Senate cannot be regarded as a "rubber stamp."

Two centuries after the first nominations to the Court, the Senate has approved most, but hardly all, presidential choices. Of 145 nominations to the Court submitted to the Senate from 1789 through 1990, 28 have failed to gain approval (twelve confirmed persons declined to serve). In the twentieth century, 6 nominations out of 54 have met defeat outright or have been withdrawn.[56] By contrast, Presidents almost always have their way with Cabinet appointments, nominees Lewis Strauss (1959) and John Tower (1989) being notable exceptions. Viewing its obligation to "advise and consent" as entailing greater scrutiny and more independence with Justices than with Cabinet heads, the Senate has rejected only nine of the latter.

Abraham demonstrates that numerous factors have shaped the appointment of individual Justices, but he notes that the political views of both the President and the nominee have probably been decisive in most situations. As shown earlier in this chapter, George Washington approached judicial selection with both caution and purpose. While the term "Court-packing" has for more than a half-century been linked with the name of Franklin Roosevelt, Abraham explains that even the first President's nominees had to meet "a veritable smorgasbord of qualifications. There were seven, to be exact, and he adhered to them religiously." Of the seven, "evidently the most important to him was advocacy of the principles of the Constitution—the more outspoken the better."

Can presidents really pack the Supreme Court? Chief Justice Rehnquist—himself twice nominated by Presidents determined to mold the Court in a particular image—has minimized the impact of any President on the Court. "Presidents who wish to pack the Supreme Court, like murder suspects in a detective novel, must have both motive and opportunity." Even with both, "a number of factors militate against a president having anything more than partial success." Chief among them is that neither Presidents nor nominees "are usually vouchsafed the foresight to see what the great issues of 10 or 15 years hence are to be."[57] Abraham describes the significance of those militating factors, but he concludes that most, although hardly all, Presidents "have had reason to be more or less satisfied."

The current political alignment may also affect a President's impact on the Supreme Court. If this pattern persists, Republicans will control the White House much more than they will control the Senate. A Democratic Senate will therefore face a Republican President's nominations in a very high proportion of the total instances of nominations. This creates a dynamic that reduces presidential ability to select nominees who have gone on record with views unacceptable to a majority of the Senate. The President must then choose someone closer to the Senate's position or someone who has not been outspoken politically. An Anthony Kennedy is confirmable, but a Robert Bork is not.

In "The Office of Solicitor General: Political Appointee, Advocate, and Officer of the Court," Rex E. Lee focuses on one of the central aspects (advocacy) and one of the key actors (the Solicitor General) in the judicial process. The question posed in Lee's chapter is the degree to which process, as represented by the work of the Solicitor General, influences the Court's product. Specifically, does (and should) the Court defer to the Department of Justice?

To say that the Solicitor General is the third-ranking official in the Department of Justice and is appointed by the President (with the Senate's approval) to represent the government in the Supreme Court only begins to describe the political and legal significance of the office. Performing tasks originally the sole responsibility of the Attorney General and, later, outside counsel from 1789 until creation of the post in 1870, the Solicitor General has been called "the highest government official who acts primarily as a lawyer" and who "can devote his time to studying the legal problems which come before him."[58] Among other duties, the Solicitor General decides which cases the federal government should appeal from lower courts and handles the government's business before the Supreme Court. "It's the most sophisticated, disciplined kind of law, a constant intellectual engagement," reports Lincoln Caplan.[59]

In this latter capacity, the Solicitor General has an impact that goes beyond that of being an attorney who appears frequently at the Court.[60] To be sure, the U.S. government is currently a party to roughly half the cases on the Court's docket. But the Justices historically have not considered the Solicitor General as merely counsel for a frequent litigant. Rather, the Solicitor General's views are accorded unusual significance, if not deference.

In the early 1960s, for example, Solicitor General Archibald Cox filed amici briefs in both *Baker v. Carr* and *Reynolds v. Sims* (discussed previously). They illustrate the role the federal government can play even when the United States is not a party to the litigation. In *Baker*, the government's brief urged federal courts to take jurisdiction of state apportionment cases. Acknowledging that "exact numerical equality of population within legislative districts is, of course, impossible," the government suggested a standard similar to the "approximately fair weight" rule originally favored by a plurality. In *Reynolds v. Sims*, the government urged affirmance of a district court reapportionment plan that combined elements of two state-sponsored plans. The Crawford-Webb Act would have allocated senators in Alabama by county, roughly on a population basis. A proposed constitutional amendment for the state House would have apportioned the 106 members by assigning one member per county with the remaining 39 seats being allocated by population. Close to "approximately fair weight," this was the version initially, but not finally, favored by the Supreme Court.

Statistics also suggest considerable influence for the Solicitor General's position. Among petitions for certiorari filed by the Solicitor General in a recent twenty-year period, 69 percent were granted. This contrasts with an overall acceptance rate of barely 5 percent. In fiscal year 1984, there were 2,861 petitions for certiorari filed in the Court seeking review of decisions by the courts of appeals. The Justices granted 6.5 percent. Yet in the 1983–84 Term of the Court, the Solicitor General called for review of 49 appeals court decisions. Of this number, 42 (or nearly 86 percent) of his petitions were granted. Recent data also show the growing role of the Solicitor General's office in filing briefs amici curiae. Once before the Court, the Solicitor General does very well, with a "win rate" substantially above 50 percent.[61]

From hands-on experience Lee explains that the Solicitor General must exercise restraint in seeking access as a way of preserving such formidable odds. As Robert Stern has argued, the Solicitor General

> is aware of the necessity from the standpoint of the effective administration of justice of the judicial system of restricting the number of cases taken to the Supreme Court to the number that the Court can hear. . . . A heavy additional burden would be imposed on the Court if the government, with its great volume of litigation, disregarded that policy and acted like the normal litigant who wants to take one more shot at reversing a decision which is obviously wrong because he lost.

But Stern notes the operation of self-interest as well. The Solicitor General wants the Court to have confidence in the government's position.

> It is hoped and believed—although no one who has not been on the Court can be sure—that the Court will realize that the Solicitor General will not assert that an issue is of general importance unless it is—and that confidence in the Solicitor

General's attempt to adhere to the Court's own standards will cause the Court to grant more government petitions.[62]

Lee's observations, coming a quarter-century later, and within only a few months of his resignation as Solicitor General, are of particular interest in light of the well-publicized attempt by the Reagan administration to advance its social agenda through the courts, especially after Congress failed to act on matters such as school prayer and affirmative action in a way pleasing to the White House. It was after Lee's departure that the administration seemed to adopt a legally more confrontational stance. Attorney General Edwin Meese, in a speech in July 1985 to the American Bar Association, referred to the Court's 1985 rulings on church and state as resting on a "bizarre" reading of the First Amendment. And in the fall of 1985, Acting Solicitor General Charles Fried, Lee's successor, asked the Court to abandon *Roe v. Wade*, even though the Justices had expressly reaffirmed the 1973 decision only two years before, and even though there had been no intervening change in personnel. In response to a question following his 1985 lecture (appearing in this volume as Chapter 3), Lee explained that one of the first things one learns as Solicitor General "is how to count to five." As he had already explained in an interview on National Public Radio, he at times found it necessary as Solicitor General to moderate the government's arguments in order to maintain the credibility of his office. "It is very damaging to the administration's position to make arguments before the Supreme Court that are not likely to succeed." On some matters, "it's simply a question of, 'Do you want to blow the bugle, or do you want to win the war?' "[63]

If advocacy is central to understanding the Court, so is another aspect of the institution's process: leadership and the relationships among the Justices. This is the aspect of process explored by James F. Simon in "Conflict and Leadership on the U.S. Supreme Court: From Marshall to Rehnquist." The Court's internal workings are of interest because the Supreme Court is a collegial body; that is, the Justices sit as a single body, not alone or in groups of three or four. They work together to reach and to explain a decision. "The data in judicial papers reveal the decisional process on the . . . Court to be far different from the mere voting by nine men of their individual value preferences."[64] Of course, individual Justices may employ different methods to decide cases, "but one cannot ignore the effect of working together or, as a psychologist would put it, the effect of social interaction."[65] And leadership is a part of social interaction.

John Marshall was the fourth, not the first, Chief Justice, but the subject of judicial leadership begins with him. His impact on the Court was so substantial that it became the custom after his death in 1835 to think of the Court's history as a series of periods, each identified by the Chief Justice's name. So one speaks of the Taft Court or the Vinson Court even though, as Simon explains, such a designation hardly guarantees that the occupant of the center chair was in fact a leader of the bench.[66] "Popular interest naturally centers in the Chief Justice as the titular head of the Court," Charles Evans Hughes wrote before being named Chief Justice himself in 1930 (but after serving as an associate justice between 1910 and 1916).

> [I]n a small body of able men with equal authority in the making of decisions, it is evident that his actual influence will depend upon the strength of his character and the demonstration of his ability in the intimate relations of the judges. . . . While the Chief Justice has only one vote, the way in which the Court does its work gives him a special opportunity for leadership.[67]

Judicial leadership as a valid subject of inquiry begins with Marshall for two reasons. First were Marshall's personal qualities, including, as Simon notes, a vision of the long-run constitutional needs of the nation and an ability to articulate that vision. These qualities led Justice Holmes a century later to refer to Marshall as the "one alone" to be chosen "if American law were to be represented by a single figure."[68] Second were the "institutional arrangements governing Supreme Court action during the first decade of its existence [which] were conducive to individuality in decision making to a degree that has probably never been approximated since 1800."[69] Significant changes in the Court's procedures occurred after Marshall took office in 1801, probably owing to the sharp political conflict between the Federalists and the Republicans (or Jeffersonians). New procedure gave Marshall "a key role in the decision making process and seriously reduced the independence of the individual justices in this process."[70]

No one since Marshall has dominated a court the way he did, but the nation has experienced influential Chief Justices. Will William H. Rehnquist be among them? To what extent can it be said in the early years of the Rehnquist Court that it is the Rehnquist Court in fact as well as in name? Simon draws on Marshall's experience and that of Charles Evans Hughes, but he looks at the careers of Associate Justices Hugo Black and Felix Frankfurter as well, as indications that leadership is sometimes not confined to the chief. He believes that effective court leadership flows from the combination of the instincts of a politician and the vision of a judicial statesman.

In "Justice Sandra Day O'Connor: An Assessment," Harold J. Spaeth examines a member of the current Supreme Court. The emphasis is on "personality" as that element contributes to the decisions of the Court.

Perhaps partly because she is the first woman Justice and partly because she was the first appointee of a recent President determined to change the policy direction of the Supreme Court, Justice O'Connor has not languished from scholarly and journalistic attention. Most studies, however, have focused on her pre-Court career in Arizona or on a particular aspect of her performance as a Justice. In his chapter, Spaeth goes beyond these to survey her ideological perspective in virtually every area of the Court's work. He accomplishes this through a statistical analysis of her "special opinions" (dissenting or concurring opinions, as contrasted to majority or plurality opinions). Spaeth thus considers process as well: the freedom Justices have to express themselves apart from the majority's statement of the decision and its justification.

The Court's procedures, Spaeth believes, allow Justices "to give free play to their personal policy preferences . . . not only when they disagree with the majority's decision, but even when they are members of the majority coalition." Because the "opinion of the Court" (majority opinion) is usually accurately viewed as a group product, Spaeth finds that special opinions are a helpful means to determine a Justice's general ideological position on questions before the Court. No Justice "can be forced to write a special opinion; no Justice can be prevented from writing one; no Justice can be forced to or be prevented from joining in the special opinion of another Justice. As a result, such an opinion tends to reflect the strongly held views of its author." Moreover, Spaeth surmises, a Justice joining another's special opinion "can reasonably be said to be persuaded of the correctness of the views presented therein."

Spaeth first examines the number of special opinions Justice O'Connor has authored and the ideological orientation of those Justices who have been "joiners."[71] (By a "liberal" or "conservative" orientation, Spaeth means a Justice's tendency to support a certain outcome in cases, as these labels are commonly used to evaluate Supreme Court Justices. For example, in the context of cases in criminal justice, First Amendment issues, and civil rights, Justices are regarded as conservative if they support the prosecution, reject the First Amendment claim, and oppose civil rights claims.) He then examines the ideological orientation of those Justices whose special opinions she has joined.

In O'Connor's case, these data suggest a strong conservative orientation. Spaeth then considers the possibility that exclusive focus on special opinions exaggerates her conservative orientation. As a check, he analyses the "directionality" of the dissents she has authored and joined. Because special opinions she has authored or joined amount to such a small percentage of the total number of cases in which she has participated, Spaeth turns for an additional indicator to an assessment of her voting over a range of issues as compared to the voting of her colleagues. To accomplish this task, the Court's business is grouped into ten fields: criminal justice, civil rights, First Amendment, due process, privacy, unions, economic activity, judicial power, federal taxation, and federalism. Finally, Spaeth probes contradictions between her voting behavior and the positions she adopts in her opinions. Throughout, where sufficient data exist, Spaeth finds that Justice O'Connor has been a consistent member of the conservative wing of the Court—a "staunch conservative."

Indeed, in only a single case did Spaeth find a discrepancy between "what she says and what she does, vote-wise."[72] This occurs in the area of judicial federalism. Here Spaeth notes that she has been willing to "subordinate considerations of federalism to the substantive aspects of her conservatism." In so doing, she is no different from other Justices on this and recent courts. "Instrumental values, such as considerations of federalism (which, when all is said and done, is nothing more than an aspect of judicial restraint), are invoked only when a Justice approves of the merits of the decision or the action under review." As Spaeth has written elsewhere, "one may defer, but never blindly."[73]

"The Constitution and the Legacy of Justice William O. Douglas" by Walter F. Murphy treats one of the most intriguing figures to sit on the Court in the twentieth century. Moreover, because of the length of Douglas's record service on the Court—more than thirty-six years—and the relevance of many of Douglas's opinions to issues confronting the Court nearly two decades after his retirement, Murphy's contribution highlights a second element—the impact of the past on the present.

The chapter is organized in four parts: Douglas the man, his constitutional jurisprudence, the right to privacy, and Douglas's judicial and constitutional legacies. Drawing on his own relationship with Douglas as well as the experience and insights of others, Murphy attempts to connect Douglas's upbringing, background, and outlook on life to his way of looking at constitutional issues and the role of the Supreme Court. This is not an easy task because a decade after his death Douglas remains, as Murphy says, "an enigmatic and frustrating figure." Moreover, "in each of his roles, whether as father, husband, administrator, or judge, Douglas was a loner. He saw himself as an outsider, an alien, at times even a pariah."

Murphy finds that Douglas typically approached constitutional questions in a pragmatic or even ad hoc fashion. That is, he tended to use whatever technique or mode of analysis he thought best to decide the case at hand. "With personal liberty as his lodestar, the result that best fit the problem was usually crystal clear in his mind." This attitude meant that Douglas never explained his legal philosophy in terms of a general theory, a failing that long troubled fellow Justices and scholars alike. Partly that was because Douglas, as a Realist, had a distrust of grand theories that purported to assure the objectivity of the law. Moreover, he was impatient. His intelligence made it difficult for him to understand how an argument clear to him was not necessarily clear to others. In

Murphy's view, Douglas also possessed a Calvinist perspective that required recurring evidence of his self-worth. One needing constant reassurance of his place among the elect does not have time to wait out the months and even years that development of a grand theory consumes. Finally, a general restlessness and a talent for quickly cutting to the heart of a question probably added to his reluctance to theorize.

These traits are reflected, Murphy finds, in the part Douglas played in developing a broad constitutional right to privacy. He did not create such an idea but built on the thinking of others, notably Justice Louis Brandeis. Still, it was Douglas who, over about three decades, did as much as anyone to elevate privacy to the constitutional status it enjoys today. Reviewing a series of cases on this issue, Murphy reveals Douglas's passion for liberty, his willingness to use his position as a judge to defend individual rights, his ability to "begin to articulate a theory of constitutional interpretation," followed by a tiring or impatience with careful argument, and the "frustrations he could inflict on those who expect a learned and brilliant jurist to explain and defend a coherent jurisprudence." Throughout his chapter, Murphy juxtaposes Douglas with colleagues such as Felix Frankfurter and, especially, Hugo Black. Black was in some respects an ally and in others an adversary, and his positivist approach to constitutional interpretation stands as a relief against which Douglas's ideas appear more clearly.

Even with the absence of a general theory of jurisprudence in Douglas's opinions, Murphy sees a "broader unity in his constitutional interpretation." This unity is Douglas's constitutional legacy. He was more of a Jeffersonian and more of a constitutionalist than Black. Whereas the latter thought that Americans had only those rights enumerated in the Constitution, the former subscribed to the view that Americans retained all those rights they had not expressly surrendered to government. As a judge, Douglas remained both a Realist and an idealist. He was a Realist "in that he cared not for the appearance of what the Court was doing but for its actual effect on litigants, the political system, and on the Constitution." He was an idealist "in his vision of America as a city on a hill, of the Constitution as the polity's sacred scripture, and the Court as guardian of both the image and reality of America." These were parts of a vision Douglas pursued throughout his professional life.

In the series of lectures at Franklin and Marshall College from which these chapters derive, Murphy's presentation on Douglas preceded William M. Beaney's on the second Justice Harlan: "John Marshall Harlan: A Modern Conservative Justice." The scheduling was fortuitous and instructive. Like Murphy's survey, Beaney's turns a study of an individual Justice into a vehicle that displays the importance of constitutional legacy in understanding the Supreme Court.

In many respects Justice Harlan was the antithesis of Douglas. Douglas had a poverty-stricken childhood; Harlan came from a comfortable background. Douglas was a Democrat who at times harbored presidential ambitions; Harlan was a lifelong Republican who never sought elective office. Douglas's public employment prior to his Court service consisted of his work at the Securities and Exchange Commission; Harlan's included appointment as an assistant United States Attorney, special assistant attorney general of New York state, and chief counsel of the New York State Crime Commission, as well as a short tenure on the U.S. Court of Appeals for the Second Circuit. Douglas practiced law for barely two years, while much of Harlan's professional life was spent in private practice, including several leadership positions with bar associations. Douglas prided himself on being "anti-establishment," seemed to relish tweaking the nose of privilege, and appeared to be more at home in hiking clothes than in a judicial gown. Harlan made no apologies when he was called a "patrician."As a former clerk to Harlan explained to an undergraduate doing an independent paper on Harlan in 1972, "the Justice ate more lunches with millionaires than you've eaten lunches." Douglas's tenure on the Supreme Court exceeded thirty-six years, Harlan's only sixteen. While they were Associate Justices together on the Court, Douglas unhesitatingly espoused an activist posture in defense of individual liberties and was usually part of the majority during the second half of the Warren Court; Harlan was an articulate apostle of judicial restraint and the values of federalism, and in the latter Warren Court he was often in dissent. General theory and the fine points of opinion writing were not important to Douglas; Harlan by contrast placed high value on legal craftsmanship, being known by some as a "judge's judge."

Being more controversial and certainly more colorful, Douglas seems to be the more appealing subject for a lecture. As Professor Beaney apologetically explained in his lecture on Harlan, "it is more difficult to lecture in an interesting fashion on a judicial conservative like Harlan than on a judicial liberal like Douglas. Douglas was always doing attention-getting things off the Court like touring Russia or falling off a horse. Harlan was not. It is easy to be passionate about William O. Douglas. How does one become passionate about John Marshall Harlan?" Harlan was a passionate conservative because he was passionate about federalism.

The connection between judicial conservatism and federalism is central to understanding Harlan's constitutional jurisprudence, Beaney believes. Simply labeling him a conservative does not capture "the richness of the Justice's approach to the Constitution." The fundamental charter provided guidance but was not a straitjacket. Primary responsibility for policy-making lay with the people's representatives in legislative chambers. Most constitutional strictures applied to the national government, not to the states, since the limitations of the Fourteenth Amendment were general, not particular as in the Bill of Rights. Moreover, federalism deserved judicial recognition and support because it combatted the centralizing tendencies of the age. In centralization Harlan saw a threat to liberty and to the system the framers had designed.

Barely a decade after his appointment to the Supreme Court, Harlan warned that some of the Warren Court's pioneering decisions restricting the discretion of the states and expanding constitutionally protected liberties came at the expense of principles that lay "at the root of our constitutional system." "We are accustomed," he observed, "to speak of the Bill of Rights and the Fourteenth Amendment as the principal guarantees of personal liberty. Yet it would surely be shallow not to recognize that the structure of our political system accounts no less for the free society we have." The framers "staked their faith that liberty would prosper in the nation not primarily upon the declaration of individual rights but upon the kind of government the Union was to have.... No view of the Bill of Rights or interpretation of any of its provisions which fails to take account of [federalism and separation of powers] can be considered constitutionally sound."[74] Harlan was echoing Alexander Hamilton's observation in *The Federalist*, No. 84, that the Constitution, even without amendments, "is itself, in every rational sense, and to every useful purpose, a Bill of Rights."

Harlan's legacy also lies in his craftsmanship, according to Beaney. No reader of his opinions can fail to note his tendency to "lay out all the elements necessary to the resolution of the case at hand." Teachers and students alike have come to recognize that "appreciation of a case is greatly strengthened by Harlan's opinions, whether for the Court, concurring or in dissent." His vision of a federal union coupled with his judicial skills allowed him to "play a significant role as a conservative Justice of the highest calibre."

Jesse H. Choper's "Affirmative Action and the Supreme Court" moves beyond emphasis on a single Justice such as Harlan or Douglas and that Justice's legacy. Rather, Choper's interest is the members of the contemporary Court and their response to one of the most divisive and significant policy questions of our time: affirmative action. He emphasizes the effect of the Court's past and its personnel on its product.

Since the nineteenth century, much litigation under the equal protection clause of the Fourteenth Amendment has been aimed at halting practices deemed harmful to certain minorities, especially blacks. The focus in those cases has been on what the Constitution prohibits. In contrast, within the past two decades, various institutions—themselves not necessarily guilty of racial discrimination—have voluntarily established remedial programs. Their efforts are broadly aimed at correcting what is often termed "societal discrimination." This is discrimination that is reflected in various aspects of life, but that cannot be directly attributed to specific laws or official policies. Measures to combat societal discrimination have been challenged in court as also being a violation of the ban on racial discrimination in the Constitution or in the Civil Rights Act of 1964. (Gender-based affirmative action programs have been contentious, too, but most of the affirmative action litigation has involved race-based programs.) The question today has become one of determining what the Constitution and the laws permit.

For instance, if a state university makes a special effort to recruit and admit members of certain racial groups and to apply different criteria in assessing their qualifications, has the equal protection clause been compromised? Opponents of affirmative action argue that such programs are certainly not in the spirit of keeping the Constitution "colorblind," as the first Justice Harlan asserted in his famous dissent against racial discrimination in *Plessy v. Ferguson.*[75] Proponents reply that a cessation of discrimination is not enough. Positive measures are needed to overcome the residual effects of generations of discrimination.

In situations where institutions have practiced discrimination, courts have ordered remedial programs in hiring and promotions. Even with a demonstrated record of past discrimination by an institution, opponents have attacked these remedial plans as well because they are said to be too extreme: They reward those who may not have been actual victims of prior discrimination and deny rights to racial majorities.[76] The catch is that jobs and seats in medical school classes, for example, are finite. To give to one means to withhold from someone else. It may also be the case that those non-minority individuals who claim to be hurt by affirmative action are in many situations those least able to bear the burden. They may even have benefited least from the effects of invidious discrimination that do remain. Given the extent of the controversy surrounding both voluntary and involuntary affirmative action, it is not surprising that the issue has reached the Supreme Court. The turmoil of litigation proves Alexis de Tocqueville correct once again: Another political issue in the United States has transformed itself into a judicial dispute. The turmoil shows little sign of subsiding.

Choper's objective in his chapter is not to propose a particular resolution of the affirmative action debate. Rather, his objective is to analyze the current Supreme Court and to explore where each member stands on the question, especially in cases where a Justice has expressed himself or herself in a judicial opinion or in other writings. The result is not a broad-stroke view that labels one or another Justice "for" or "against" affirmative action, but a finely tuned presentation that seeks to discover the variables distinguishing one case from another and consequently those characteristics of affirmative action programs a certain Justice will be inclined to approve or disapprove. Thus, Choper does not pretend to lay bare the Court's undisclosed views on affirmative action but to determine plainly the common ground that is presently shared by at least a bare majority of the bench. He does this by identifying "the important pieces of the puzzle," concluding that those "who presently claim that there is clarity in this area . . . are either deluded or deluding."

Affirmative action and other issues figure prominently in the concluding chapter, Martin Shapiro's survey of "Chief Justice Rehnquist and the Future of the Supreme Court." William H. Rehnquist has been part of the Supreme Court for two decades, although he has been Chief Justice only since 1986. He is a member of that very small club of Chief Justices who were named from the ranks of Associate Justice. The only other members have been Edward D. White and Harlan F. Stone. Abe Fortas came close to being a member, but opposition in the Senate to his nomination in 1968 led to the Justice's withdrawing his name from consideration. Chief Justices John Rutledge and Charles Evans Hughes do not qualify because each resigned from the bench as Associate Justice to pursue other objectives.[77] In both cases nomination to the office of Chief Justice occurred later.

Rehnquist is distinctive among successful nominees to the Court in recent decades in having engendered substantial opposition to his appointments, both as Associate Justice in 1971 and as Chief Justice in 1986. Because of close identification with some of the controversial policies of the Nixon administration, and thus supposedly lacking in "judicial temperament," and because he was thought by some to be too conservative, Rehnquist garnered twenty-six negative votes before joining the Court initially. President Reagan's announcement in 1986 that he wanted Rehnquist to succeed Warren Burger as Chief Justice provoked even more controversy. Now the Senate had a rare second chance: Senators could vote on the results of a Justice's career, not just on its prospects. Other Senators, perhaps reluctant to pass judgment openly on a nominee's ideology, directed questions to surrogate issues that cast doubt on Rehnquist's fitness to serve. Hearings by the Judiciary Committee consumed four days, and Senate floor debate five. This time thirty-three Senators voted "no," sixty-five "yes." Not since 1836, when the Senate confirmed Roger Taney, had a nominee for Chief Justice been approved by a ratio of less than two to one.[78]

In the first of a projected several-volume study of Rehnquist (completed just prior to his appointment as Chief Justice), biographer Donald Boles shows that Rehnquist's professional record both before and during his tenure as Associate Justice contains ample evidence for those senators who opposed his nomination in 1986 on ideological grounds. Boles found that Rehnquist tended to resolve conflicts between the government and the individual in favor of the former, conflicts between state and national authority in favor of the former, and conflicts over the extent of federal jurisdiction in favor of the states.[79] Boles is not surprised by Owen Fiss and Charles Krauthammer's contention that Rehnquist "is no conservative as that term is ordinarily understood in the law, but rather a revisionist of a particular ideological bent."[80]

Will Rehnquist prove to be one of the most influential American jurists of the last quarter of this century? Will he be recognized "as a catalyst to many of [the Supreme Court's] great struggles"?[81] To understand Rehnquist as a Justice and to evaluate his impact on the Court, Martin Shapiro first places the present Court in perspective. This perspective is the realignment of American constitutional law, which began after the electoral realignment of 1932 and was all but completed by 1942. A Court sympathetic to the values of the newly ascendant Democratic Party read out of the Constitution "Republican constitutional law"—an interpretation of the Constitution that had offered some federal judicial protection for private property and that had provided some limits on the growth of national power with respect to the states. In its place came "Democratic constitutional law," which removed federal judicial protection for private property but which embraced protection for civil liberties and civil rights. Moreover, states now enjoyed little federal judicial protection from national power, and the virtually complete application of the Bill of Rights to the states further reduced local autonomy.

In recent years, judges with a Republican orientation "are reflecting a major unresolved tension within the Republican Party." Are they to be conservative in the sense of protecting the individual's autonomy from big government? Or are they to be conservative in the sense of promoting "traditional values?" The former would be inclined to keep the liberties created by the post–1937 Court and to restore property interests to the status of constitutionally protected rights. The latter would be as anxious to erode the first group of rights as they would be to enshrine the second. Rehnquist's place in this battle over the dominant construction of the Constitution will be shaped by how well he "understands the dynamics of the constitutional campaigns that have been unfolding since 1932 and the degree to which he is able to influence their outcomes."

Rehnquist's most active leadership role in the constitutional arena has been an attempted reconstruction of federalism. Shapiro explores cases in such fields as traditional nation-state relations, criminal justice, property rights, and free expression. So far, attacks on New Deal and post–New Deal constitutional law have succeeded only in piecemeal fashion because Justices of Rehnquist's persuasion have been in a distinct minority. "In the final analysis," Shapiro maintains, "great judicial craftsmanship comes from winners or judges who are willing to lose in glorious dissents. If you are trying to win without the votes, judicial life is harder. Chief Justice Rehnquist is in pursuit of the conservative agenda, but he is not yet, and may never be, playing on the winning team." The record will be made by the staying power of the long-dominant "Democratic agenda" and the perseverance of Justices pursuing constitutional values long out of fashion.

In its look ahead, Shapiro's chapter on the future of the Rehnquist Court is a fitting conclusion to a volume intended to illustrate five elements that this introduction has suggested are helpful in understanding the Supreme Court. From various perspectives the eight authors portray facets of the Court's political and intellectual environment, its personalities, its past, its process, and its product. The intent throughout is a better grasp of an institution that has evolved a role as "essential safeguard" in a political system now in its third century.

NOTES

1. R. Jackson, address, February 1, 1940. 84 L. Ed. 1428.
2. J. Madison, *The Federalist*, No. 51.
3. 60 U.S. (19 How.) 393 (1857).
4. *Osborn v. Bank*, 22 U.S. (9 Wheat.) 738, 866 (1824).
5. *The Federalist*, No. 78.
6. J. Bassett, *The Federalist System 1789–1801* (1906), p. 21.
7. W. Taft, "Criticisms of the Federal Judiciary," 29 *American Law Review* 641, 642–43 (1895).
8. 1 C. Warren, *The Supreme Court in United States History* (1926), p. 31.
9. C. Hughes, *The Supreme Court of the United States* (1928), p. 49.
10. B. Murphy, *Fortas* (1988).
11. Warren, *The Supreme Court in United States History*, p. 31.
12. J. Stevens, "Reflections on the Removal of Sitting Judges," 13 *Stetson Law Review* 215, 217 (1984).
13. B. Cardozo, *The Nature of the Judicial Process* (1921), p. 168.
14. *Furman v. Georgia*, 408 U.S. 238 (1972).
15. *Gregg v. Georgia*, 428 U.S. 153 (1976).
16. 57 U.S.L.W. 4705 (1989); 427 U.S. 160 (1976).
17. 57 U.S.L.W., p. 4707.
18. Max Lerner, as quoted in H. Abraham, *The Judicial Process* (5th ed., 1986), p. 348.
19. 279 U.S. 655, 689.
20. *Youngstown v. Sawyer*, 343 U.S. 579, 610–11 (1952) (concurring opinion).
21. F. Frankfurter, "Some Observations on the Nature of the Judicial Process of Supreme Court Litigation," 98 *Proceedings of the American Philosophical Society* 233, 238 (1954).
22. However, as Justice John B. Gibson admonished, "To say... that the power is to be exercised but in perfectly clear cases, is to betray a doubt of the propriety of exercising it at all." *Eakin v. Raub*, 12 Serg. & Rawle 330, 352 (Pa. 1825) (dissenting opinion).
23. *United States v. Butler*, 297 U.S. 1, 87 (1936) (dissenting opinion).
24. R. Jackson, address, p. 1429.
25. *Id.*, p. 1428.

26. 2 Warren, *The Supreme Court in United States History*, pp. 748–49.
27. C. Hughes, speech at Elmira, N.Y., May 3, 1907.
28. Cardozo, *The Nature of the Judicial Process*, p. 20.
29. *Thornburgh v. American College of Obstetricians and Gynecologists*, 476 U.S. 747, 786–87 (1986) (dissenting opinion).
30. 476 U.S., p. 787. Dissenting in *South Carolina v. Gathers*, Justice Scalia elaborated:

> I had thought that the respect accorded prior decisions increases, rather than decreases, with their antiquity, as the society adjusts itself to their existence, and the surrounding law becomes premised upon their validity. The freshness of error not only deprives it of the respect to which long-established practice is entitled, but also counsels that the opportunity of correction be seized at once.

57 U.S.L.W. 4629, 4634 (1989).
31. 57 U.S.L.W. 4132 (1989).
32. 448 U.S. 448 (1980).
33. 448 U.S., p. 484.
34. *Id.*, p. 490.
35. Justice Rehnquist, however, slipped away in *Metro Broadcasting v. F.C.C.*, 58 U.S.L.W. 5053 (1990), where a majority of five upheld two minority preference policies adopted by the Federal Communications Commission for the purpose of promoting programming diversity rather than remedying past discrimination. Whether this decision will long survive the retirement of Justice Brennan in July 1990 is problematical.
36. 369 U.S. 186 (1962).
37. 376 U.S. 1 (1964).
38. 377 U.S. 533 (1964).
39. B. Schwartz, *Super Chief: Earl Warren and His Supreme Court* (1983).
40. *Id.*, p. 415.
41. *Id.*, pp. 417–18.
42. *Id.*, p. 423.
43. *Id.*, p. 503.
44. J. Howard, "On the Fluidity of Judicial Choice," 62 *American Political Science Review* 43, 43 (1968).
45. 418 U.S. 683 (1974).
46. *Marbury v. Madison*, 5 U.S. (1 Cranch) 137, 177 (1803).
47. T. Jefferson, letter to William C. Jarvis, Sept. 28, 1820. 15 *The Writings of Thomas Jefferson* (A. Lipscomb, ed., 1903), p. 278.
48. 2 J. Richardson, *A Compilation of the Messages and Papers of the Presidents* (1908), p. 581.
49. *Cooper v. Aaron*, 358 U.S. 1, 18 (1958).
50. 6 Richardson, *A Compilation of the Messages and Papers of the Presidents 1789–1902*, p. 9.
51. 410 U.S. 113 (1973); 57 U.S.L.W. 5023 (1989).
52. Remarks before the Senate Judiciary Committee, September 13, 1990. Quoted in N. Lewis, "Souter Deflects Senators' Queries on Abortion Views," *New York Times*, September 14, 1990, p. A1.
53. *Mapp v. Ohio*, 367 U.S. 643 (1961).

54. *United States v. Leon*, 468 U.S. 897 (1984).

55. Because Rutledge had already assumed some of the duties of his office prior to action by the Senate, most authorities count him among the total number of sixteen Chief Justices to date.

56. The Seventeenth Amendment, providing for the popular election of the Senate, may have removed some of the basis for political differences between the President and the Senate.

57. Quoted in A. Mason and D. Stephenson, Jr., *American Constitutional Law* (8th ed., 1987), p. 10.

58. R. Stern, "The Solicitor General and Administrative Agency Litigation," 46 *American Bar Association Journal* 154 (1960).

59. Quoted in L. Greenhouse, "Justice," *New York Times*, June 2, 1989, p. A11. Caplan is author of *The Tenth Justice* (1987), a book about the Solicitor General.

60. For data on this point, see J. Segal, "Supreme Court Support for the Solicitor General: The Effect of Presidential Appointments," 43 *Western Political Quarterly* 137 (1990).

61. G. Uelman, "The Influence of the Solicitor General upon Supreme Court Disposition of Federal Circuit Court Decisions . . . ," 69 *Judicature* 360, 361–62 (1986).

62. Stern, "The Solicitor General . . . ," p. 156.

63. Quoted in "Reagan vs. Court: A Continuing Crusade," *Congressional Quarterly Weekly Report*, July 20, 1985, p. 1463.

64. W. Murphy and J. Tanenhaus, *The Study of Public Law* (1972), p. 155.

65. R. Seddig, "John Marshall and the Origins of Supreme Court Leadership," 36 *University of Pittsburgh Law Review* 785, 787 (1975).

66. "We seem incapable of possessing our past save in temporal segments. . . . No one man puts his exclusive stamp on the Court, but among all the men who do not, it is least invidious to regard the Chief Justice as if he did." A. Bickel, *The Supreme Court and the Idea of Progress* (1970), p. 3.

67. C. Hughes, *The Supreme Court of the United States*, pp. 56–58.

68. O. Holmes, Jr., *Collected Legal Papers* (1952), p. 270.

69. J. Schmidhauser, *The Supreme Court: Its Politics, Personalities, and Procedures* (1964), p. 105.

70. *Id.*

71. This is not Max Lerner's use of the term, when, in his apology for Hugo Black's membership in the KKK, he wrote of Black's tendency "from the very beginning" to be "a 'joiner.' " "Hugo Black—A Personal History," *The Nation*, October 9, 1937, p. 368.

72. *Michigan v. Long*, 463 U.S. 1032 (1983).

73. H. Spaeth and S. Teger, "Activism and Restraint: A Cloak for the Justices' Policy Preferences," in S. Halpern and C. Lamb, eds., *Supreme Court Activism and Restraint* (1982), p. 297.

74. Quoted in Mason and Stephenson, *American Constitutional Law*, pp. 135–36.

75. 163 U.S. 537 (1896).

76. For example, see *United States v. Paradise*, 480 U.S. 149 (1987).

77. See note 55.

78. The Senate voted 52 to 26 (eighteen senators did not vote) to confirm

Charles Evans Hughes as Chief Justice in 1930. The vote in the Senate to confirm Melville Fuller as Chief Justice in 1888 was 41 to 20.

79. D. Boles, *Mr. Justice Rehnquist, Judicial Activist: The Early Years* (1987).

80. O. Fiss and C. Krauthammer, "The Rehnquist Court: A Return to the Antebellum Constitution," *The New Republic*, March 10, 1982, p. 20.

81. A. E. D. Howard, "Justice Rehnquist—A Key Fighter in Major Battles," *ABA Journal* 49 (June 1986).

2

Can Presidents Really Pack the Supreme Court?

Henry J. Abraham

"Can Presidents really pack the court?" is not only an intriguing but a constantly recurring question, posed in either fear or hope or a variant of each—not infrequently comprising a mélange of both sides, the negative and the positive. There are but nine seats on the Supreme Court of the United States, and vacancies occur, on the average, only once every eight years, with the average tenure of Justices now approaching twenty years. Yet it is axiomatic that the role of the Court is so seminal in our constitutional constellation that it hardly requires a course in Political Science 1, let alone anything more elevated, to recognize the crucial nature of the identity of those who are fortunate enough to receive the presidential call to serve on what the great Oliver Wendell Holmes, Jr., with half-tongue in half-cheek, styled "Mount Olympus."

It is also axiomatic that the forty Presidents (counting all repeaters as well as the split dual presidency of Grover Cleveland only once) who, collectively, have appointed the 105 individuals having served to date on the highest tribunal in the land—which incidentally is assuredly also the most powerful in the entire democratic world—would endeavor to select future Justices whose general weltanschauung dovetailed at least generally with their own. One would hope, however, that choices would, above all, be meritorious—and merit *is* identifiable. It is at once a flippant oversimplification and a disservice to the principle involved to insist that merit lies only in the eye of the beholder. It may well lie there, but it *is* objectively identifiable within acceptable limits. To put it somewhat differently, while any set of criteria (which we will discuss later) for the selection of future members of the Supreme Court is quite naturally both informed and discountable by eye-of-the-beholder conceptualizations, by subjectivity, it is not impossible to advance certain standards that—at least in theory—ought to govern eligibility, regardless of the degree to which a President's motivation may permit them to play a governing role in his decision to make a particular appointment. Ergo, antecedent to any attempt to answer this chapter's stated question, it seems appropriate to elaborate on the contention that merit is indeed identifiable. Thus, Professor Sheldon Goldman, a close observer of the judicial selection process—particularly at the trial and intermediate appellate levels—identified, in a recent *Annals* article, "eight qualities, characteristics, or traits that most," or so he argued warmly, "would agree are associated with the ideal type of a judge."[1] The eight are, in his language, (1) neutrality as to the parties in litigation; (2) fair-mindedness; (3) being well versed in the law; (4) ability to think and write logically and lucidly; (5) personal integrity; (6) good physical and mental health; (7) judicial temperament; and (8) ability to handle judicial power sensibly. It is hard to argue with the octet. To apply it to specific instances of selection, however, makes for considerably more complexity and introduces controversy in at least some of the stated components. The same observation may well apply to the somewhat shorter roster of six components of merit that I suggested as *de minimis* qualification guidelines in the Seventh Annual Address to the Supreme Court Historical Society in 1982:

> One, demonstrated judicial temperament. Two, professional expertise and competence. Three, absolute personal as well as professional integrity. Four, an able, agile, lucid mind. Five, appropriate professional educational background or training. Six, the ability to communicate clearly, both orally and in writing, especially the latter.[2]

Others have amply voiced similar requirements and qualifications. But the latter may also be expressed quite differently, as for example by Bruce E. Fein, a top Justice Department official in the early days of the Reagan administration. He set forth five more subjective requirements for the selection of a Supreme Court Justice, requirements that seek merit yet concurrently present a clarion call for jurisprudential commitments. His quintet was:

> [1.] An understanding that the Supreme Court is not the nation's moral conscience, does not monopolize the nation's concern for minority interests and is not infallible. . . . [2.] A conviction that the express language of the Constitution and intent of the framers are the only legitimate guides to constitutional inter-

pretation. . . . [3.] An understanding of the constitutional scheme of federalism; a tolerance of divergent policies among the 50 states. . . . [4.] Knowledge of the network of nonjudicial mechanisms that safeguard against abuse of government power. . . . [and 5.] A recognition that the paramount federal judicial role is to decide on concrete cases, not gratuitously to pronounce on the constitutionality of action taken by Congress, the President, or the states.[3]

Did the Founding Fathers prescribe qualifications? Beyond James Madison's often-repeated fond wish that the bench be "happily filled," a call for meritorious designees, the framers were essentially occupied with questions of the methodology of appointments to the bench. Monday, May 14, 1787, was the date agreed upon for the opening of the Federal Constitutional Convention in the Old Independence Hall, called the State House, at Fifth and Chestnut Streets in Philadelphia. But since only two states—Virginia and Pennsylvania—were represented on that historic day, the Convention was compelled to adjourn for lack of a quorum. This procedure continued daily, until Friday, May 25, at last saw the requisite majority of the thirteen constituent states in their seats. Some four months later, on Tuesday, September 17, 1787, the Convention adjourned, having signed the historic document—the nascent Constitution of the United States—on the preceding day, highlighted by Benjamin Franklin's magnificent closing address to the assemblage (which was read for him by his fellow Pennsylvanian, James Wilson). As the most authoritative accounts, records, and interpretations of the events of that historic period demonstrate reliably—for example, James Madison's *Notes of Debates in the Federal Convention of 1787*,[4] *The Federalist*,[5] Charles Warren's *The Making of the Constitution*,[6] and Joseph P. Harris's *The Advice and Consent of the Senate*[7]—while the question of the methodology to be employed for judicial appointments was subjected to intensive floor debate during twelve days in June, July, August, and September, 1787, criteria for such appointments were not debated, nor did they appear to loom as a matter of either significance or puzzlement.

Those few delegates who vocalized the issue of judicial selection criteria at all did so by assuming *viva voice* and *sub silentio* that merit, as opposed to favoritism, should—and indeed would—govern naturally. The central issue *cum* controversy concerned the degree of power to be vested in the executive and/or the degree of legislative participation. The provision finally agreed upon as a result of debates on September 6, 7, and 15 represented a compromise between (1) those who, like Benjamin Franklin, James Madison, and John Rutledge, feared "monarchical" tendencies in strong solo executive prerogatives on the issue and thus called for a potent legislative role; and (2) those who, like James Wilson, Alexander Hamilton, and Gouverneur Morris, favored broadly independent executive appointive powers. It was the latter group that did most of the compromising, resulting in the ultimate adoption of Article II, Section 2 (which was largely fashioned by James Madison), as we know that provision today.[8]

If it may be validly considered as having been raised at all, the issue of judicial qualifications was addressed, however briefly, on June 5 by Franklin in pointing to the Scottish mode of appointment "in which the nomination proceeded from the lawyers, who always selected the ablest of the profession in order to get rid of him, and share his practice among themselves."[9] If any concern about qualifications was subsequently expressed by delegates, it came all but inevitably in connection with the controversy over the role of the participatory political branch, ultimately the agreed-upon senatorial one, about which James Madison, for one, notwithstanding his support of the legislative input, raised the question of "partiality." Delegates simply assumed, perhaps a mite naively, albeit quite understandably, that those selected as federal jurists would be chosen on the basis of merit. Period.

It is thus clear—with convenient 20/20 hindsight—that the Founding Fathers did not foresee the role political parties would soon come to play in the appointment process. Only John Adams among the notable contemporary statesmen—and he, of course, was not a member of the Constitutional Convention—visualized clearly the future rise of political parties and, as Harris put it well, "that partisan considerations rather than the fitness of nominees would often be the controlling consideration of the Senate in passing on nominations."[10] Shades of contemporary Senate postures!

Little attention was given to the matter of judicial appointments in the debates surrounding the ensuing state ratifying conventions. It was assumed as a matter of course that merit would govern. Alexander Hamilton did address the appointment power in *The Federalist*, Nos. 66, 72, 76, and 77, which render patently evident that even that supreme political cognoscenti verily championed merit. Thus, in *The Federalist*, No. 66, he expressed full confidence that the Senate, whatever its stance on a particular nominee might be, would be guided by a candidate's merit.[11] In the famed No. 76, in which Hamilton so trenchantly and approbatively elucidated the judicial function, he lauded the Senate's putative role as "an excellent check upon a spirit of favoritism in the President . . . [one that] would tend greatly to prevent the appointment of unfit characters from State prejudice, from family connection, from personal attachment, or from a view of popularity."[12]

And Hamilton's No. 77 assumed without self-doubt—and, of course, quite erroneously—that individual senators would not exert influence on presidential nominations. For he, too, quite unlike Adams, failed to foresee the influence that political parties would exert on appointments; the leverage they would provide thereby to an assertive chief executive;

and the prominent role senators would soon play in dictating nominations.[13] In sum, and notwithstanding Hamilton's interest and concerns, the debates in the state constitutional conventions paid but passing heed, if any, to the appointive arrangements in general, and judicial ones in particular. Engaged by issues of far greater moment to them in their crucial decision whether or not to ratify the handiwork of the Founding Fathers, they assumed that those appointed to the bench would be qualified.

It may be instructive—perhaps even engaging—to examine the 105 successful appointees to the Supreme Court in statistical composite. (1) Of that total 104 were men; the first of President Reagan's three was its first woman, Judge Sandra Day O'Connor of Arizona. True to his campaign promise to make such an appointment, President Reagan sent O'Connor to the magnificent Marble Palace on First Street, S.E., to succeed the retired Justice Potter Stewart in 1981. There is no doubt that a "woman's seat" has now been firmly established and that there will always be at least one of that gender on the Court henceforth. (2) In longevity, only symphony conductors among identifiable professions outscore Supreme Court Justices. Perhaps writing increases circulatory flow! (3) All Presidents through George Bush, except William Henry Harrison, Zachary Taylor, Andrew Johnson, and Jimmy Carter, have been able to send nominees to the Court, Carter being the only one among that quartet to have served a full presidential term by election. (4) History permitted George Washington to appoint fourteen, although only ten actually served. Franklin D. Roosevelt, regarded by the public as the champion "Court packer," stands in second place in frequency of appointments with nine (a figure that includes his elevation of Harlan Fiske Stone, the Court's then lone Republican, to the chief justiceship to succeed the retired Charles Evans Hughes). (5) Only a little more than one-half had prior judicial experience on either the federal or state bench or both, but many of the most illustrious had none—among them eight of the sixteen Chief Justices, including John Marshall, Roger B. Taney, Charles Evans Hughes, Harlan Fiske Stone, and Earl Warren, and such illustrious Associate Justices as Joseph Story, Louis D. Brandeis, Felix Frankfurter, Robert H. Jackson, and Lewis F. Powell, Jr. (6) The leading occupations that they held prior to their selection were those of lower federal court judge (twenty-four), followed by lower state court judge and federal office holder in the executive branch (the first in twenty-three and the second in twenty-two instances). (7) They were selected from thirty-one states, led by New York's fifteen, followed by Virginia and Ohio with nine and Massachusetts with eight. (8) The leading acknowledged religion has been Protestant, with twenty-eight Episcopalians at the top, including as the most recent Justice Souter. There have been eight Roman Catholics (including the two last Reagan appointees, Justices Scalia and Kennedy) and five Jews. (9) All appointees except Thurgood Marshall have been white. But, as is assuredly true with respect to the O'Connor appointment apropos of gender, there is simply no question that there is now a non-white seat on the Supreme Court, and that there will continue to be at least one henceforth. Finally, in this apposite statistical litany, the avowed political affiliation at the time of appointment of the 105—who filled 109 slots because of promotions—was forty-nine Democrats, forty-five Republicans, thirteen Federalists, one Whig, and one Independent.[14]

Beyond these indisputable historical statistics—which, after all, merely record a profile rather than provide a guide or mandate—it is quite possible to identify what history demonstrates as the ascertainable reasons or motivations for the presidential selection of Supreme Court Justices, and thus conceivably to provide some clues to the Court-packing syndrome. A quartet of steadily occurring criteria appears to emerge quite clearly, *pace* specific assertions or analyses to the contrary. In no particular order of avowal or numerology, that quartet embraces: (1) objective merit; (2) personal friendship; (3) balancing "representation" or "representativeness" on the Court; and (4) "real" political and ideological compatibility.[15]

Obviously, more than one of these factors—and indeed sundry others—have been present in most nominations to the Court, and in some cases all four were. Yet it is entirely possible to point to one as the overriding factor. Thus, a classic and well-known illustration of presidential selection based purely on the first category, objective merit qua merit, is that of Democrat Benjamin Nathan Cardozo by Republican Herbert Hoover to succeed Justice Holmes early in 1932. That public opinion and senatorial insistence practically had put the President on a rack to prompt him to choose Cardozo is beside the point. He did—and he would ultimately be credited for it as "the finest act of his career as President."[16]

Examples abound that point to the second category (i.e., personal and political friendships) as the overriding cause for presidential choice. Among the several illustrations that come to mind quickly—yet were nonetheless unquestionably characterized by merit—are President Andrew Jackson's selections of Roger Brooke Taney for Associate Justice (unsuccessful) and Chief Justice (successful). Taney had been Jackson's longtime close friend, loyal adviser, and confidant. All of President Truman's appointments fall into this category, as do those by Taft of Horace H. Lurton and by Lyndon B. Johnson of Abe Fortas.

The third category, the representation or representativeness of a putative selectee, has become increasingly prevalent. Thus, such representative or "equitable" factors as race, gender, religion, and geography never fail to be advanced as a major consideration, sometimes as the controlling one. Among a host of illustrations are the recent selections of Thurgood Marshall (race) and Sandra Day O'Connor (gender) by Presidents Lyndon Johnson and Reagan, respectively; President Lincoln's fruitful search for "an outstanding trans-Mississippi lawyer" (whom he found in Samuel F. Miller); President Cleveland's insistence upon "geographic appropriateness" in the person of his new Chief Justice, Melville Fuller of Illinois; and President McKinley's choice of Joseph McKenna (religion).

The fourth, political and ideological compatibility, may well be *the* controlling factor, and it is here that what is generally viewed as Court packing occurs. Indeed, political and ideological compatibility has been demonstrably present in a large majority of instances, and understandably so. One of the legion of examples was President Harding's selection (inspired by Chief Justice Taft) of ex–U.S. senator and congressman George Sutherland from Utah—one of the very few of foreign birth (England) to reach the Court. An experienced lawyer as well as legislator, Sutherland began his alliance with Harding when the two served together in the U.S. Senate, the association culminating in the role of "brain truster" to the President. He could have had any position in the latter's administration, but he preferred to accept spot troubleshooting assignments at home and abroad—in the frank anticipation of a Court vacancy. It came in 1922. Had President Reagan's 1987 nomination of Judge Robert H. Bork succeeded, it would have been a pertinent contemporary illustration—and the subsequent choice of Judge Anthony M. Kennedy assuredly is.

Now, to Court packing qua court packing: Whatever the merits of the other criteria attending presidential motivations in appointments may be, what must be of overriding concern to any nominator is his perception of the candidate's "real" politics. The chief executive's crucial predictive judgment concerns itself with the nominee's likely future voting pattern on the bench, based on his past stance and commitment on matters of public policy insofar as they are reliably discernible. All Presidents have tried thus to pack the bench to a greater or lesser extent. An illuminating illustration is President Kennedy's selection of his longtime friend and ideological kinsman, Deputy Attorney General Byron J. White, to fill the first vacancy on the Court during his brief administration. As *Washington Star* reporter James E. Clayton reported the decision:

> Thinking back on the process months later, the Attorney General [Robert F. Kennedy] tilted back his chair and said: "You wanted someone who generally agreed with you on what role government should play in American life, what role the individual in society should have. You didn't think about how he would vote in a reapportionment case or a criminal case. You wanted someone who,

in the long run, you believe would be doing what you thought was best. You wanted someone who agreed generally with your views of the country." Both he and the President believed that White and Arthur J. Goldberg met that test. They could not be as sure of the others on the list [Paul A. Freund of Harvard University and Judge William H. Hastie of the U.S. Court of Appeals for the Third Circuit].[17]

In the public eye, Court packing has been most closely associated with Franklin D. Roosevelt. Having had not a single opportunity to fill a Court vacancy in his first term (1933–37), and seeing his domestic programs consistently battered by the Court, the frustrated President attempted to get his way all at once. His "Court-packing bill," however, died a deserved death in the Senate by being recommitted.

It is not surprising that Court packing and the name of President Roosevelt have become synonymous. Yet even such popular heroes as Jefferson, Jackson, and Lincoln followed similar courses of action in the face of what they considered "judicial intransigence and defiance." Their approach was not as radical as Roosevelt's, but they very likely would have been sympathetic to his efforts. George Washington, although broadly regarded as far removed from "politics," had insisted that his fourteen nominees to the Court meet a veritable smorgasbord of qualifications. There were seven, to be exact, and he adhered to them religiously: (1) support and advocacy of the Constitution; (2) distinguished service in the Revolution; (3) active participation in the political life of state or nation; (4) prior judicial experience on lower tribunals; (5) either a "favorable reputation with his fellows" or personal ties with Washington himself; (6) geographic "suitability"; and (7) "love of our country."[18] Of these criteria, evidently the most important to him was advocacy of the principles of the Constitution—the more outspoken the better. Perhaps more than many of his contemporaries he recognized the potential strength and influence of the judicial branch, keenly sensing the role it would be called on to play in spelling out constitutional basics and penumbras. In letters of commission to his initial six nominees to the first Supreme Court in September and October of 1789, he wrote: "The Judicial System is the chief Pillar upon which our national Government must rest." That pillar needed strong men—proponents of the Federalist philosophy of government. Indeed, seven of those the President sent to the bench had been participants in the Constitutional Convention of 1787. He knew most, if not all, of his appointees intimately.

In fact, every President who has made nominations to the Supreme Court has been guilty of Court packing in some measure. It is entirely understandable that a President will choose those who will share his own philosophy of government and politics, at least to the extent of giving him a sympathetic hearing. Theodore Roosevelt, for example, in discussing the potential candidacy of Horace H. Lurton with Henry Cabot Lodge, put the issue well:

> The nominal politics of the man has nothing to do with his actions on the bench. His real politics are all important.... He is right on the Negro question; he is right on the power of the federal government; he is right on the Insular business; he is right about corporations, and he is right about labor. On every question that would come before the bench, he has so far shown himself to be in much closer touch with the policies in which you and I believe than even [Associate Justice Edward D.] White because he has been right about corporations where White has been wrong.[19]

Lodge concurred in substance, but he replied that he could see no reason "why Republicans cannot be found who hold those opinions as well as Democrats."[20] Consequently, he strongly urged the candidacy of a Republican, whom Roosevelt then duly nominated—William H. Moody, Attorney General of Massachusetts.

Thus, concern with a nominee's real politics is a fundamental issue, and examples abound. It prompted Republican Taft to give half of his six appointments to Democrats who were kindred souls, Republican Nixon to appoint Democrat Powell, Democrat Roosevelt to promote Republican Stone, and Democrat Truman to appoint Republican Burton. Yet there is no guarantee that what a President perceives as real politics will not fade into a mirage. Hence, Charles Warren, eminent chronicler of the Court, observed that "nothing is more striking in the history of the Court than the manner in which the hopes of those who expected a judge to follow the political views of the President appointing him are disappointed."[21]

Few have felt the truth of that statement more keenly than Teddy Roosevelt did with Oliver Wendell Holmes, Jr., whose early "anti-administration" opinions in antitrust cases (notably in *Northern Securities v. United States*)[22] were entirely unexpected. A bare 5 to 4 majority in that case upheld the government's order under the Sherman Anti-Trust Act, dissolving the Northern Securities Company, brainchild of E. H. Harriman and J. J. Hill, the wealthy and powerful owners of competing railroads who had organized the company in order to secure a terminal line into Chicago. Roosevelt had won that important litigation, but he was furious about his recent appointee's "anti-antitrust" vote in the case. He stormed: "I could carve out of a banana a judge with more backbone than that!"[23] Holmes reportedly merely smiled when told the President's remark, referred to him as "a shallow intellect," and noted his intentions to "call the shots as I see them in terms of the legal and constitutional setting." Later, during Roosevelt's second term of office (1905–1909), Holmes expressed his sentiments to a labor leader at a White House dinner: "What you want is favor, not justice. But when I am on my job, I don't give a damn what you or Mr. Roosevelt want."[24]

James Madison, having refused to heed his political mentor, Thomas Jefferson, was similarly chagrined with his appointment of Justice Joseph Story. Jefferson had warned him that Story was an inveterate Tory who would become a rabid supporter of Chief Justice Marshall, and he was right: Story not only instantly joined Marshall's approach to constitutional adjudication and interpretation, but he even out-Marshalled Marshall in his nationalism. Perhaps even more chagrined was Woodrow Wilson when his appointee James C. McReynolds proved himself at once to be the antithesis of almost everything his nominator stood for and believed in.

More recently, Harry Truman observed that "... packing the Supreme Court simply can't be done.... I've tried and it won't work.... Whenever you put a man on the Supreme Court he ceases to be your friend. I'm sure of that. Lord knows I've tried!"[25] And he had. But not only did he fail to be pleased in his expectations, he appointed a group of four that would not make the list of "greats" or "near-greats" on any of the several formal ratings or rankings of Supreme Court Justices: Burton, Vinson, Clark, and Minton.[26] Ironically, Truman reserved his most bitter attack of "non-support" for the best of the four, his one-time Attorney General, Tom C. Clark. The President was furious with Clark for his "anti-Truman" vote in the Steel Seizure Case of 1952.[27] There, in a carefully crafted concurring opinion, Clark joined five other colleagues in disallowing Truman's seizure of the struck steel mills; all six, in diverse compass, objected to executive usurpation of legislative authority in the presence of ascertainable congressional intent. Truman was not amused; in fact, he was livid, calling Clark "[t]hat damn fool from Texas" and "my biggest mistake," adding, "well, it isn't so much that he is a *bad* man. It's just that he is such a dumb son of a bitch. He's about the dumbest man I think I have ever run across."[28] Clark was hurt, but the deep personal friendship between the two men continued, their closeness apparently unaffected.

The story of President Dwight D. Eisenhower's disenchantment with two of his five appointees, Chief Justice Earl Warren and Associate Justice William J. Brennan, Jr., is well known. Sparring with reporters aboard Air Force One on one of his last days in office, Ike was asked whether he had ever committed any serious mistakes in office. "Oh sure," he replied. "Yes, Mr. President, but did you ever make any 'beauts,' Sir?" "Yep," he intoned, "and they are both on the Supreme Court!" His reference was to Warren and Brennan.

His successor, Richard M. Nixon, was initially delighted with the voting pattern of the second of his four appointees, Associate Justice Harry Blackmun, whom the press soon derisively dubbed "the Minnesota twin" because he was so frequently recorded on the same side as his close old personal friend and fellow Minnesotan, Chief Justice Warren Burger. But gradually—or, indeed, not so gradually—Blackmun began to assert his independence and commenced a steady journey to the liberal or left side of the Court, where he became a now usually predictable ally (except in certain criminal justice cases) of Justices Brennan, Marshall, and, recently, Stevens. Nixon filled the air with expletives after the controversial Blackmun-authored opinion in the 1973 abortion cases of *Roe v. Wade* and *Doe v. Bolton.*[29] Nixon had been similarly disenchanted with Justice Lewis F. Powell, Jr.'s surprise authorship, for his unanimous brethren, in *United States v. United States District Court for the Eastern District of Michigan* in 1972,[30] just shortly after the Virginia Brahmin had joined the Court. As a private citizen Powell had publicly supported the Nixon administration's claim of constitutional authority for wiretapping of radical domestic groups without a warrant; yet when the issue reached the Court, the Powell opinion declared that contention and practice to be an unconstitutional invasion of Fourth Amendment guarantees as well as being unauthorized under the applicable statute. And, of course, Nixon did not garner a single supportive vote in the Court's unanimous (8 to 0) ruling against him in *United States v. Nixon*,[31] also known as the Nixon Tapes Case of 1974, including the votes by Nixon appointees Burger, Blackmun, and Powell (Justice Rehnquist having recused himself).

Well, then, can our chief executives really pack the Court? The tentative, perhaps equivocal, answer suggested here is both "yes" and "no." To the extent that a President can reliably ascertain his nominees' "real politics" (to re-utilize the fortunate Theodore Roosevelt–Henry Cabot Lodge term), the answer is affirmative. Examples are legion—not perhaps 100 percent (what is?), yet with a comfortable degree of majoritarian reliability. FDR needed to be certain of a person who would supply a "safe" vote for his New Deal program when he at last gained a vacancy in 1937: He took no chances whatsoever with Senator Hugo Lafayette Black of Alabama. Nor did he with William O. Douglas. Ike's selection of New York's patrician John Marshall Harlan was similarly safe. So was Lyndon B. Johnson's of Thurgood Marshall. So was Richard Nixon's of Chief Justice Warren Burger. With some qualifications, so was President Ronald Reagan's choice of Sandra Day O'Connor—although she has manifested some interesting departures from the proverbial reservation. His appointment of Antonin Scalia and that of Anthony Kennedy—following the dramatic rejection of his controversial nominee, Robert Bork—have generally lived up to his administration's expectations.

Nothing is certain, however, and examples of assertions of judicial independence abound even among those appointments that can be categorized as generally safe. As a rule, most, albeit not all, presidents have had reason to be more or less satisfied. To at least some degree Court packing is plausible, even if only marginally. Yet the presence of major "anti-nominator" on-Court stances—as, for example, Eisenhower's appointees Warren and Brennan; Nixon's Blackmun; Madison's Story; and Wilson's James Clark Reynolds—tempers that earlier judgment. Tempers, yes; but arguably, in each of these admittedly extreme "anti-nominator" instances, more careful, more reflective, more assiduous prenomination research might well have cast considerable doubt on the nomination's political safeness or wisdom. Thus, Ike had been warned about Warren's progressivism; Madison's mentor, Thomas Jefferson, had told him that Story would "out-Marshall" Marshall—and he assuredly did; Wilson had had ample opportunity to observe his cabinet member McReynold's mercurial characteristics. The more intriguing, and far less clear, instances of attempted Court packing gone awry are the very considerable number in which the yeasty independence of a Justice's on-bench existence releases the kind of unpredictable and nominator-maddening votes that have been delivered by many a Justice (e.g., John Marshall Harlan, the Elder; Holmes; Stanley Reed; Felix Frankfurter; White; Blackmun; and Powell).

Future Presidents may be well advised to heed the admonition of Zecharia Chafee, Harvard's famed expert on the judicial process, who contended that to forecast the behavior of a future jurist it is wiser to consider the books in his library than the list of clients in his office. That may or may not serve as a yardstick. It is not quite so simple. Yet there is indeed a considerable element of unpredictability in the judicial appointing process, and so be it. To the often-heard "Does a person become any different when he puts on a gown?", Justice Frankfurter's sharp retort was always, "If he is any good, he does!" In the words of Alexander M. Bickel, "You shoot an arrow into a far-distant future when you appoint a Justice and not the man himself can tell you what he will think about some of the problems that he will face."[32] And late in 1969, reflecting on his sixteen years as Chief Justice of the United States, Earl Warren pointed out that he, for one, did not "see how a man could be on the Court and not change his views substantially over a period of years . . . for change you must if you are to do your duty on the Supreme Court."[33] It is a duty that, in many ways, represents the most hallowed in the governmental process of the United States.

NOTES

1. S. Goldman, "Judicial Selection and the Qualities that Make a 'Good' Judge," 462 *Annals* 112 (1982).

2. Abraham, "Address," Restored Supreme Court Chamber, U.S. Capitol,

April 30, 1982. Somewhat shortened and adapted, the address was published in 66 *Judicature* 7 (1983).

3. B. Fein, *National Journal*, July 6, 1985, p. 1563.

4. Introduction by Adrienne Koch (1966).

5. H. Lodge, ed., *The Federalist* (1888).

6. (1937).

7. (1953).

8. J. Madison, *Notes of the Debates in the Federal Convention of 1787* (1966), pp. 67–68; 112–13; 314–17; 343–46; 517; 525; 575.

9. *Id.*, pp. 67–68.

10. J. Harris, *The Advice and Consent of the Senate*, pp. 28–30; 34.

11. *The Federalist*, pp. 416–17.

12. *Id.*, pp. 474–75.

13. *Id.*, pp. 476–80.

14. For a detailed analysis, see Abraham, *Justices and Presidents: A Political History of Appointments to the Supreme Court* (2d ed. 1985).

15. See Abraham, *The Judicial Process: An Introductory Analysis of the Courts of the United States, England, and France* (5th ed. 1985).

16. *New York Times*, March 2, 1932, quoting Senator Clarence Dill (R.-Wash.).

17. As quoted in J. Clayton, *The Making of Justice: The Supreme Court in Action* (1964), p. 52.

18. Abraham, *Justices and Presidents*, pp. 71–72.

19. 2 H. Lodge, *Selections from the Correspondence of Theodore Roosevelt and Henry Cabot Lodge, 1884–1918* (1925), pp. 228; 230; 241.

20. *Id.*, p. 229.

21. 2 C. Warren, *The Supreme Court in United States History* (rev. ed. 1926), p. 22.

22. 193 U.S. 197 (1904).

23. As quoted by Clayton, *The Making of Justice*, p. 47.

24. As quoted by Arthur Krock, *New York Times*, October 19, 1971, p. 43.

25. H. Truman, Lecture at Columbia University, New York, N.Y., October 19, 1971.

26. See Appendix A in Abraham, *Justices and Presidents*, pp. 377–79.

27. *Youngstown v. Sawyer*, 343 U.S. 579 (1952).

28. Quoted by Merle Miller in his oral history biography of Truman, *Plain Speaking* (1974), p. 242. Margaret Truman Daniel has consistently challenged the authenticity of the quote, yet it is widely reported and would appear to be accurate.

29. 410 U.S. 113 and 410 U.S. 179 (1973), respectively.

30. 407 U.S. 297 (1972).

31. 418 U.S. 683 (1974).

32. As quoted in *Time* magazine, May 23, 1969, p. 24.

33. Comment to Anthony Lewis, "A Talk with Warren on Crime, the Court, and the Country." *New York Times Magazine*, October 19, 1969, pp. 128–29.

3

The Office of Solicitor General: Political Appointee, Advocate, and Officer of the Court

Rex E. Lee

This chapter is about a law firm. It has the world's most interesting cases and is, on balance, the world's most attractive place to practice law. It is not a very big firm. Presently it has about twenty lawyers, and at times it has had only one. It has always had high-quality lawyers; probably no other firm anywhere has as much talent, lawyer for lawyer. It is unlike other good firms, however, in its high rate of attrition; most of its lawyers leave after about two to five years in the office. This law firm is highly specialized. It does only appellate work; its lawyers appear in only one court—the Supreme Court; and they have only one client.

The firm is the Office of Solicitor General of the United States. And it is more than just a law firm. It is also an important institution of government. The "senior partner" in this firm not only has exclusive rights of representation of all U.S. interests in the United States. That individual—and not the department heads whose cases are involved—also decides which cases the government will ask the Supreme Court to review, and his or her approval is required before any federal litigant can appeal a case it has lost in any court. This includes, for example, appeals from federal district courts to courts of appeals.

First, this chapter will discuss how the office came into existence. Then it will mention some of the peculiar functions and problems of the office.

The history of the Office of Solicitor General actually begins at least eight decades before that office came into existence. It begins with the

Solicitor General's boss, the Attorney General. The Attorney General was one of the first four Cabinet offices established by the first Congress. But the Attorney General differed from the other three Cabinet officers in several respects that are germane to this discussion. First, his office was created by the Judiciary Act of 1789. Thus, while the Attorney General is beyond question a member of the executive branch of government, from the very beginning the closeness of his office and his function to the Article III branch has been reflected in the statutes. A second difference, of lesser relevance but nonetheless interesting, is that the Attorney General's annual salary of $1,500 was half that of the other Cabinet officers. The assumption was that this was appropriate because he would continue to carry on a private practice.

The Judiciary Act of 1789 required that the Attorney General be "[a] meet person, learned in the law," whose statutory duties were "(1) to prosecute and conduct all suits in the Supreme Court in which the United States shall be concerned, and (2) to give his advice and opinion upon questions of law when required by the President of the United States, or when requested by the heads of any of the departments, touching any matters that may concern their departments."[1]

Thus, from the beginning, the Attorney General's first responsibility, identified by statute, was to represent the United States in the Supreme Court. In those early years that was not quite the demanding task that it is today. The Court did not render a decision on the merits until 1792.[2]

The very first case of very great importance to come before the Supreme Court[3] was *Chisholm v. Georgia*.[4] That case, appropriately enough, was argued by the very first Attorney General, Edmund Randolph. But he argued it in his private capacity, not as Attorney General. Indeed, he represented the non-governmental client, Chisholm, and helped convince the Justices the states could be sued in the federal courts—a point which the people reversed by the Eleventh Amendment to the Constitution.[5] Easby-Smith, in "Edmund Randolph, Trailblazer," wrote that

> Randolph made a brilliant argument in support of his motion [to enter a default judgment against Georgia, which did not appear] and the Supreme Court sustained all his contentions, holding that under the second section of Article III of the Constitution a State might be sued by an individual citizen of any other State, and in such suit judgment might be entered in default of an appearance. The argument of Randolph and the decision of the court brought down upon both a shower of abuse from the anti-federalists throughout the country, and in answer to popular clamor the Congress, on December 2nd, 1793, adopted the Eleventh Amendment to the Constitution, which was subsequently ratified.[6]

Perhaps the foremost case from the early years is *McCulloch v. Maryland*.[7] That case, argued by Attorney General William Wirt,[8] with assistance from Daniel Webster, established the fundamental proposition that the powers of Congress are not to be construed narrowly. Chief Justice Marshall wrote for the Court: "Let the end be legitimate, let it be within the scope of the constitution, and all means which are appropriate, which are plainly adapted to that end, which are not prohibited . . . are constitutional."[9]

To those whose personal acquaintance with the Justice Department is limited to this century, it is astounding to learn that for the first twenty-seven years those early Attorneys General performed their tasks with no help of any kind. Not even a clerk. Randolph described himself in 1790 as "a sort of mongrel between the State and U.S.; called an officer of some rank under the latter, and yet thrust out to get a livelihood in the former."[10] Apparently the first request for a clerk came from Randolph in a letter to President Washington dated December 26, 1791:

> I might . . . add, that the opinions which the Attorney General gives are many in number and often lengthy. From this consideration, united with the foregoing, the reasonableness of allowing him a transcribing clerk will, I hope, be obvious.[11]

President Washington sent Randolph's letter to Congress, but to no avail. "Congress took no action. Twenty-seven years elapsed before any allowance was made for a clerk."[12] The difficulties faced by the early Attorneys General can be appreciated from Easby-Smith's account:

> No quarters were provided for the Attorney General, and he was expected to furnish his own quarters, fuel, stationery, and clerk. For this reason the Attorneys General after [Charles] Lee [who succeeded William Bradford, Randolph's successor who died in 1795] and until 1814 did not reside permanently in Washington, but remained at their homes and transmitted their advice and opinions by mail, going to Washington only when it became necessary to appear before the Supreme Court.[13]

It was not until 1853 that Congress finally established a salary for the Attorney General equivalent to that of the other Cabinet officers, thereby bringing to an end the tradition of part-time Attorneys General who kept up a private law practice.[14]

At the end of the Civil War, the nation's legal business, and consequently the demands on the Attorney General, increased manyfold. The aftermath of the Civil War marks the single point in our nation's history when the place of federal law vis-à-vis the laws of the states experienced its greatest expansion. Homer Cummings and Carl McFarland, in their book *Federal Justice*, describe the situation as follows:

> As the war came to a close and reconstruction began, the legal business of the government increased. In April 1866, James Speed, who had been Attorney General for less than a year and a half, had written nearly as many opinions as

his predecessor had written during three years. For many months the employees in his office worked more than double the official number of hours, and Sundays and holidays were unknown to them.[15]

In December 1867, Attorney General Stanbery was asked by the Senate to report on the affairs of his office, and he responded:

As to the mere administrative business of the office, the present force is sufficient, but as to the proper duties of the Attorney General, especially in the preparation and argument of cases before the Supreme Court of the United States and the preparation of opinions on questions of law referred to him some provision is absolutely necessary to enable him properly to discharge his duties. After much reflection, it seems to me that this want may best be supplied by the appointment of a Solicitor General. With such an assistant, the necessity of appointing special counsel in the argument of cases in the Supreme Court of the United States, would be, in a great measure, if not altogether dispensed with.[16]

Stanbery's letter appears to contain the first mention of the term "Solicitor General." The name, like so much else in the U.S. legal system, is of English origin. At first glance that seems strange, given the well-known distinction between English barristers and solicitors, and the equally well-known fact that the dominant characteristic of the solicitor is that he is the fellow who does not appear in court. Further research discloses, however, that the phrase is of ancient origin, and that for at least two reasons it fairly aptly describes the relationship that Stanbery envisioned the Solicitor General of the United States would bear to the Attorney General.

In the early common law, the parties prosecuted their own suits and had to be present at all legal proceedings. "The idea that one man can represent another is foreign to early law. When first it is introduced it is regarded as an exceptional privilege, and the first representative must be solemnly appointed."[17] Only gradually were agents allowed to appear for the parties to represent their interests in litigation.[18] These were "attorneys."

A "solicitor," as Holdsworth explains, was a legal practitioner, similar to an attorney, whose earliest function appears to have been to assist the attorney in the preparation of cases for litigation. Solicitors were defined in 1589 as persons who, " 'being learned in the Laws, and informed of their Master's Cause, do inform and instruct the Counsellors in the same.' "[19] Originally nothing more than a servant or agent of the attorney or his client, the solicitor came into his own, professionally speaking, with the rise of non–common-law courts—especially the Court of Chancery, where attorneys, who were authorized to practice only in common-law courts, could not appear.[20] Given their humble origins as attorneys' assistants, solicitors were long regarded as " 'but ministerial persons and of an inferior nature.' "[21] In 1750, solicitors were finally given admission as attorneys, and "[f]rom that time onwards we can say that this new class of practitioners has become substantially amalgamated with the attorneys."[22]

Similarly, the English Solicitor General, both originally and also today, was and is one who assists the Attorney General in the discharge of his responsibilities. In the English system, which is a parliamentary system, both are members of Parliament and are "law officer" members of the Cabinet. Thus, while there are necessarily differences in their functions, owing principally to the differences between parliamentary and separation of powers systems of government, the significant similarity is that on both sides of the Atlantic, the Attorney General was and is the nation's chief legal officer, and the Office of Solicitor General was created to assist him in that task.

As Stanberry's letter suggests, the practice of hiring private counsel to argue the government's cases had been growing in the post-war years. In 1867 alone, the Attorney General reported, the government had spent more than $6,000 for such services.[23] Thus, it was partly out of frugality,[24] and not entirely out of concern for the effectiveness of the Attorney General's operations, that Congress in 1870 enacted legislation establishing the Department of Justice and creating the Office of Solicitor General. The Act provided in part that

> there shall be in said Department an officer learned in the law, to assist the Attorney General in the performance of his duties, to be called the Solicitor General, and who, in case of a vacancy in the office of Attorney General, or in his absence or disability, shall have power to exercise all the duties of that office.[25]

The distinction between the responsibilities of the Attorney General and the Solicitor General appears not to have been as cleanly defined in the early years as it is today. The evidence is strong that the first two Solicitors General—Benjamin Bristow, who served from 1870 to 1872, and Samuel Phillips, who served from 1872 to 1885 (longer than any other Solicitor General)—probably functioned more as the Attorney General's Chief Deputy, with no particular responsibility for any one phase of the Attorney General's work. At that time, duties were not narrowly defined, as they are today, as the chief—or indeed (acting under supervision of the Attorney General) exclusive—Supreme Court litigator for the United States. Several facts support this general conclusion.

First, far from having the near-monopoly enjoyed by their modern counterparts over Supreme Court litigation, early Solicitors General shared this responsibility in about equal portions with the Attorneys General and with the Assistant Attorneys General. This early practice—and the extent to which special counsel were displaced by regular government counsel after the creation of the Office of Solicitor General—

can be seen from the following statistics. In the Supreme Court's unusually heavy December 1866 Term,[26] some twenty-four cases were argued by the Attorney General, either alone or with the help of an assistant, and roughly five cases by the Attorney General with the help of what appears to have been outside counsel. Another sixteen cases were argued alone by assistants to the Attorney General and two by special counsel, also arguing alone.[27] In the 1867 Term,[28] there were about thirteen cases argued by the Attorney General, some with help from assistants; and, as it appears from the reports, another four with help from special counsel. Nine additional cases were argued by the Attorney General's assistants, and two by special counsel arguing alone. The December 1868 Term showed a similar pattern: eighteen cases argued by the Attorney General and/or his assistants, four by special counsel (two with the Attorney General and two without). There was an apparent increase in the use of special counsel in the 1869 Term,[29] when eighteen cases were argued by the Attorney General and/or his assistants, and fifteen with some apparent involvement of outside counsel.

The picture begins to change a bit in the December 1870 Term,[30] when the Solicitor General first appeared on the scene. The nature of the change can be best understood against the background of a fundamental difference between nineteenth-century oral arguments and today's experience. Today, the sharing of arguments by several lawyers representing the same client is virtually nonexistent. The Court still hears divided arguments, but only when the oral advocates represent different clients in the same case. A hundred years ago, however, arguments lasted for many hours, sometimes days, and dividing the oral presentation for a single client was common.

In only two cases during the 1870 Term did special counsel assist in arguing the federal government's case, as compared with thirteen cases argued by the new Solicitor General, Benjamin Bristow (three by Bristow alone, five shared with Attorney General Ackerman, and five shared with Assistant Attorneys General). Another seven cases were argued by the Attorney General and/or the Assistant Attorneys General without the Solicitor General's involvement. In the December 1871 Term,[31] Bristow came more into his own, arguing some twenty-six cases (seven solo, five with the Attorney General, and fifteen with the Assistant Attorneys General). Special counsel was used only once that term. In the December 1872 Term[32] (the last of the December terms, 1873 being the first of the October terms), there is not trace of special counsel in the reports, but Bristow, too, was gone, and his successor, Samuel F. Phillips, had been in office only long enough to argue some seven cases.[33] The Attorney General and his assistants carried the load that term, with some thirty arguments among them.

These numbers seem to show that at least in those very early days the

Solicitor General, while an actor of some importance in the Supreme Court, shared the honors to a greater degree than we have come to expect today with the Attorney General and Assistant Attorneys General. Moreover, a quick spot check of the records of the government's briefs and motions in the Supreme Court in the late 1800s and early 1900s reveals a surprising number of submissions bearing the names of Attorneys General or Assistant Attorneys General and *not* the Solicitors General. It appears not to have been standard practice to stamp the imprimatur of the Solicitor General on all submissions until roughly the 1920s, judging by a very unscientific survey of the old, dusty books in the Justice Department's attic.

The different relationship of Attorney General to Solicitor General is also reflected in the $7,500 salary. During the term immediately preceding Bristow's appointment, the government paid $6,000 for outside counsel. Thus, it is fair to infer a congressional anticipation that this new person at the Justice Department would have responsibilities other than Supreme Court litigation. And thus it came to pass. In 1871, Bristow went to Oxford, Mississippi, to help prosecute Ku Klux Klan members under the Enforcement Act of 1870.[34] These prosecutions were apparently very important in combating the terrorism of the Klan at a time when state authorities in the South were powerless to do so, as is reflected by the fact that the task was vested personally in the Justice Department's second-ranking law officer.

Today, the distinction between the Attorney General and the Solicitor General is much more cleanly defined. It has been defined by 120 years of history and also by formal Department of Justice regulation. Neither in 1870 nor in any subsequent enactment has Congress ever specified any Supreme Court litigation responsibilities—nor any other responsibilities—for the Solicitor General. Then as now, he is required to assist the Attorney General but is given no statutory responsibility.[35]

One hundred and twenty years of history have pretty well taken the Attorney General out of the business of arguing cases for the United States in the Supreme Court and have vested that responsibility exclusively in the Solicitor General, subject to whatever supervision the Attorney General wants to assert. But those same 120 years have also preserved the original basic relationship between the two. The Solicitor General does what he does in the context of assisting the Attorney General, who has the statutory responsibility for all litigation on behalf of the United States, and who was arguing cases in the Supreme Court eight decades before there was a Solicitor General of the United States.

Since Benjamin Bristow took the oath of office in 1870, thirty-nine men have held the office of Solicitor General of the United States. The longest tenure, thirteen years, belongs to Samuel F. Phillips, who succeeded Bristow, and the shortest, about three months, belongs to Walter J. Cummings, Jr., formerly Chief Judge of the United States Court of Appeals for the Seventh Circuit. Most of the thirty-nine have been easterners. Only five have come from states west of the Mississippi. The list includes some interesting people. Among them are a President, four U.S. Supreme Court Justices, and a defeated candidate for President.[36]

Over the 120 years of its existence, the Solicitor General's office has not only become a specialized and successful law firm, it is also an important institution of government. Its special status as a law firm and as a governmental entity is rooted in the unique relationship it enjoys with the Court where its lawyers practice. Its continuing professional success as well as its continuing stature depend on striking just the right balance between, and reaching the right accommodation of, the Solicitor General's two roles. These two roles are (1) advocate for his clients and causes, some of which are quite political, and (2) officer of the Supreme Court.

The Solicitor General is a litigating advocate. He represents clients, and his job is to win cases in a way that best serves the interests of those clients. More than that, he is a presidential appointee, a member of the executive branch team. He can make a contribution toward implementing the program of the President who appointed him. It is a contribution that no one else can make because as long as he holds the office, no one else—not even other persons appointed by the President—appears in the Supreme Court representing any federal client.

One of the President's most important powers is the power of appointment, including the power to appoint the person who will serve as steward over the government's Supreme Court advocacy. And the success of any president's program depends in large part on his selection of persons who will direct particular programs implementing the purposes for which he was elected.

A President who wants to implement policy changes must do so principally through changes in—or incremental additions to—existing law. One of the ways that this can be done is through changes in statutes. Another is through changes in administrative regulations and procedures. Much of the law in our country, however, is made by the courts. Ostensibly, this is accomplished by interpretation of other substantive law sources—statutes, regulations, and the Constitution. But even if the courts were scrupulously faithful (and often they are not) to the judicial duty to interpret the will of the Constitution makers, or the legislators, or the regulation draftsmen, they nevertheless would not be free of the duty to make law. The reason is that many of the laws that the judge is called upon to interpret in carrying out his or her constitutional obligation to decide cases or controversies are so broad in scope and general in terms that interpretation requires filling in some of the details. Not only the opportunity but also the responsibility for judicial lawmaking are thus created in part by the policymakers themselves when they build ambiguity into the written provision that the judges must interpret.

The highest authority in this judicial lawmaking process is the U.S. Supreme Court. The person vested with the exclusive authority to advance the administration's arguments before the Court occupies a crucial position: As long as he or she holds the office, no one else can appear before the nation's highest court as advocate for the programs of the nation's chief executive. One of the Solicitor General's two roles, therefore, is that of advocate for his clients. Those clients include the President who appointed him. They also include other presidential appointees whose programs may depend in substantial part on their being defended in the Supreme Court. It necessarily follows that the Solicitor General has a duty to advance the President's programs by defending them in the Supreme Court. His responsibility to the President who appointed him demands as much.

He also has a responsibility to the court before which he practices. The relationship between the U.S. Supreme Court and the Solicitor General is not only important, it is unique. It is a relationship for which there is no counterpart between any other court and any other lawyer in the world. First, in no other court of general jurisdiction does one law firm appear in over half of its cases.[37] Second, no other court, as a regular matter, seeks the views of a lawyer who practices before the court in cases not involving that lawyer's client.[38] Third, the national average for persuading the Supreme Court to grant certiorari is less than 3 percent and the national average for success in cases the Court takes is 50 percent. The Solicitor General's average in both of these categories is in the 70 percent range. Fourth, while every member of the Supreme Court Bar is an officer of that Court, only six are so listed in the United States Reports. Four of the six are Court employees. The other two are executive branch officers who for the better part of two centuries have advocated the government's causes before the Supreme Court: the Attorney General, and the man who for 120 years has served as the Supreme Court equivalent of the Attorney General's designated hitter.

Beyond these specific examples there is a widely held—and probably substantially accurate—impression that the Solicitor General's office provides the Court with advocacy that is more objective, dispassionate, competent, helpful, and respectful of the Court as an institution than is true of Supreme Court practitioners as a whole. In return, the office enjoys a stature and credibility unmatched by other lawyers. Of the tens of thousands of officers of the Supreme Court, this office stands alone.

In the great majority of instances these two roles—officer of the Court and advocate for a client—are not only mutually compatible, but mutually enhancing. Three examples support this conclusion. The first is quite obvious. An advocate who enjoys the special status that the Solicitor General has with the Supreme Court is bound to be taken seriously by the Court, and that, in turn, should lead to greater success. Over the long run, therefore, the single most important factor contributing to the success of a president's litigating objectives is the preservation of the Solicitor General's unique standing with the Supreme Court.

A second example concerns the restraint traditionally exercised by Solicitors General in taking the government's cases to the Supreme Court for review. Each term the Court decides about 150–160 cases on the merits, after full briefing and oral argument. Roughly 40 percent of these, about sixty, are federal government cases. Selecting those sixty cases involves some screening by the Court, but even more by the government itself. And the key screener—the final screener—is the person required by statute to be learned in the law. Given the government's success rate at the certiorari/jurisdiction statement stage (about 70 percent), and allowing for the fact that a few government cases will be taken over by the government's opposition, the Solicitor General each year will file about 70–80 petitions for certiorari and jurisdictional statements. Those filings represent a culling from requests by clients—departments, agencies, commission, U.S. attorneys, and litigating divisions within the Department of Justice that have lost cases before the lower courts—amounting to five or six times that number. In other words, for every time the Solicitor General accedes to a request to seek Supreme Court review, he says no about five times.

What if he said no less often? What if he doubled or tripled the number of government petitions for certiorari? Or what if he started applying the same standards as most private practitioners: As long as the legal arguments are respectable, and the client understands the risks and is willing to pay the costs, the lawyer will file.

Probably, over the short run, a dramatic increase in the number of certiorari petitions filed by the government would result in an increase in the number of government cases taken for review. This would mean that the government would consume a larger share of the Supreme Court's decisional capacity. But it is equally likely that over the longer run—probably not much more than two or three years—the government's share of the Court's merits cases would settle back to about where it is now. It might even go a little lower because of the Court's diminished confidence in the Solicitor General's assurances. The net result would be harmful to both the Article II and the Article III branches of our government. The harm to the executive branch would be that the screening of its cases would be performed by the judiciary rather than the executive. The executive would therefore lose the opportunity to make comparative judgments concerning which cases are more important and which are less important to the President's program. The harm to the judicial branch would be a significant additional drain on the Supreme Court's resources.

There would also be another, more subtle, loss to both branches—the Supreme Court's diminished confidence in the lawyer who appears before it with greatest frequency and represents the largest, and most important, consumer of its resources. Because the Solicitor General is not only a Supreme Court litigator but also an official in the same government of which the Supreme Court is part, his duties include a shared responsibility with the Court itself for the optimum allocation of the Court's limited capacity to decide cases.

The third example pertains more to narrow interests of the administration currently in office. All other things being equal, the Solicitor General provides a comparatively safer harbor within which controversial decisions can be made. The main reason is that not only courts and lawyers but also journalists understand the high professional standards traditionally exercised by the Office. Frequently, when a politically sensitive decision is made, the only question reporters ask is whether the decision was the Solicitor General's or was made by someone in the White House. Once reporters are assured that the decision has been made by the Solicitor General (as it almost always is), the inquiry ends.

There are instances in which the adversarial and officer-of-the-Court roles come into conflict, so that one of them can be served only at a potential cost to the other. Where this happens, there are two possible approaches. The first is to assume categorically that one role is more important than the other, and that the lesser must always yield whenever the two conflict.[39] The second is a case-by-case approach.

The case-by-case approach is probably better. Both roles are too important and the consequences on them vary too much from one case to another to permit an all-encompassing preference for either. The only real advantage offered by a categorical approach—either categorical approach—is that it would be easier to apply.

Moreover, a categorical preference for either role would actually disserve the interests of its own advocates. A per se preference for the adversarial role, for example, would make the government's litigation efforts less successful because of the diminution of the Court's respect over the longer run for the advocate. The other side of that proposition is more difficult to demonstrate, but a categorical downplaying of the adversarial role—even in the narrowest sense of advocate for the President's particular philosophically based positions—would diminish his effectiveness as a member of the executive branch team. In time, this would also diminish the stature of the Office itself.

Reaching just the right accommodation between his two roles on a case-to-case basis is the most difficult thing the Solicitor General does. It is also one of the most important. One reason it is so difficult is that it frequently requires him to say no to the very people who are his clients and his fellow presidential appointees (and sometimes, his executive branch superior officers), whose substantive objectives he shares.

The context in which the inter-role conflict arises with most frequency is the decision to participate or not participate in someone else's lawsuit as amicus curiae, or "friend of the court." In some cases the choice is fairly easy. There is little downside risk to participation in cases involving the interpretation of federal statutes or other cases that will affect the federal government's ability to carry out its law enforcement or program-defending responsibilities. Even here, some discretion must be exercised, because if the government participated in every private antitrust case or civil rights case, its views in any particular case would be less persuasive. But as long as there is an identifiable federal interest linked to the government's ongoing litigating responsibilities, participation in one Title VII or securities case rather than another is not likely to present a serious problem.

The hard choices and the big risks come where the case involves neither the interpretation of a federal statute nor any other ongoing federal enforcement or litigational interest, but does involve an issue, probably of constitutional dimension, that is important to the President as a policy matter. It is not only legitimate for a Solicitor General to participate in such cases; a categorical refusal to do so would be a breach of his professional duty to the man who appointed him and who is his client. But it must be done with selectivity. This is one instance in which precedent may work in reverse. The fact that it has already been done may be a reason against doing it again.

The factors that enter into the decision whether to participate in amicus cases where there is no traditional federal interest should include: (1) the likelihood that a filing by the government will help the Court and influence the decision (subsidiary questions go to the quality of the parties' lawyers and whether the government would offer some additional argument not presented by the parties); (2) the importance of the issue to the administration; and (3) whether there is at least a decent possibility of a successful result. In most Supreme Court cases, the outcome cannot be predicted with confidence. But in some it can, and there are large costs to a Solicitor General's taking a position he knows the Court will reject. At the very least, a precedent will come into existence. That precedent will make it more difficult for future litigants who share the same substantive objectives to achieve those objectives before a later Court with other personnel, which, absent the precedent, might be willing to give the argument serious consideration. Moreover, if it is obvious to the Solicitor General that the Court will reject his argument, it will be equally obvious to the Court that this lawyer knows what he is doing.

While the effect of this fact on his credibility with the Court is impossible to quantify, it is not going to be positive.

NOTES

1. Chapter 20, § 35, 1 Stat. 73, 93 (1789).

2. *Georgia v. Brailsford*, 2 U.S. (2 Dallas) 402 (1792).

3. J. Easby-Smith, "Edmund Randolph, Trailblazer," 12 *Journal of the Bar Association of the District of Columbia* 415, 426 (1945).

4. 2 U. S. (2 Dollas) 419 (1793).

5. H. Cummings and C. McFarland, *Federal Justice: Chapters in the History of Justice and the Federal Executive* (1937), p. 31. Another landmark early case argued by an Attorney General in his private capacity was *Dartmouth College v. Woodward*, 17 U.S. (4 Wheat.) 518 (1819), in which William Wirt appeared for the college along with Daniel Webster. The Court in that case, again led by Chief Justice Marshall, held that an act of the New Hampshire legislature purporting to make the college a state institution materially changed the charter of the college, impaired the obligation of the charter, and thus was unconstitutional and void.

6. Easby-Smith wrote that Randolph "ignored personal abuse and quietly accepted an amendment to the Constitution which was aimed at him and nullifed one of his greatest victories in the Supreme Court." Easby-Smith, "Edmund Randolph, Trailblazer," p. 416.

7. 17 U.S. (4 Wheat.) 316 (1819).

8. Wirt, himself a Marylander by birth, was "[p]robably the most active of the early Attorneys General, one who held the office for a longer period than any other in the history of the Government." *Origin and Development of the Office of the Attorney General*, H. R. Doc. No. 510, 70th Cong., 2d Sess. 14 (1929). He was our ninth Attorney General, was appointed by President Monroe in 1817, and served until 1829. See J. Easby-Smith, *The Department of Justice: Its History and Functions* (1904), p. 45.

It was Wirt who first began the practice of keeping a record of the Attorney General's opinions and who decided that the Attorney General's opinions should not be given to all who asked, but only to the President and other Cabinet-level officers. See Easby-Smith, *The Department of Justice*, pp. 10–11; H. Cummings and C. McFarland, *Federal Justice*, pp. 78–92. After Wirt's death, John Quincy Adams remarked that "the duties of the Attorney General of the United States . . . were never more ably or more faithfully discharged than by Mr. Wirt." H. Cummings and C. McFarland, *Federal Justice*, p. 78.

9. 17 U.S., p. 419.

10. Quoted in H. Learned, *The President's Cabinet: Studies in the Origin, Formation, and Structure of an American Institution* (1912), p. 159. It should be pointed out that Randolph, after leaving the government (having served as both Attorney General and Secretary of the State), was Aaron Burr's chief defense counsel in Burr's 1807 treason trial, over which Chief Justice Marshall presided as Circuit Justice. Easby-Smith wrote: "What a scene this trial presented, the most famous in the annals of American criminal jurisprudence! A former Vice President of

the United States on trial for his life, charged with treason; the great Chief Justice presiding; and [Caesar A.] Rodney and [William] Wirt, present and future Attorneys General, pitted against Randolph, former Attorney General; all the chief actors including the defendant himself; who took part in the arguments, being among the greatest lawyers of their day." "Edmund Randolph, Trailblazer," p. 429.

11. *Id.*, p. 424.

12. *Id.*, p. 425.

13. J. Easby-Smith, *The Department of Justice*, p. 8.

14. A major preoccupation of the Attorneys General in the years leading up to the Civil War was "[t]he task of supervising appeals in public litigation over the three great bodies of private land claims, in the Louisiana Territory, the Floridas, and California." Large parcels of lands in these territories, which were acquired from France, Spain, and Mexico, respectively, were claimed by settlers under grants purportedly given by the French, Spanish, and Mexican governments. Documentation was scarce and many extravagant and fraudulent claims were made. Among these were some eight claims filed by a Frenchman named Linmantour covering a thousand square miles of California, including the entire city of San Francisco. Linmantour's claims were later exposed as frauds through the combined efforts of Attorney General Jeremiah Sullivan Black and Edwin M. Stanton, a "[b]rilliant, industrious, painfully thorough and precise" lawyer, who was hired by Black as special counsel in the California case and later succeeded Black as Attorney General. These land cases, a number of which reached the Supreme Court, are described in detail in Cummings and McFarland, *Federal Justice*, pp. 120–41.

15. The *New York Tribune* and *Harper's Weekly* said of Jeremiah Black that "though you never meet the Attorney General at a ball or *soirée*, you can find him all day in the Supreme Court, and nearly all night at his office." H. Cummings and C. McFarland, *Federal Justice*, pp. 120, 159–60.

16. *Id.*, pp. 222–23.

17. W. Holdsworth, *A History of English Law* (7th ed. 1956), p. 432.

18. See Bellot, "The Origin of the Attorney General," 25 *Law Quarterly Review*, 400–401 (1909); 7 W. Holdsworth, *A History of English Law*, pp. 432–33.

19. Quoted in 7 W. Holdsworth, *A History of English Law*, pp. 449–50.

20. *Id.*, pp. 449–51. (Attorneys eventually did gain access to the Court of Chancery as well. See *Id.*, pp. 455–56.) The other two courts where solicitors practiced were the Court of Requests and the Star Chamber. Holdsworth described how the solicitors came to prominence in the Court of Chancery, and he noted that "[n]o doubt we should have seen a similar phenomenon in the case of the Court of Requests and the Star Chamber if those courts had survived. But they did not survive. Therefore the solicitor came to be associated mainly with the Court of Chancery." *Id.*, pp. 455–56.

21. Quoted in 7 W. Holdsworth, *A History of English Law*, p. 440.

22. *Id.*, p. 457.

23. *Congressional Globe*, 40th Cong., 2d Sess. 3038 (April 27, 1870).

24. Congress's fiscal motivation is reflected in the fact that legislation establishing the Department of Justice originated in the Committee on Retrenchment,

"a joint committee of the two houses to find ways of reducing government expenditures." H. Cummings and C. McFarland, *Federal Justice*, p. 223.

25. Act of June 22, 1870, ch. 150, § 2, 16 Stat. 162, 162.

26. 71 U.S. and 72 U.S., volumes 5 and 6 of Wallace's Reports.

27. These statistics are somewhat debatable because it is not always possible to tell from either the U.S. Reports or the Lawyers' Edition Reports whether certain individuals were arguing as special counsel or as assistants to the Attorney General.

28. 73 U.S. (7 Wall.).

29. 76 U.S. and part of 77 U.S. (9 and 10 Wall.).

30. Latter portion of 77 U.S. and all of 78 U.S. (11 Wall.).

31. 80–81 U.S. (13–14 Wall.).

32. 82 through part of 84 U.S. (15–17 Wall.).

33. Today, seven oral arguments per term would be about normal for a Solicitor General, but a hundred years ago the Supreme Court's docket was not discretionary, many of the cases were less difficult to prepare, and, I suspect, there were fewer other demands on the time of the Solicitor General. It would be quite unrealistic for anyone now to argue twenty-six cases in a single term, as Bristow did in the 1871 term.

34. Bristow apparently undertook this task at some personal risk. Drawing upon his experience there, he later advised the U.S. Attorney in North Carolina that "[t]he higher the social standing and character of the convicted party, the more important is a vigorous prosecution and prompt execution of judgment." See H. Cummings and C. McFarland, *Federal Justice*, pp. 235–37.

35. "You will note that the Solicitor General is required by statute to be learned in the law. This was true of the Attorney General as well under the Act of 1789 creating that office; but curiously enough when the Solicitor General came into being in 1870, the requirement of legal learning on the part of the Attorney General was dispensed with, and no longer appeared in the statutes. It is reassuring, however, that the impetus of earlier statutory law has prevailed and the Attorneys General have remained learned in the law regardless of statute." C. Fahy, "The Office of the Solicitor General," 28 *American Bar Association Journal* 20, 22 (1942).

Judge Fahy, who was the Solicitor General from 1941–45, also remarked that the great variety of legal questions that come to the Solicitor General "should insure that, regardless of his legal learning at the time of entry upon his duties, a reasonably attentive Solicitor General should be 'learned in the law' if he remains very long in office." *Id.*

36. John W. Davis, who was the Democratic nominee for President in 1924, served as Solicitor General from 1913 to 1918. He is probably the best-known Supreme Court advocate of the twentieth century, and possibly of all time. In numbers of Supreme Court oral arguments, Davis ranks third, with 140. Another well-known lawyer, Daniel Webster, argued over 200 Supreme Court cases. First place, according to Davis's biographer, belongs to a person unknown to most twentieth-century lawyers and, I suspect, even to most historians. His name is Walter Jones, and he practiced during the first half of the nineteenth century. Given the easier accessibility of Washington, D.C., in this century, and the greater proclivity of lawyers throughout the country to argue their own cases, Jones's

record of over 317 oral arguments is likely to be secure for all time. See W. Harbaugh, *Lawyer's Lawyer: The Life of John W. Davis* (1973), p. 531.

37. The Solicitor General in a typical term will participate in the briefing and argument of about 60 percent of the cases the Supreme Court decides on the merits. About one-fourth to one-third of these are cases in which the government appears as amicus curiae.

38. This happens about two dozen times a year. It usually, although not always, occurs at the stage when the Court is considering whether to take the case on the merits (grant certiorari or note jurisdiction) and invariably involves a case potentially affecting federal government interests.

39. There are some who go even further, contending, at one extreme, that the Solicitor General's *only* job is to advocate the current administration's position, or, at the other, that such advocacy is totally foreign to his stewardship. Both of these positions have been advocated with some fervor.

4

Conflict and Leadership on the U.S. Supreme Court: From Marshall to Rehnquist

James F. Simon

William H. Rehnquist was confirmed by the Senate as the nation's sixteenth Chief Justice on September 17, 1986. A half-decade later, one may fairly ask the question: What are the qualities of leadership for a Justice of the U.S. Supreme Court? Put more boldly, is Chief Justice Rehnquist the leader of the Rehnquist Court?

To answer the questions, this chapter will discuss four Justices who have led or attempted to lead the Supreme Court, beginning with Chief Justice John Marshall. The chapter will then discuss three Justices of the modern era—Chief Justice Charles Evans Hughes and Associate Justices Hugh Black and Felix Frankfurter—before addressing the qualities of leadership exhibited by Chief Justice William Rehnquist since he took his seat as an Associate Justice in 1972.[1] Throughout, the chapter will refer to the qualities of leadership that Chief Justice Rehnquist has endorsed in his own writings.

The Chief Justice is primus inter pares—first among equals. Whether John Marshall or William Rehnquist, the Chief Justice is assured of holding only the most tenuous reins of Court leadership. Formal powers include presiding at judicial conferences, stating the facts and legal issues of the cases, and assigning the opinions when in the majority. Yet for the extraordinary Chief Justice, even those modest duties may become the subtle instruments for leadership. This possibility may explain why John Quincy Adams once rated the office of Chief Justice as more important than that of the President. More often than not in American constitutional history, however, Chief Justices have found the tools inadequate to lead their fiercely independent colleagues.

Chief Justice William Rehnquist has made the point this way: "The chief justice presides over a conference not of eight subordinates, whom he may direct or instruct, but of eight associates who, like him, have tenure during good behavior, and who are as independent as hogs on ice. He may at most persuade or cajole them."[2]

Even one of the most successful Chief Justices, Charles Evans Hughes, often had problems with his colleagues. It was Chief Justice Hughes's policy to convene Court precisely at the noon hour. One day at noon all the Justices stood ready except the crusty septuagenarian, Justice James Clark McReynolds. Hughes sent word to McReynolds's office that the Court was ready to convene. The attendant returned from McReynolds's office with the message: "Mr. Justice McReynolds says he doesn't work for you."[3]

Not surprisingly, scholars have placed the mantle of greatness on precious few Justices. It is significant that most chiefs placed in that rarefied category have come to the Court from positions of political leadership, often high in national office. Chief Justice Marshall, for example, was John Adams's secretary of state.[4] Roger Taney served as Andrew Jackson's secretary of the treasury. Charles Evans Hughes was nominated for the presidency by the Republican party in 1916. Earl Warren was thrice elected governor of California.

Each of them possessed a special quality of leadership that comes from a sure political instinct, an ability to deal successfully with people of all backgrounds, intellects, and temperaments. In Rehnquist's words, "the chief justice must be not only a jurist, but interlocutor of the judicial minstrel show, a planner, and occasionally a statesman. Surely his training in the rough and tumble of politics is no hindrance to the performance of these tasks."[5] For Rehnquist, part of a chief's political task is to serve as judicial statesman. To be a successful leader of the Court, a chief must be equipped with political skills not only to deal effectively with his independent colleagues on the bench but also to exercise statesmanship in presenting the Court to the nation.

Experience suggests, therefore, that Chief Justice Rehnquist will succeed as leader of the Court only if he is adept at the political aspects of the job. First, he must be able to work effectively with his colleagues. Second, he must understand that to lead he must identify and be able to articulate the long-range constitutional goals of the nation. He must, in other words, be a judicial statesman. This theme—the Justice as political leader—begins with Chief Justice John Marshall.

John Marshall is considered "the great Chief Justice" as though it is biologically impossible to create another of his talents. Without denigrating the wonders of genetic engineering, one would be hard pressed to imagine a more effective leader of the Supreme Court in the first third of the nineteenth century. Of course, Marshall enjoyed a distinct advantage over his successors. In Marshall's day the Justices resided in the same boardinghouse, wined and dined together, and trundled en masse to and from their courtroom in the Capitol basement. Quite naturally, Marshall's dominant personality and sure political instincts began to have their effect on his colleagues. During his thirty-four years as Chief Justice, Marshall wrote more than half of the Court's opinions and almost all of the Court's constitutional opinions. He dissented only nine times.

Equally important to his greatness, Marshall had a clear vision of the constitutional needs of the nation. He believed firmly in a strong national government and a critical role for the United States Supreme Court in the constitutional system. Marshall presented this vision in opinion after magisterial opinion, beginning with *Marbury v. Madison* in 1803, which articulated the Court's authority to declare an act of Congress unconstitutional.[6] *Marbury* asserted that it was the Court's role to decide what the Constitution means. His *Marbury* opinion was all the more remarkable because the Marshall Court was vulnerable to attacks by a hostile President Thomas Jefferson and the Republican-controlled Congress. But in *Marbury*, as in so many later opinions defining the contours of American constitutional government, Marshall showed not only the instincts of a politician but the vision of a judicial statesman. He adroitly avoided conflict, all the while taking a position that in time augmented the Court's powers.

A century after Marshall's tenure, Charles Evans Hughes became Chief Justice. Like Marshall, Hughes has been considered one of the great Chief Justices by scholars and colleagues alike. Indeed, Justices as diverse in temperament and philosophy as Hugo Black and Felix Frankfurter fully recognized and appreciated Hughes's leadership qualities.[7]

William Rehnquist has also acknowledged Hughes as one of the preeminent leaders in Supreme Court history. In making that point, Rehnquist has referred to Hughes's political skills within the Court as well as his ability to represent the Court as an institution to the outside world. As to his internal political skills, it is conceded that Hughes was without peer, at least in this century, in presenting the facts and legal issues to his colleagues in judicial conference. He had a talent for narrative and also showed consummate skill in moving his colleagues, even the most contentious ones, along in meaningful discussion.

That is not something to be taken for granted. Hughes's successor as Chief Justice, Harlan Fiske Stone, was a source of particular frustration to his colleagues because he allowed Justices to ramble. Chief Justice Rehnquist has written approvingly of the ability of a chief to move discussions in judicial conference ahead expeditiously. "Certainly conference discussion should not be throttled. Even the most junior justice should be given the impression that he is entitled to make the fullest statements of his views. But the realistic alternatives are not gag rule or full and free discussion. Instead, the choice is between orderly, relevant discussion, on the one hand, and stream of consciousness reflections or seriatim lectures, on the other."[8] The nation's present Chief Justice has left no doubt that he favors the first choice.

More than his effectiveness with his colleagues, Chief Justice Hughes is remembered for his reverence for the Court as an institution and his ability to project that reverence to the nation. He was Chief Justice in the mid-1930s, a time of crisis in the Court's history. It was Hughes's difficult task to try to give some semblance of authority to a philosophy articulated by a five-man conservative majority that declared one piece of New Deal legislation after another unconstitutional. Rather than make the Court appear unnecessarily divided, Hughes chose to support the majority view. When President Roosevelt introduced a so-called reform plan that would have packed the Court and overwhelmed the conservative majority in the guise of helping the Court do its work more efficiently, Hughes wrote a letter to the Senate Judiciary Committee about the legislation and countered, point by point, the argument that the President had made.[9]

It is important to Hughes's effectiveness as Chief Justice that he was not particularly wedded to preserving the philosophy of the conservative majority. Rather, his purpose was to protect the Court as an institution from the impingement of another coequal branch. And he was successful. FDR's Court-packing plan failed. The fact that Hughes supported a new Court majority that rejected the old majority's anti–New Deal opinions lends further credence to the view that Hughes placed the prestige of the Court as an institution above any individual view of correct constitutional policy that he might have held.

Like Marshall's, Charles Evans Hughes's skills as Chief Justice transcended his talents as an opinion writer, although those talents were considerable. Both Marshall and Hughes understood the inner workings of the Court, were sensitive to their colleagues' strengths and weaknesses as jurists, and were able with political as well as intellectual talent effectively to lead the Court. Besides dealing effectively with colleagues, each kept a steady eye on the Court's role in promoting the essential constitutional needs of the nation.

Neither Hugo Black nor Felix Frankfurter was Chief Justice and, therefore, neither had the modest tools of authority that Marshall and Hughes possessed. Black and Frankfurter are included in this discussion, nonetheless, because their debate over the proper role of the Court in protecting civil liberties has special relevance today in assessing the leadership potential of Chief Justice Rehnquist. As with Marshall and Hughes, an evaluation of Black and Frankfurter begins with their effectiveness with their colleagues as well as their abilities as judicial statesmen.

Given their backgrounds, it was assumed that Frankfurter, a champion of civil liberties and a well-known constitutional scholar, would lead the liberal wing of the Court after his appointment in 1939. Surprisingly, however, Hugo Black, who had come on the Court two years earlier, replaced Frankfurter as leader in a very short time.[10] To understand that unpredictable result, one must look to the political skills of the two Justices, skills that may be as relevant today as in the 1940s.

Understanding the political skills of Black and Frankfurter should begin with a brief sketch of the backgrounds of the two men in order to grasp better the unique perspectives and talents they brought to their jobs as Associate Justices of the U.S. Supreme Court.

Felix Frankfurter immigrated from his native Vienna in 1894 at the age of twelve, not speaking a word of English.[11] Young Felix came home to his parents' lower East Side cold water flat one day and said, "This man Laundry must be a very rich man since he has so many stores."[12] Frankfurter learned the English language quickly and well, graduating third in his class at City College. He then entered the Harvard Law School, where he ranked first in his class all three years. His performance was so outstanding that Harvard professors read his exams aloud to classes for years after his graduation.

As a young lawyer, Frankfurter worked for Henry Stimson, first as an assistant U.S. attorney in New York and later as counsel for the Bureau of Insular Affairs in the War Department when Stimson was secretary of war. Under Stimson, Frankfurter was arguing cases in front of the U.S. Supreme Court before he was thirty years old. In 1914, Frankfurter was called to the Harvard law faculty and became a nationally recognized scholar in the fields of constitutional and administrative law. At the same time, Frankfurter was establishing a reputation as one of the country's most prominent civil libertarians. He was a founding member of the American Civil Liberties Union as well as a contributing editor of the *New Republic*, writing numerous articles defending civil liberties. Finally, and most impressively, Frankfurter became the public defender of Sacco and Vanzetti, publishing a devastating attack on the criminal justice system in which the two Italian immigrants were convicted and sentenced to death.

Frankfurter always had 200 best friends from the time he was a young man at City College and, as it turned out, many of those best friends became very prominent in government. One was Franklin Delano Roosevelt. When Roosevelt was elected governor of New York, Frankfurter became an unofficial but very insistent and welcomed advisor to Roosevelt. And when Roosevelt was elected President of the United States, he looked to Frankfurter for ideas and advice on a regular basis. FDR offered Frankfurter the position of Solicitor General of the United States, but Frankfurter turned it down. However, when Roosevelt called Frankfurter in his Cambridge apartment and asked if he would agree to become his nominee as an Associate Justice of the U.S. Supreme Court, Frankfurter's reply was very different. "All that I can say is that I wish my mother were alive," he told the President.[13]

Frankfurter was appointed to the Court two years after Roosevelt's first nominee, Hugo Lafayette Black of Alabama. Black had none of the polish of a Harvard Law School education nor had he advised U.S. Presidents in any informal capacity. Hugo Black, nonetheless, was a man of remarkable background and talents. He was born in the raw hill country of northern Alabama, the eighth child of William and Martha Black. Hugo attended Clay County, Alabama schools and then completed a two-year course at the University of Alabama Law School, where he graduated with honors in a class of twenty-three.[14]

Shortly after graduation Black sought his legal fortunes in big, booming Birmingham. Slowly, Black began to build a clientele among the laborers in Birmingham's iron and steel industry who had been injured at their workplace. Interspersed with his private practice, Black served in the public sector, first as a police court judge and later as an aggressive county prosecutor. After World War I, Black practiced law privately and quickly became one of the most successful trial lawyers in the state. "I'll take the jury in the box," he would tell the judge, so sure of his powers of advocacy that he expected to persuade any man of the rightness of his cause.[15] And he usually did.

In 1925 Black declared his candidacy for a seat in the U.S. Senate. Relatively unknown, Black nonetheless defeated three more experienced politicians in the race. He did it by taking a stand for the common man against the established corporate and political interests in the Democratic party. He also did it with hard work, visiting every county in the state in a Model T Ford and shaking every hand in sight.

Once in the Senate, he concentrated on furthering the interests of his Alabama constituents and, more generally, of common men and women who he believed were victimized by the vested corporate and political interests in the nation. In sum, he was an unabashed populist. By his second term in office, Black was also one of the most skilled legislators in the Senate in support of Roosevelt's New Deal. And he was one of the Senate's most feared investigators, uncovering widespread waste and corruption in the shipping and public utilities industries.

In 1936, when President Roosevelt needed support for his ill-fated Court-packing plan, Hugo Black offered his services in speech and radio broadcasts alike. Black defended the President's action, saying that it was within the framework of the Constitution and that it was an essential response to a conservative Supreme Court majority that was overturning the social and economic legislation of the people. When FDR was finally given the opportunity to replace one of the conservative Justices on the Court, he appointed Hugo Black.

Although Black's appointment predated Frankfurter's by two years, almost every knowledgeable observer of the Supreme Court, including Felix Frankfurter himself, expected that Frankfurter, the celebrated civil libertarian and constitutional scholar, would lead the liberal wing of the Court after his appointment. He had even been called upon by Justice Harlan F. Stone to "tutor" Hugo Black on the intricacies of constitutional law before he, Frankfurter, had been appointed.[16] Black, on the other hand, was considered a bright enough fellow and certainly hard working, but no match for Felix Frankfurter.

At first, all seemed to go according to script. In the first dramatic challenge to Frankfurter's leadership in 1940, the former Harvard professor prevailed impressively. The case involved two elementary school children of William Gobitis, a Jehovah's Witness in Minersville, Pennsylvania. Gobitis and his children were raised to believe that the worship of false idols condemned them to eternal annihilation. When the Minersville school board insisted that all public school children salute the American flag before each school day, the Gobitis children refused, saying that it was a violation of their religious beliefs. The children were expelled from school and their father later brought suit against the school board, arguing that the policy was a violation of their First Amendment rights to expression and the free exercise of religion.

The Gobitis children's position was accepted by the trial and appellate courts, and the case was set for argument in the U.S. Supreme Court in 1940. At the time, Adolf Hitler's troops had already devoured large chunks of Europe and were preparing for the Battle of Britain. On this side of the Atlantic, many, including Frankfurter, feared that the Nazis would soon be setting their sights on the United States itself. It was, therefore, a particularly poignant time to raise the issue of patriotism in the United States.

At the judicial conference on the Gobitis case all of the Roosevelt appointees—Black and William Douglas, Stanley Reed, and Frank Murphy—looked to Frankfurter for leadership. And he spoke passionately—but not on behalf of the Gobitis children's First Amendment rights. Rather, he emphasized the need for patriotism, particularly on the eve of World War II. He also stressed his philosophy of judicial restraint, of the limited role that the Court must play in the constitutional process. Liberals, after all, had been critical of Justices who only recently had declared so many of Roosevelt's New Deal programs unconstitutional. Deference to elected officials was the stance the Court should take now. The First Amendment claim, he said, must therefore fail.

Seven members of the Court, including every Roosevelt appointee, voted with Frankfurter. Not just Hugo Black, but Reed, Murphy, and Douglas. Frankfurter wrote the majority opinion for the Court. It would be the last major opinion he would write in the First Amendment area in which he carried all of the Roosevelt appointees. Only Harlan Stone, a Coolidge appointee, dissented.[17]

But Frankfurter's *Gobitis* opinion was only partially successful. Frankfurter led the Court, but he could not persuade the nation that his opinion embodied the nation's highest constitutional ideals. One hundred and seventy-one newspapers across the country and almost every law review opposed the Frankfurter majority opinion. "We think this decision of the United States Supreme Court is dead wrong," an editorial in the *St. Louis Post Dispatch* declared.[18] "If patriotism depends upon such things as this—upon violation of the fundamental rights of religious freedom—then it becomes not a noble emotion of love for country, but something to be rammed down our throat by law."

Two years later, Black, Murphy, and Douglas publicly rejected the position they had taken in *Gobitis* and said that the First Amendment rights to the free exercise of religion and expression must take precedence. In 1943 the Court explicitly reversed the holding of *Gobitis*.[19] Felix Frankfurter dissented. He no longer led the liberal wing of the Court.

In two other First Amendment cases, Hugo Black openly and aggressively took the reins of liberal leadership away from Felix Frankfurter. The first case involved the radical longshoreman leader, Harry Bridges, who had threatened in a telegram, which was later published, to call a strike if a state court judgment in a labor dispute was upheld. The second case involved the *Los Angeles Times*, which, in a series of editorials, demanded a harsh sentence from a state court judge in the roughest verbal terms. The question in both cases was whether the California courts, which had cited for contempt both Bridges and the *Times* for their threatening expressions, violated the First Amendment's right to free expression.[20]

Justice Black wrote the majority opinion overturning the contempt citations, and he was joined by Roosevelt appointees Douglas, Murphy, Reed, and newly appointed Justice Robert Jackson. The California courts had no right to inhibit speech, said Black: "The assumption that respect for the judiciary can be won by shielding judges from published criticism wrongly appraises the character of American public opinion. For it is a prized American privilege to speak one's mind, although not always with perfect good taste, on all public institutions."[21] With his *Bridges* opinion,

Black effectively announced his view that First Amendment rights were preferred freedoms under the Constitution. That conviction would grow in the years to come.

Felix Frankfurter dissented in *Bridges*, declaring that the contempt power had been a necessary tool for courts to protect the integrity of the judicial process through centuries of Anglo-American law. It was, he said, a matter of balancing First Amendment rights against those of the state. Unlike Black, Frankfurter refused to recognize that First Amendment freedoms held a preferred position in the constitutional hierarchy.

Bridges came down two years after the Court appointment of Felix Frankfurter. Within that relatively short span, Frankfurter had not only lost his liberal majority and leadership, but he had been unceremoniously replaced in that position by Hugo Black. How, one must ask, did this happen so quickly?

To answer the question, recall the discussion of the qualities of leadership on the Court. First consider Black and Frankfurter's political effectiveness with their colleagues. Both Frankfurter and Black had the powerful intellects to take a leadership position on the Court, although Frankfurter was slow to recognize that Black's intellect was as formidable as his own. Others on the Court did.

So when Black began to carve out his own strong position on the First Amendment, colleagues like Douglas and Murphy came under the influence of Black. They listened to Frankfurter's lectures on the balancing of constitutional demands, but they voted with Hugo Black. They voted with him not only on principle but also because Black, with his political skills, was better equipped to influence his colleagues. True, Frankfurter had been an advisor to U.S. Presidents. But Hugo Black had worked in the trenches, speaking plainly to juries and Alabama's voters as well as U.S. senators. He knew how to talk to them persuasively without lecturing them as a Harvard professor might. The more Frankfurter lectured, the less influential he became with his colleagues.

It was also a nasty Frankfurter habit to talk deprecatingly about colleagues who did not agree with him. In conversations with his colleagues and friends, he belittled Frank Murphy for his limited intelligence and castigated both Black and Douglas for what he perceived to be their bald political maneuvering. For his part, Hugo Black never tired of promoting his view of the First Amendment, but he did so directly and relied on the force of his argument, not personal insults.[22]

But Black's success with his colleagues was only half of the story. He, like Marshall, had a sense of institutional mission. For Black, the Court's primary role was to protect the individual liberties guaranteed in the Bill of Rights. In this respect, Black—more than Frankfurter—understood the elemental constitutional needs of the American people in the modern era. Central to those needs in a time of big government and high technology is the protection of individual liberties.

This brings the discussion to William Rehnquist and this question: Does the present Chief Justice have the political skills of a Marshall or a Hughes or a Hugo Black to lead the Court? These political skills, as shown here, have to be demonstrated in two areas, one within the Court, the other outside.

In their own distinct ways, Marshall, Hughes, and Black worked effectively with their judicial colleagues to develop broad support on important constitutional issues. Marshall and Hughes, in particular, willingly gave up their own ideological positions upon occasion in the interests of a broader Court agreement. They were, in other words, willing to compromise and saw compromise as a part of leadership.

We have little indication so far that Chief Justice Rehnquist will emulate Marshall or Hughes in this respect. In his writings Rehnquist has noted, with less than total admiration, Chief Justice Hughes's tendency to shift doctrinal directions to accommodate shifting Court majorities.[23] Compromise as yet does not seem to be a word in Chief Justice Rehnquist's vocabulary.

At his confirmation hearings in 1971, when Rehnquist's record was being reviewed for his appointment as an Associate Justice of the Supreme Court, the point was made that the nominee had an undiluted record as a conservative ideologue. As a private attorney and later as a high-level official in Richard Nixon's Justice Department, William Rehnquist had consistently favored government interests over those of individual rights and liberties. Moreover, he had been critical of judicial decisions protecting individual rights and was likely, it was suggested, to continue that criticism as a member of the Supreme Court.[24]

After his appointment to the Court, Associate Justice Rehnquist fulfilled the predictions perfectly. He was precisely the conservative ideologue on the Court that he had been in the Justice Department before his Court appointment. He consistently favored government interests over individual rights and often did so in outspoken and sometimes lone dissent. His dissents sometimes savagely attacked Court majority opinions that protected civil liberties and interpreted the Fourteenth Amendment's equal protection clause to prevent race- and sex-based discrimination.[25]

Based on Chief Justice Rehnquist's past record, it is likely that he will lead the Court only if his colleagues are brought closer to his ideological views. The model, then, for his internal leadership on the Rehnquist Court may, ironically, be that of civil libertarian Justice Black. For Black developed a very strong libertarian position for himself in his early years on the Court and was able to persuade other liberal colleagues to follow his lead. Moreover, he was successful in influencing more moderate members of the Court to come closer to his philosophical position. As a result, the Court majority gradually moved toward Hugo Black's position in many civil liberties issues as well as his position that the provisions of the Bill of Rights were incorporated through the Fourteenth Amendment to the Constitution and applied to the states.[26]

It may be that William Rehnquist will be able to accomplish a similar task. By force of his extraordinary intellect and his ability to articulate his views, he may well be able to bring a majority of the Court irrevocably toward his conservative position. He has already been greatly assisted by President Reagan's appointments to the Court of two men, Antonin Scalia and Anthony Kennedy, whose conservative views are closely akin to the Chief Justice's.[27] Justice David Souter's impact on the Court's alignment will soon be seen.

What, then, are Chief Justice Rehnquist's chances of leading the Court in the eyes of the nation? Is he likely to be a Court leader who can defend the institution to the outside world and understands, in defending it, that the Court should play a crucial role in setting an example to the nation? Marshall and Hughes understood this well. So did Hugo Black. Marshall knew that the task at hand was to build a nation with a strong national government that included a critical role for the Supreme Court. Hughes was sensitive to the threat from both extremes of the political spectrum—first, from the anti–New Deal majority that was trying to impose its views on a more liberal electorate, but also from an immensely popular President, Franklin Roosevelt, who wanted to impose his will on the Court.

Hugo Black viewed the primary mission of the modern Supreme Court as protecting individual rights and liberties in this country. In doing so, Black showed that he, more than Felix Frankfurter, understood the constitutional needs of the American people in the modern era.

Will William Rehnquist fulfill the role of national leader as Chief Justice of the United States? To answer the question, we must look to the dominant constitutional values in the country today and what they are likely to be later in the last decade of this century. It is also true that the two most recent occupants of the White House, Ronald Reagan and George Bush, have been political conservatives. It is also true that we have had a Supreme Court majority, following the liberal Warren Court majority, that it was commonly presumed would cut back on liberal judicial initiatives. The Court under Chief Justice Warren Burger worked for thirteen of the Burger Court's seventeen years under Republican Presidents.

And yet, neither the people's choice of Republican Presidents nor President Nixon's choice of Warren Burger as Chief Justice caused the Supreme Court majority to backtrack significantly on individual rights and liberties. There was no retreat, for example, from *Brown v. Board of Education.*[28] In fact, the Burger Court issued decisions allowing busing to promote desegregation and introduced some constitutionally protected forms of affirmative action. And the Burger Court majority sometimes trod where the Warren Court did not. The Court, for example, established a constitutional test that gave greater protection against sex-based discrimination than ever existed during the Warren Court years. Moreover, this Court, which was expected to be more cautious than its predecessor, announced in 1973 that a woman's control of her body was a constitutionally protected right to privacy.[29]

This is not to suggest that those decisions were necessarily correct or that they perfectly reflected the dominant constitutional values in the country at the time. It is to suggest, however, that the pattern was unmistakable and noteworthy: The Burger Court majority affirmed an expectation that has dominated Supreme Court jurisprudence for fifty years—that our Constitution and our people place individual rights and liberties very high in the hierarchy of constitutional values.

A Chief Justice who leads a Court majority in the opposite direction does so at considerable institutional risk. For the Court has never, for very long, been able to resist the dominant political trends in the nation. When it attempts to do so, its own prestige and power are placed in considerable jeopardy. That was true with the Court's *Dred Scott* decision[30] in the last century and the anti–New Deal Court decisions in the earlier part of this century.[31] If the lessons of history still apply, then Chief Justice Rehnquist, to be the leader of the Court, must acknowledge those lessons.

All of the Court leaders discussed here—Marshall, Hughes, and Black—were successful largely because they were able to anticipate the long-range constitutional needs of the nation. Perhaps the new Chief Justice will follow in this tradition. To do so he will have to put the Court's and nation's interests above his own ideological convictions. So far, the Chief Justice has exhibited a firm determination to reverse the modern Supreme Court's consistent pattern of protecting individual rights and liberties. He succeeded impressively during the 1988 and 1989 Court Terms primarily because he could count on the votes of the two newest appointees, Justices Scalia and Kennedy, as well as Justices O'Connor and White. But reaction to the newly emerging conservative majority could immediately be seen in the nation at large. After the five-member conservative majority, led by Chief Justice Rehnquist, used *Webster v. Reproductive Health Services*[32] to attack the analysis of *Roe v. Wade* and placed additional obstacles in the way of a pregnant woman's freedom to obtain an abortion, pro-choice forces began a counterattack, generally successful so far in the political arena.[33]

The record of the Rehnquist Court and its Chief Justice is, of course, incomplete. Although Chief Justice Rehnquist has occasionally shown an inclination to compromise with his more liberal brethren,[34] he more typically has worked skillfully to build a new conservative majority that appears to cut back on major precedents in the areas of civil liberties and civil rights.[35] It is not too early to observe, however, that Chief Justice Rehnquist is attempting to steer the Court toward his conservative positions. In doing so, he is making a risky assumption, namely, that his conservative philosophy represents the long-range constitutional need of the nation. That is an assumption with potentially far-reaching historical consequences.

NOTES

1. The Senate confirmed Rehnquist as Associate Justice by a vote of 68 to 26 in December 1971. The vote to confirm as Chief Justice was 65 to 33 in 1986, one of the largest percentages of negative votes ever received by a successful nominee to the chief justiceship.

2. W. Rehnquist, "Chief Justices I Never Knew," 3 *Hastings Constitutional Law Quarterly* 637, 637 (1976). See generally W. Rehnquist, *The Supreme Court: How It Was, How It Is* (1987).

3. J. Simon, *In His Own Image: The Supreme Court in Richard Nixon's America* (1973), pp. 52–53.

4. For background on Chief Justice Marshall and the Marshall Court, see generally, 1 C. Warren, *The Supreme Court in United States History* (1923), pp. 169–540; R. McCloskey, *The American Supreme Court* (1960), pp. 54–80; W. Rehnquist, *The Supreme Court*, pp. 99–122.

5. W. Rehnquist, "Chief Justices," p. 639.

6. *Marbury v. Madison*, 5 U.S. (1 Cranch) 137 (1803).

7. On Chief Justice Hughes's political skills, see W. Rehnquist, "Chief Justices," pp. 642–45; J. Simon, *The Antagonists: Hugo Black, Felix Frankfurter, and Civil Liberties in Modern America* (1989), p. 106; E. McElwain, "The Business of the Supreme Court as Conducted by Chief Justice Hughes," 63 *Harvard Law Review* 5 (1949).

8. W. Rehnquist, "Chief Justices," p. 646. As an example of Hughes's support for the conservative majority, see *Schechter Corp. v. U.S.*, 295 U.S. 495 (1935); *Carter v. Carter Coal Co.*, 298 U.S. 238 (1936).

9. 2 M. Pusey, *Charles Evans Hughes* (1951), p. 756. For commentary on FDR's Court-packing plan, see S. Hendel, *Charles Evans Hughes and the Supreme Court* (1951), pp. 250–54; 2 M. Pusey, *Charles Evans Hughes*, pp. 753–60. On Hughes's later rejection of the anti–New Deal majority, see, for example, *NLRB v. Jones & Laughlin Steel Corp.*, 306 U.S. 1 (1937).

10. J. Simon, *The Antagonists*, pp. 16–18.

11. For a more detailed account of Frankfurter's background, see *id.*, pp. 21–65.

12. H. Phillips, ed., *Felix Frankfurter Reminisces* (1960), p. 4.

13. *Id.*, p. 283.

14. For a review of Black's background, see J. Simon, *The Antagonists*, pp. 66–100.

15. H. Black, Jr., *My Father* (1975), p. 46.

16. A. Mason, *Harlan Fiske Stone, Pillar of the Law* (1956), p. 469.

17. *Minersville School District v. Gobitis*, 310 U.S. 586 (1940); see also J. Simon, *The Antagonists*, pp. 106–14.

18. *St. Louis Post Dispatch*, June 4, 1940.

19. *West Virginia Board of Education v. Barnette*, 319 U.S. 624 (1943).

20. *Bridges v. California* and *Times-Mirror Co. v. Superior Court*, 314 U.S. 252 (1941).

21. 314 U.S., p. 270.

22. See J. Simon, *The Antagonists*, p. 116.

23. W. Rehnquist, "Chief Justices," pp. 642–45.

24. For Rehnquist's background and a review of his 1971 confirmation hearing, see J. Simon, *In His Own Image*, pp. 229–40.

25. For example, see *Frontiero v. Richardson*, 411 U.S. 677 (1973); *Sugarman v. Dougall*, 413 U.S. 634 (1973); *Bob Jones University v. United States*, 461 U.S. 574 (1983).

26. See J. Simon, *The Antagonists*, and G. Dunne, *Hugo Black and the Judicial Revolution* (1977), pp. 250–73.

27. President Reagan's assistance to Chief Justice Rehnquist came with the Court appointments of Associate Justices Antonin Scalia (1986) and Anthony Kennedy (1989), who have joined, with remarkable consistency, Chief Justice Rehnquist and Associate Justices Sandra Day O'Connor and Byron White to forge a fragile conservative majority; see the *National Law Journal* analysis of Justices' voting records, August 21, 1989, p. 52.

28. *Brown v. Board of Education*, 347 U.S. 483 (1954).

29. On the Burger Court's protection of civil rights and liberties, see, for example, on busing, *Swann v. Charlotte Mecklenburg Board of Education*, 402 U.S. 1 (1971); on affirmative action, *Regents of the University of California v. Bakke*, 438 U.S. 265 (1978); on sex-based discrimination, *Frontiero v. Richardson*, 411 U.S. 677 (1973); on a woman's control of her body, *Roe v. Wade*, 410 U.S. 113 (1973).

30. *Dred Scott v. Sandford*, 60 U.S. (19 How.) 393 (1856).

31. Noteworthy anti–New Deal Court decisions include *Schechter Poultry Corp. v. United States*, 295 U.S. 495 (1935); *Carter v. Carter Coal Co.*, 298 U.S. 238 (1936); and *United States v. Butler*, 297 U.S. 1 (1936).

32. 57 U.S.L.W. 5023 (1989).

33. For political reaction to the Court's *Webster* decision, see *U.S. News & World Report*, July 31, 1989, p. 26; *Los Angeles Times*, October 29, 1989, p. M1; *The Washington Post*, November 10, 1989, p. B1.

34. For example, see *Falwell v. Flynt*, 485 U.S. 46 (1988).

35. See, for example, *Webster v. Reproductive Health Services*, 57 U.S.L.W. 5023 (1989); *Richmond v. J. A. Croson Co.*, 57 U.S.L.W. 4132 (1989); *Wards Cove Packing Co. v. Atonio*, 57 U.S.L.W. 4583 (1989).

5

Justice Sandra Day O'Connor: An Assessment

Harold J. Spaeth

As she is the first woman to sit on the United States Supreme Court, assessments of Justice O'Connor are not in short supply. However, those that do exist either assess her pre-Court career[1] or concentrate—albeit intensively—on only a portion of her Supreme Court decisions.[2] This assessment, by contrast, will attempt to specify Justice O'Connor's ideological position on the major issues confronting the Court. It will do so, first, by identifying the Justices with whom she tends to associate when she articulates her position on various issues, as well as the Justices who associate with her; and second, by analyzing her voting record in order to identify her position on the major issues during her first five years on the Court, which correspond with the last five years of the Burger Court: October 1981 through July 1986. There will also be references to votes cast in cases in subsequent years. Finally, this chapter will specify such evidence of deviation between her voting behavior and her opinions as may exist.

Although I have not considered the matter at any length or in depth, for purposes of this assessment I assume that gender is without biologically determined behavioral effects.[3] This is not to say that environmental factors lack such effects, but only that Justice O'Connor's gender, as such, does not cause her to act differently from her male colleagues.

To a greater extent than in other courts, the rules under which the U.S. Supreme Court operates allow the Justices to give free play to their

Table 5.1
Justices Joining O'Connor's Special Opinions

term	81	82	83	84	85	total
Rehnquist	5	8	7	6	6	32
Burger	4		3	5	3	15
Powell	2	2	6	2	2	14
Stevens		4	2		2	8
Brennan	1	2	2	1	2	8
Blackmun	4		1	1	1	7
Marshall	1		1	2	2	6
White		3			1	4
total	17	19	22	17	19	94

personal policy preferences.[4] As the Court of last resort, whose members serve until they resign, retire, or die, the individual Justices are free agents in the sense that they may vote as they please and express their personal opinion, not only when they disagree with the majority's decision, but also even when they are members of the majority coalition.

Justices voice their personal opinion by writing special opinions—that is, dissents or concurrences. Although the opinion of the Court may also be viewed as expressing the personal opinion of its author and that of the other members who subscribe to it, the opinion of the Court is more accurately considered to be a group product, in the sense that a majority of the participating Justices must agree with its contents.

A good way to determine a Justice's general ideological position is to ascertain with whom he or she agrees insofar as special opinions are concerned. Such agreement is much more instructive than an analysis of majority opinions for the following reasons: No Justice can be forced to write a special opinion; no Justice can be prevented from writing one; no Justice can be forced to join or prevented from joining in the special opinion of another Justice. As a result, such an opinion tends to reflect the strongly held views of its author. In addition, any Justice who joins another's special opinion can reasonably be said to be persuaded of the correctness of the views presented therein.[5]

Given the foregoing, we observe who joins Justice O'Connor when she writes special opinions and, conversely, whose special opinions she joins. These results provide strong evidence of her overall ideological position. In compiling these data, I have excluded from consideration the memorandum cases—typically denials of requests for writs of certiorari—which appear in the back of the volumes of the *United States Reports*.

Tables 5.1 and 5.2 display the term-by-term frequency with which

Table 5.2
Special Opinions Joined by O'Connor

term	81	82	83	84	85	total
Rehnquist	8	7	9	2	6	32
Powell	7	8	4	2		21
Blackmun	4	2	1	1	2	10
White	2		2	2	2	8
Burger	2	3			1	6
Stevens	1	1	1	2	1	6
Brennan	1	1		1	1	4
Marshall		1		2		3
total	25	23	17	12	13	90

Justice O'Connor's colleagues joined her special opinions and the frequency with which she joined theirs. As an author, she gained 94 joiners for her 98 Burger Court special opinions, a proportion that places her a standard deviation above the Justices' average (.71) for the twelve terms of the Burger Court that antedated her arrival.[6] Her most frequent joiner by far was Rehnquist, with 34. He more than doubled the number of her next most frequent joiner, Burger, who had 15. Indeed, five of her colleagues—White, Marshall, Brennan, Stevens, and Blackmun—collectively joined her only one more time than did Rehnquist alone. Inasmuch as Rehnquist was the Court's most conservative member, we may assume that he joined O'Connor's special opinions because he found them compatible with his own conservative policy preferences.

Table 5.2 shows that in joining her colleagues' special opinions O'Connor did so in a fashion roughly reciprocal of the frequency with which they joined her. Although all of the Justices joined her as or more often than she joined them with the exceptions of White, Blackmun, and Powell, she favored Rehnquist with 32 of her 90 joins. At the other extreme, O'Connor joined the Court's two liberals—Marshall and Brennan—a total of only seven times. The results of Table 5.2 are affected, of course, by the frequency with which any given Justice writes special opinions. Because the Court's two liberals are in the minority more often than any other Justice, from which position they regularly articulate their views, O'Connor did not lack opportunities to join far more than seven of their special opinions if she had been so inclined.

Inasmuch as Justice O'Connor wrote only 98 special opinions during her first five terms and joined those of her colleagues in only 90 instances, it is quite possible that the evidence adduced above concerning her conservative orientation may be overstated. The opinions that she wrote and joined represent a small fraction of her overall decision-making behavior. A good supplementary indicator of her orientation may be obtained by analyzing the "direction" of the dissents she authored and joined.

Direction refers to whether a vote supports a liberal or conservative outcome, as these terms are commonly used to describe Supreme Court decisions. Accordingly, in the context of criminal procedure, civil rights, and First Amendment litigation, a conservative may be said to support the prosecution, to oppose civil rights claimants, and to support the government's action in due process matters. In the context of labor relations and economic activity, a conservative supports employers, business, and union members, while opposing unions, injured persons, debtors, and consumers. With regard to the exercise of judicial power, federalism, and federal taxation, a conservative opposes the exercise of judicial power and supports the states and federal taxpayers. In miscellaneous cases and those concerning interstate relations, direction is not assigned.

One cannot reliably determine the direction of concurring votes and opinions because, by definition, they agree with the disposition the majority makes. Hence, the focus here is limited to dissenting opinions. Justice O'Connor wrote 43 such opinions, while joining 65 written by others. One of her dissenting opinions concerns the apportionment of fish among three states,[7] an issue to which direction does not apply. Thirty-five of the other 42 take a conservative position, as do 54 of the 65 dissents that she joined. Interestingly, both proportions equal 83 percent.

Although these dissents comprise a subset of what itself is a small subset of all of O'Connor's votes, they nonetheless encompass the totality of her decisional disagreement with the majority. As such, their direction cannot be dismissed as irrelevant to her ideological orientation. Because they constitute exceptions to the rule, a specification of the issue that occasioned a liberal dissent may shed further light on Justice O'Connor. Two of her seven liberal dissenting opinions pertain to issues in which her position is arguably conservative: *Shepard v. National Labor Relations Board*,[8] in which she alone dissented from a ruling that victims of a secondary boycott need not be provided a "make-whole" remedy, and *Ruckelshaus v. Monsanto Co.*,[9] in which she, again alone, held that EPA disclosures effected a taking of appellee's property. Three other liberal opinions concerned the Freedom of Information Act, securities regulation, and state taxation.[10] Only two of her dissenting opinions directly concerned matters high in the panoply of liberal concerns: Miranda warnings and the free exercise clause.[11]

The eleven liberal dissents that O'Connor joined display a similar pattern: two tort actions,[12] two statutory constructions of criminal laws,[13] liability under the civil rights laws,[14] comity,[15] judicial review of agency action,[16] secondary union activity,[17] and state regulation of Indians.[18] The only two that address concerns central to liberals are *Ralston v. Robinson*,[19] which concerned the status of juveniles under the Youth Correction Act, and *Bowen v. American Hospital Ass'n*,[20] which dealt with the provision of health care to handicapped infants.

O'Connor's conservative dissents, both the 35 that she authored and the 54 that she joined, span the spectrum of civil rights, criminal procedure, First Amendment, economic regulation, and federal-state relations. No particular issues manifest themselves disproportionately. Proportionately more of them appear to concern major issues than is true of her liberal dissents.[21]

We may parenthetically note that Justice O'Connor has evidenced a marked degree of stability in authoring special opinions. In each of her first five terms she wrote either 19 or 20 such opinions. This, coupled with other indicators,[22] suggests that she "was very quick to adapt to her new environment . . . that she comes to the Court with a clear orientation in terms of ideology and policy."[23] Nor has the position she has taken in her special opinions distanced her from her colleagues. As noted above, these have garnered an average of .96 joiners per special opinion, which places her a standard deviation above the Justices' mean during the first twelve terms of the Burger Court.[24]

Although the foregoing analysis suggests that Justice O'Connor has established a conservative track record, we do not know how conservative she is relative to her colleagues; neither do we know if her conservatism—if such it be—extends across all of the Court's major policy areas. Given that special opinions—especially dissents—comprise such a small portion of her overall decisional behavior, it is entirely possible that her behavior may differ in cases in which she neither wrote nor joined a special opinion from those in which she did. To consider this possibility, we assess her voting issue by issue and compare hers to that of her colleagues. Previous research has identified several dozen "issue areas" into which the decision making of the Burger Court may be divided.[25] The position of each Justice on each issue may be specified by use of scale scores ranging from +1.00 to −1.00.[26] Justices score +1.00 if they always vote in favor of the hypothesized attitude or value that motivates the Justices to vote as they do in the issue area under consideration. Conversely, Justices score −1.00 if all their votes oppose the underlying attitude or value.

Although this assessment of Justice O'Connor is based on her performance during the Burger Court, she did not participate in enough cases in all issue areas to enable one to calculate a reliable scale score and thereby specify her position on that issue relative to those of her colleagues. The issue areas into which the Court's decisions have been divided encompass the entirety of the Burger Court. Justice O'Connor served for less than a third of that period (five out of seventeen terms). If, for example, she cast six votes in an issue area constituting twenty decisions, the first of which unanimously supported a civil rights claimant while the last unanimously opposed such a claimant, we would not know if her support ended after the third case, immediately before the seventeenth case, or at some point between these extremes. Voting distributions such as these prevent us from identifying her position in a number of issue areas. However, she has participated in enough cases and voted sufficiently consistently to allow inferences to be made where data are missing.

The issue areas into which previous research has divided the decision making of the Burger Court may be gathered for convenience into ten generic fields: criminal procedure, civil rights, First Amendment, due process, privacy, unions, economic activity, judicial power, federal taxation, and federalism. We discuss each in turn.

In several areas of criminal procedure, Justice O'Connor's position is indeterminate either because she cast no votes—for example, contempt of court, line-ups, and search and seizure in Crime Control Act litigation—or because her votes are so badly skewed that no judgment can be made as to her position—for example, involuntary confessions and the right to trial by jury. But in those aspects of criminal procedure in which she can be positioned, she staunchly supports the prosecution while concomitantly opposing persons accused or convicted of crime. As such, she may properly be labeled a conservative. The Justices with whom she associates most closely are Rehnquist and Burger; she typically ranks as the Court's penultimate conservative, with Rehnquist anchoring the scale. The right to counsel and double jeopardy cases are illustrative. In both sets, O'Connor scored a strongly conservative −.76, Rehnquist −.80, and Burger −.61 and −.75, respectively. Similar patterns emerge in the death penalty cases, discovery and inspection, cases involving extra-legal jury influences, the Federal Rules of Criminal procedure, habeas corpus (where she ties Burger as the Court's most conservative member), search and seizure, self-incrimination, the retroactive application of newly announced individual rights, statutory construction of criminal laws, and subconstitutional fair procedure.

In five other areas O'Connor's voting clearly establishes her as supportive of law and order, but we are unable to specify how supportive she is relative to her associates. In cruel and unusual punishment cases that do not involve the death penalty, only Rehnquist and Burger may be as or more conservative than she; in plea bargaining and speedy trial litigation, only Rehnquist, Burger, and Powell may be as or more conservative; in vehicular search and seizure, only Rehnquist, Burger, and Blackmun; and in grants of immunity from self-incrimination, only Stevens. Of a total of 28 votes in these five areas, 27 rejected the accused's contentions.

O'Connor breaks her pattern of staunchly conservative voting in two areas of criminal procedure: confrontation clause and Miranda warning cases. Although she displays a conservative score of −.30 in the confrontation cases, she nonetheless ranks ahead of Rehnquist, Burger, White, and Powell, and cast a liberal vote that decided the outcome of *Lee v. Illinois*,[27] which held that out-of-court confessions by alleged accomplices are "presumptively unreliable." In the Miranda cases, O'Connor showed herself tied with White, with a marginally moderate score of −.19, less conservative than Rehnquist (−.69), Blackmun (−.59), Powell (−.44), and Burger (−.31). O'Connor's relative moderation is best exemplified by her opinion in *New York v. Quarles*,[28] in which she disagreed with the breadth of the public safety exception that the majority created in this case. This exception allows the police to question suspects in custody without reading them their Miranda rights when justified by "overriding considerations of public safety."[29]

As with criminal procedure, certain civil rights issues do not allow for an identification of O'Connor's position. She cast no votes involving debtors' rights. Her votes are too badly skewed to specify a position in deportation, poverty law, court costs of indigents, armed forces, juveniles, and illegitimates. Seven of the 26 votes cast in these cases upheld the civil rights claimant (27%). In attorneys' fees, she voted against an award in 12 of 14 cases, thereby establishing that only Rehnquist, White, and Burger may be as conservative as she or more so.

The Voting Rights Act, employment discrimination, desegregation, reapportionment, and affirmative action illustrate O'Connor's lessened conservatism relative to criminal procedure. In voting rights, her score of +.23 made her less conservative than Rehnquist (−.38), Burger, and Powell. She also ranked less extremely than this trio in reapportionment, desegregation, and employment discrimination. She tied Justice White in the last of these sets with a score of +.03. In affirmative action, Rehnquist (−.61), Stevens, Burger, and White were all less supportive of such programs than she (+.39), although Stevens's support of the programs at issue in four such cases during the early years of the Rehnquist Court placed him to her left.

The strongly conservative position she occupied in most criminal procedure issues manifests itself in six areas of civil rights, even though she maintains a distance from Rehnquist in score, if not in rank order, in two of them. She anchors the scale, tied with Rehnquist and Burger, in immigration and naturalization. She also anchors the ballot access scale, tied here with Rehnquist and Powell, with a score of −.50. She garnered the same score in handicapped persons' rights, which gained her a position exceeded only by Burger and Rehnquist. This same pair also surpassed her conservatism in the areas of liability under the civil rights acts and Indians, as did Rehnquist in residency requirements. She scored a relatively moderate −.18 and −.14, respectively, in these last two areas, as compared with Rehnquist's −.55 and −.62. Twenty points separated them in liability under the civil rights acts: −.42 to −.62.

Three civil rights areas produce voting that enable us only to approximate her position. In school desegregation, she is less conservative than Rehnquist and more or less as conservative as Burger and Powell. In the employability of aliens, she is again less conservative than Rehnquist and more or less as conservative as Burger, Powell, and White. In voting, she is not as conservative as Rehnquist, Powell, or Stevens.

Justice O'Connor displays a moderately liberal score in two areas: state regulation of Indians (+.22) and gender discrimination (+.30). She ranked as less liberal than only Marshall, Brennan, and Blackmun in the former area, and as the swing Justice in the gender discrimination cases in which she participated. She always voted with the majority here, and in two cases she provided the decisive vote: *Mississippi University for Women v. Hogan* and *Arizona Governing Committee for Tax Deferred Annuity and Deferred Compensation v. Norris*.[30] The former held that a state university's policy to exclude males from its professional nursing school violated the equal protection clause; the latter that state retirement plans paying lower benefits to women than to men because of women's longer life expectancy violated Title VII of the 1964 Civil Rights Act. Eight of O'Connor's 13 state regulation of Indians votes opposed the states and upheld Indian autonomy, while seven of her 11 gender discrimination votes supported the victim of disparate treatment.

In the general area of First Amendment freedoms, a paucity of votes precludes determination of Justice O'Connor's position on several issues: state and federal regulation of obscenity, libelous invasions of privacy, legislative investigations, security risks, protest demonstrations, and conscientious objectors. Ten of her eleven votes in these areas opposed the claimed First Amendment violation.

Although her position is also indeterminate in two other First Amendment areas, federal internal security legislation and free exercise of religion, her vote in one case in each area may prove to be instructive. She was one of the five justices in *Regan v. Wald*,[31] who upheld the validity of the Reagan administration's regulation curbing U.S. tourist travel to Cuba. Conversely, she joined Marshall, Brennan, and Blackmun in dissent from the majority's decision that an Air Force regulation that prohibited headgear while indoors applied to an Orthodox Jew's wearing of a yarmulke.[32]

In the First Amendment areas where O'Connor can be ranked with considerable precision, she tends to act more compatibly with her civil rights behavior than with that displayed in criminal procedure. In defamatory libel, she is fourth least supportive of the media's exercise of freedom of communication with a score of −.36, ahead of White (−.73) and Rehnquist and Burger (tied with −.55). She occupied the same position in cases involving aid to parochial schools and other establishment clause issues, ahead of the same three Justices. In establishment clause litigation, she was tied in rank with Powell and cast the deciding vote in two cases: *Lynch v. Donnelly*[33] and *Bender v. Williamsport Area School District*.[34] *Lynch* upheld a city's inclusion of a nativity scene in its annual Christmas display, while *Bender* held that a school board member lacked standing to appeal from a federal district court's decision that denied the request of a group of high school students who wished to meet during regularly scheduled school activity periods for the purpose of praying.

An essentially moderate position also characterized her activity in litigation on aid to sectarian schools, which, of course, is closely connected constitutionally with the other establishment clause cases. Although she cast no deciding votes, she joined five colleagues in the liberally decided "moment of silence" case, which declared unconstitutional a state law that authorized a one-minute period of silence at the beginning of each school day for "meditation or voluntary prayer."[35] On the other side, she was one of four dissenters from the liberal decision that declared shared time to be unconstitutional—that is, programs in which classes for nonpublic school students were financed by the public school system and taught by public school teachers on nonpublic school premises.[36]

A conservative position characterizes her actions in freedom of communication and commercial speech, even though she cast the deciding vote in *Federal Communications Commission v. League of Women Voters of California*,[37] which declared unconstitutional an act of Congress that banned editorializing by federally funded public broadcasting stations. Although she ranked third most conservative in freedom of communication with a score of −.37, ahead of Rehnquist and Burger, and penultimately so in commercial speech with a score of −.30, she distanced herself from Rehnquist in both sets (−.65 and −.80).

In a final First Amendment set, campaign spending, she tied Stevens, with a score of −.43, as least willing to sanction or impose accountability on persons and organizations who exceeded legislatively mandated spending limits. Closest to her and Stevens were Burger (−.29), Blackmun (−.14), and Rehnquist (.00).

Justice O'Connor can be ranked with confidence in only two of the seven components of due process: the residual due process set and impartial decision maker. In the other categories, only 10 of her 36 votes supported a violation of due process. O'Connor positions herself between Rehnquist (−.43) and Burger (−.28) on the conservative side of the Court in residual due process with a score of −.32. In the impartial decision maker set, however, only Marshall, Brennan, and Stevens voted more liberally than she did. Her inconsistent behavior precludes determination of her position toward the takings clause. In *Ruckelshaus v. Monsanto*,[38] she was the only Justice to rule that disclosure by the Environmental Protection Agency of a pesticide manufacturer's data amounted to an unconstitutional taking of its property. On the other hand, she comprised part of a five-member majority in *MacDonald, Sommer & Frates v. Yolo County*,[39] which held that landowners failed to prove that local land use restrictions precluded all development of the property. As a result, the county need not pay compensation for "taking" the property.

In the field of privacy, as in due process, O'Connor's votes produce a mixed record. Given her vote in *F.B.I. v. Abramson*,[40] she appears to be more liberal than all but Marshall and Brennan in the interpretation of the provisions of the Freedom of Information Act.[41] But in the much more salient matter of abortion, she displays strong opposition to the right thereto. Her six Burger Court votes give her a score no higher than −.76, while Rehnquist and White score −.82. Unlike Rehnquist and White, each of whom cast two supportive votes, O'Connor's six Burger Court votes were all anti-abortion.[42]

In the field of labor union activity, O'Connor shows herself to be no friend of organized labor. Although her votes are too widely scattered to specify a position in union shop cases, arbitration of disputes between labor and management, or those involving the Fair Labor Standards and the Occupational Health and Safety Acts, she compiled a strongly anti-union record in antitrust litigation, as her vote and opinion in *Shepard v. National Labor Relations Board* establish.[43] Only Rehnquist by the narrowest of margins displayed less support for unions in their assertion of rights against management than she did (−.43 versus −.40). In disputes between unions and their members, only Stevens appeared to be less supportive of unions (−.40) than O'Connor (−.15). Rehnquist, by contrast, preferred unions to union members, as his +.40 score indicates. O'Connor moderates her anti-union animus in the remaining set in this field—management's assertion of rights against labor unions. Here she scored −.13, less hostile than Burger, Stevens, Rehnquist, and Powell, who ranged from −.47 to −.20.

In the wide-ranging field of business activity and non-union economic regulation, Justice O'Connor again displays conservative proclivities that arguably are as strong as those manifest in the labor union field. As in the other fields, O'Connor's votes are too widely scattered to establish her position relative to her colleagues on a number of issues: corporate and business mergers, legal remedies available to injured persons, the evidentiary sufficiency of jury verdicts in tort actions, the liability of persons acting in non-governmental capacities, public utilities regulation, consumer protection, and zoning regulations.

Only Rehnquist supported competition less than she under the antitrust laws (−.35 versus −.02). Only Rehnquist and Burger were more willing to immunize government from the consequences of its actions (−.60 versus −.25). And only Powell opposed governmental regulation of transportation more than she and Stevens, with whom she was tied in score (+.11 versus +.19). Rehnquist located himself next to her and Stevens at +.26. The uniformly high scores occur here because 16 of the 27 cases unanimously upheld governmental regulation. Although somewhat indeterminate, O'Connor appears to tie Burger for second place, next to Rehnquist, in supporting business in bankruptcy matters. And again, although her position in natural resources and environmental protection is indeterminate, it is clear that she falls in the range of strongly to moderately conservative in this area, not appreciably distant from either Rehnquist or Powell. Finally, she is second least willing to impose accountability on those involved in governmental corruption with a score of −.25. Even Rehnquist is a notch more willing to do so in this small set of cases.

In the remaining pair of business issues, patents and copyrights and securities regulation, O'Connor occupied a decidedly moderate to liberal position. She was the swing Justice in patents and copyrights and the only member of the Burger Court always to vote with the majority. Thus, she cast the deciding vote in *Sony Corp. of America v. Universal City Studios*,[44] which held that neither consumers nor the makers of video cassette recorders infringe the copyrights of television programs when they tape them for their own use. Similarly, she cast the deciding vote in *Mills Music, Inc. v. Snyder*,[45] which held that music publishers could continue to receive royalties from a song even though the copyright holder revoked the publishing arrangement under which the song was recorded. As for securities regulation, her position vis-à-vis her colleagues cannot be specified. Nonetheless, her dissenting opinion in *Securities Industry Ass'n v. Board of Governors of the Federal Reserve System*,[46] which was joined by Brennan and Stevens, suggests that only they may be more anti-business than she in this area of economic activity.[47]

In half the fields constituting judicial power, Justice O'Connor either cast no votes (venue) or her votes were too widely scattered to determine her position (mootness; the jurisdiction and authority of the various federal courts, including the Supreme Court; and the use of comity and the abstention doctrine in criminal and First Amendment freedom cases). In these three areas, 32 of her 42 votes opposed the exercise of judicial power.

On the matter of judicial review of administrative agency action, O'Connor tied Powell as second most opposed to judicial review with a score of −.33. Rehnquist was a notch less opposed at −.29. She was third most supportive of the use of comity in civil proceedings with a score of −.63, slightly behind Rehnquist (−.71) and Burger (−.66). These two Justices, plus Powell, also surpassed her reluctance (−.53) to award plaintiffs standing to sue.

Justice O'Connor, however, switched gears by dropping her opposition to the exercise of judicial power insofar as the Federal Rules of Civil Procedure were concerned. Eight of her eleven votes upheld an activist position and produced a score of +.14. Only Marshall and Brennan were more activist than she. No other member of the Burger Court always voted in the majority. But this orientation did not survive the end of the Burger Court. During the early Rehnquist Court, her only activist votes came in unanimously decided cases.

In the three areas of federal taxation, Justice O'Connor groups herself with other Justices who oppose the government and support taxpayers. In the priority of federal fiscal claims and in the taxation of gifts and personal and professional expenses, no Justice exceeds her support of taxpayers. She ties Rehnquist and Stevens in priority, and Blackmun in gifts and personal and professional expenses. In the residual federal taxation category, she is tied in score with Rehnquist and Burger, somewhat less supportive of taxpayers than Powell and Stevens.

The final field into which the decisions of the Burger Court have been divided is federalism. Although O'Connor's position cannot be specified in the areas of state regulation of business and Submerged Lands Act litigation, she displays in unwavering support for the states in the four other areas that comprise this field. Furthermore, in these areas she locates closest to Rehnquist and is either penultimately or most supportive of the states. Thus, in state taxation, her pro-state score of +.43 is exceeded only by Rehnquist's +.60. Similarly, in national supremacy, only Rehnquist's +.76 surpasses her +.36. In the two preemption sets, she matches Rehnquist in cases involving state court jurisdiction with a pro-state score of +.65, while in preemption of state regulation her score of +.38 surpasses Rehnquist's +.33.

We turn now to the final portion of this assessment of Justice O'Connor: evidence of deviation between her voting behavior and positions espoused in her opinions. She is no less reluctant than her colleagues to spell out her position on various matters. See, for example, her opinion for the Court in *Allen v. Wright*,[48] dealing with standing to sue under Article III of the Constitution, and her special concurrence in *Davis v. Bandemer*[49] on the subject of the reapportionment of partisanly gerrymandered legislative districts. Although one may cavil that she states her position legalistically (which is certainly true of her Burger and Rehnquist Court colleagues), she occasionally minimizes their legalistic content. In this regard, note may be made of her concurrence in the affirmative action case *Wygant v. Jackson Board of Education*,[50] and her dissenting opinion in *Akron v. Akron Center for Reproductive Health*,[51] which

Rehnquist and White joined, and which she identifies as her authoritative position on abortion regulation.[52] These opinions, however, accord with her voting behavior. Indeed, in only one of her opinions has a marked discrepancy occurred between what she says and what she does, votewise: her opinion of the Court in *Michigan v. Long*.[53]

Long concerned an otherwise run-of-the-mill vehicular search and seizure case in which the Court upheld a protective search of those portions of the passenger compartment of an automobile in which a weapon could be placed or hidden. The police had stopped to investigate after Long's car swerved into a ditch. The search yielded a pouch containing marijuana.

In the course of upholding the constitutionality of the search, the Court created a presumption that it had jurisdiction to review state court decisions in cases that contain intermixed questions of state and federal law. Prior to *Long*, the Court had consistently adhered to a self-imposed policy that it would not review a state court decision that rested on adequate and independent non-federal grounds, even though the case also involved a federal question, and even though that federal question had been wrongly resolved. The reason for this policy is that the federal courts—including the Supreme Court—are courts of limited jurisdiction, and that their only authority over the state courts is to correct the latters' judgments to the extent that they incorrectly adjudge federal rights.[54]

Accordingly, the crucial inquiry for the Justice in every state court case that contains both state and federal issues is twofold: (1) does the state court decision rest on non-federal grounds, and, if so, (2) is that non-federal ground adequate to support the state court's decision? If the answer to both questions is "yes," the Supreme Court would refuse to review the case.

Prior to *Long*, the Court presumed such decisions to rest on an independent and adequate state ground unless the party petitioning the Supreme Court for review persuaded the Justices to the contrary. But in *Long*, the Court reversed itself and ruled that when

> a state court decision fairly appears to rest primarily on federal law, or to be interwoven with the federal law, and when the adequacy and independence of any possible state law ground is not clear from the face of the opinion, we will accept . . . that the state court decided the case the way it did because it believed that federal law required it to do so.[55]

To overcome this presumption, a state court "need only make clear by a plain statement in its judgment or opinion that the federal cases are being used only for the purpose of guidance, and do not themselves compel the result that the court has reached."[56]

If the foregoing language were not enough to belie deference to state court decisions, the paragraph from which this quote comes ends as follows: "If the state court decision indicates clearly and expressly that it is alternatively based on *bona fide separate*, adequate, and independent grounds, we, of course, will not undertake to review the decision" (italics added).[57] To avoid the possibility of Supreme Court review, not only must state courts provide a plain statement abjuring reliance on federal law in arriving at their decisions, but presumably they must also satisfy the Justices that this reliance is "bona fide." The addition of the word "separate," along with "adequate" and "independent," would seem to make it still easier for the Justices to review most any state court decision even if only passing reference is made to federal law.[58]

Given her support for considerations of federalism, why did Justice O'Connor and her like-minded colleagues refuse to continue the Court's policy of deference to state court decisions? A survey of the use that the Burger Court has made of *Long* in its remaining three years may prove instructive.

In ten cases, the Justices used *Long* as authority to establish jurisdiction to review state court decisions.[59] Eight of these overturned decisions of state supreme courts that had upheld the contentions of persons accused or convicted of crime: five did so in the context of Fourth Amendment claims;[60] one concerned instructions given to a jury at the penalty phase of a capital punishment case;[61] another pertained to double jeopardy;[62] and the remaining case involved the due process rights of prisoners.[63] Two cases that utilized *Long* to justify Supreme Court review of state court decisions produced a liberal outcome: *Caldwell v. Mississippi*,[64] a death penalty case, and *Three Affiliated Tribes of the Fort Berthold Reservation v. Wold*,[65] in which a federally recognized Indian tribe uncharacteristically sought to subject itself to the jurisdiction of North Dakota's courts for the purpose of resolving a dispute with a non-Indian. The Supreme Court ruled that federal law did not preclude North Dakota jurisdiction over the tribe's suit. Apart from the pro-Indian result in this case, the decision also indicates that the scope of *Long* is not limited to matters of state criminal procedure, but that it also extends to other areas in which state courts may apply federal law.

On the other hand, *Long*'s existence has not precluded the Justices from occasionally ruling that independent and adequate state grounds for judgment exist. Paramount in point is *Colorado v. Nunez*,[66] a confrontation clause case in which the writ of certiorari was dismissed. Three Justices, however, including O'Connor, signed a concurring opinion giving reasons why the Colorado Supreme Court's decision rested solely on state-law grounds, and Justice Stevens, also concurring, wrote a rejoinder faulting the *Long* majority for enlarging the Court's power to review state court decisions.

This survey of the early legacy of *Long* indicates its use as a means whereby the Court's conservative majority—which includes O'Connor—may overturn liberal state court decisions.[67] As the author of *Long*, O'Connor clearly indicated her willingness to subordinate considerations of federalism to the substantive aspects of her conservatism. In this respect, she behaves no differently from her colleagues and their predecessors on the Warren and Burger Courts. Instrumental values, such as considerations of federalism (which, when all is said and done, is nothing more than an aspect of judicial restraint), are invoked only when a Justice approves of the merits of the decision or the action under review. As has been said elsewhere, "one may defer, but never blindly."[68]

In conclusion, Justice O'Connor's service on the Burger Court shows her to be a staunch conservative who, upon confirmation, promptly acclimated herself to the Court and its workways. Indications are that this posture continues in the first years of the Rehnquist Court. Although she is the first woman to hold the position of Associate Justice of the U.S. Supreme Court, nonetheless she clearly appears to be—in Shakespeare's famous phrase—"to the manner born."

NOTES

1. S. Weisman, "Reagan Nominating Woman, an Arizona Appeals Judge, to Serve on Supreme Court," *New York Times*, July 8, 1981, pp. 1, 8; "The Brethren's First Sister," *Time* magazine, July 20, 1981, pp. 8–12, 17–19; L. Greenhouse, "High Court Nominee Hearings Open; Confirmation Termed Almost Certain," *New York Times*, Sept. 10, 1981; S. Mann and D. Fiduccia, "Sandra Day O'Connor: The Making of a Precedent," 16 *Stanford Lawyer* 4–9 (1981); B. Cook, "Women as Supreme Court Candidates: From Florence Allen to Sandra Day O'Connor," 65 *Judicature* 314 (1981–82).

2. N. Lewis, "Justice O'Connor's First Six Months," *New Republic*, Mar. 10, 1982; L. Greenhouse, "Justice O'Connor Finds a Theme in States' Rights," *New York Times*, June 4, 1982; K. Sylvester, "Justice O'Connor Makes Her Mark on High Court," *National Law Journal*, July 19, 1982; S. Sherry, "Civic Virtue and the Feminine Voice in Constitutional Adjudication," 72 *Virginia Law Review* 543 (1982); R. Duncan, "Justice O'Connor, the Constitution, and the Trimester Approach to Abortion: A Liberty on a Collision Course with Itself," 29 *Catholic Lawyer* 275 (1984); B. Bruckman, "Justice Sandra Day O'Connor: Trends toward Judicial Restraint," 42 *Washington & Lee Law Review* 1185 (1985); R. Cordray and J. Vradelis, "The Emerging Jurisprudence of Justice O'Connor," 52 *University of Chicago Law Review* 389 (1985); J. Scheb and L. Alshie, "Justice Sandra Day O'Connor and the 'Freshman Effect,' " 69 *Judicature* 9 (1985); M. Miller, "Justice Sandra Day O'Connor: Token or Triumph from a Feminist Perspective?" 15 *Golden Gate University Law Review* 493 (1985); M. Glennon, "Democrat with a Small 'd', " 72 *A.B.A. Journal* 55 (June 15, 1986); Elder Witt, *A Different Justice* (1986).

3. See A. Fausto-Sterling, *Myths of Gender* (1986).

4. H. Spaeth, *Supreme Court Policy Making* (1979), pp. 109–18.

5. M. Altfeld and H. Spaeth, "Measuring Influence on the U.S. Supreme Court," 24 *Jurimetrics Journal* 238–39 (1984).

6. *Id.*, p. 242.

7. *Idaho ex rel. Evans v. Oregon*, 462 U.S. 1017 (1983).

8. 459 U.S. 344 (1983).

9. 467 U.S. 986 (1984).

10. *F.B.I. v. Abramson*, 456 U.S. 615 (1982); *Securities Industry Ass'n v. Board of Governors of the Federal Reserve System*, 468 U.S. 137 (1984); and *Metropolitan Life Ins. Co. v. Ward*, 470 U.S. 869 (1985).

11. *New York v. Quarles*, 467 U.S. 649 (1984), and *Goldman v. Weinberger*, 475 U.S. 503 (1986).

12. *Welding v. Gray*, 470 U.S. 414 (1985), and *United States v. James*, 478 U.S. 597 (1986).

13. *Dickerson v. New Banner Institute*, 460 U.S. 103 (1983), and *United States v. Yermian*, 468 U.S. 63 (1984). In *Dickerson*, Rehnquist wrote the liberal dissenting opinion that O'Connor, along with Brennan and Stevens, joined. The majority held that disabilities imposed by the 1968 Gun Control Act could not be removed because a state expunged the ex-convict's record.

14. *Carpenters v. Scott*, 463 U.S. 825 (1983).

15. *Fair Assessment in Real Estate Ass'n v. McNary*, 454 U.S. 100 (1981).

16. *Lindahl v. Office of Personnel Management*, 470 U.S. 768 (1985).

17. *National Labor Relations Board v. Longshoremen*, 473 U.S. 61 (1985).

18. *South Carolina v. Catawba Indian Tribe*, 476 U.S. 498 (1986).

19. 454 U.S. 201 (1981).

20. 476 U.S. 610 (1986).

21. For example, *Maine v. Moulton*, 474 U.S. 159 (1985), and *Michigan v. Jackson*, 475 U.S. 625 (1986), which extended the right to counsel; *Sheet Metal Workers' Int'l. Ass'n. v. EEOC*, 478 U.S. 421 (1986), a major affirmative action case; *Maryland v. Munson Co.*, 467 U.S. 947 (1984), which held a state statute that limited charities' expenses to 25 percent of the monies raised to be unconstitutionally overbroad; *Pulliam v. Allen*, 466 U.S. 522 (1984), which subjected judges to a small measure of liability; *Solem v. Helm*, 463 U.S. 277 (1983), which held that a parolee's life sentence for a repeat violation of a nonviolent felony violates the Eighth Amendment; *Akron v. Akron Center for Reproductive Health*, 462 U.S. 416 (1983), a leading abortion decision; and *Washington v. Seattle School District*, 458 U.S. 457 (1982), a major busing case.

22. Scheb and Alshie, "Justice Sandra Day O'Connor," pp. 9–12.

23. *Id.*, pp. 10, 12.

24. Altfeld and Spaeth, "Measuring Influence on the U.S. Supreme Court," p. 242.

25. Spaeth, *Supreme Court Policy Making*, pp. 118–25.

26. The procedure and formula for calculating scale scores are provided in D. Rohde and H. Spaeth, *Supreme Court Decision Making* (1976), p. 141.

27. 476 U.S. 530 (1986).

28. 467 U.S. 649 (1984).

29. *Id.*, p. 660.

30. 458 U.S. 718 (1982); 463 U.S. 1073 (1983).

31. 468 U.S. 222 (1984).

32. *Goldman v. Weinberger*, 475 U.S. 503 (1986).

33. 465 U.S. 668 (1984). In *Allegheny County v. A.C.L.U.*, 57 U.S.L.W. 5045 (1989), O'Connor found acceptable a menorah displayed next to a Christmas tree, but found a nativity scene in a second display unacceptable.

34. 475 U.S. 534 (1986). Through the end of the 1980s, O'Connor functioned as the swing voter in the Rehnquist Court's establishment clause cases, voting in the majority in all ten such cases. For example, see *Lyng v. Northwest Indian Cemetery Protective Ass'n.*, 56 U.S.L.W. 4292 (1988).

35. *Wallace v. Jaffree*, 472 U.S. 38 (1985).

36. *Grand Rapids School District v. Ball*, 473 U.S. 373 (1985).

37. 468 U.S. 364 (1984).

38. 467 U.S. 986 (1984).

39. 477 U.S. 340 (1986).

40. 456 U.S. 615 (1982).

41. She accused the majority of redrafting the statute's language to exempt law enforcement records that were not compiled for such purposes. Ambiguities in the Act, she said, should "be resolved in favor of disclosure." *Id.*, p. 637.

42. Strictly speaking, White's pro-privacy votes occurred in contraception, rather than abortion, cases: *Eisenstadt v. Baird*, 405 U.S. 438 (1972), and *Carey v. Population Services*, 431 U.S. 678 (1977). Following Powell's retirement at the end of the 1986 Term, O'Connor's vote became crucial to the outcome of abortion cases. See *Webster v. Reproductive Health Services*, 57 U.S.L.W. 5023 (1989), where her position was essential to the state's victory.

43. 459 U.S. 344 (1983).

44. 464 U.S. 417 (1984).

45. 469 U.S. 153 (1985). Early Rehnquist Court decisions show her to be solidly conservative, however. See, for example, *K Mart Corp. v. Cartier, Inc.*, 56 U.S.L.W. 4219, 4478 (1988).

46. 468 U.S. 137 (1984).

47. The majority ruled that federal law did not allow banks to underwrite commercial paper, the short-term debt of major corporations. Such paper is a "security" and thus not within the authority of the Federal Reserve Board to regulate. O'Connor argued that the Court should defer to the Board's "expertise and experience in this area of law." *Id.*, p. 161. But her conservative votes in early Rehnquist Court decisions indicate that her position in this case was out of character. See, for example, *Shearson/American Express, Inc. v. McMahon*, 482 U.S. 220 (1987), and *Basic Incorporated v. Levinson*, 56 U.S.L.W. 4232 (1988).

48. 468 U.S. 737 (1984).

49. 478 U.S. 109, 144 (1986).

50. 476 U.S. 267, 284 (1987). Also see Lauter, " 'Affirmative Action': What's Allowed, What's Not," *National Law Journal*, June 2, 1986, pp. 5, 22.

51. 462 U.S. 416, 452 (1983).

52. As she stated in her dissent in *Thornburgh v. American College of Obstetricians and Gynecologists*, 476 U.S. 747, 814 (1986).

53. 463 U.S. 1032 (1983).

54. R. Stern and E. Gressman, *Supreme Court Practice* (5th ed. 1978), pp. 230–32.

55. 463 U.S. 1032, 1040–41 (1983).

56. *Id.*, p. 1041.
57. *Id.*
58. See R. Collins, "High Court Asserts Its Authority," *National Law Journal*, Aug. 1, 1983, p. 5, for support for this analysis.
59. Long's substantive nonjurisdictional ruling served as authority to uphold searches in several other cases: *United States v. Jacobsen*, 466 U.S. 109 (1984); *Hudson v. Palmer*, 468 U.S. 517 (1984); *United States v. Hensley*, 469 U.S. 221 (1985); and *New Jersey v. T.L.O.*, 469 U.S. 325 (1985).
60. *Maine v. Thornton*, 466 U.S. 170 (1984); *Florida v. Meyers*, 466 U.S. 380 (1984); *Massachusetts v. Upton*, 466 U.S. 727 (1984); *California v. Carney*, 471 U.S. 386 (1985); and *New York v. Class*, 475 U.S. 106 (1986).
61. *California v. Ramos*, 463 U.S. 992 (1983).
62. *Ohio v. Johnson*, 467 U.S. 493 (1984).
63. *Ponte v. Real*, 471 U.S. 491 (1985).
64. 472 U.S. 320 (1985).
65. 467 U.S. 138 (1984).
66. 465 U.S. 324 (1984).
67. Quite clearly, a liberal majority could just as easily use *Long* as a means to overturn conservative state court decisions.
68. H. Spaeth and S. Teger, "Activism and Restraint: A Cloak for the Justices' Policy Preferences," in S. Halpern and C. Lamb, eds., *Supreme Court Activism and Restraint* (1982), p. 297.

6

The Constitution and the Legacy of Justice William O. Douglas

Walter F. Murphy

A biographical sketch of William Orville Douglas can be terse. He was born in 1898 in Minnesota; grew up in Yakima, Washington, a small town in the Cascade Mountains; graduated from Whitman College in Walla Walla, then Columbia Law School; practiced law on Wall Street for a brief period; returned to Columbia to teach; moved to the faculty at Yale; was appointed in 1936 as a member and then later as chairman of the Securities and Exchange Commission; was a friend and confidant of Franklin D. Roosevelt, who nominated him as an Associate Justice of the Supreme Court of the United States in 1939; retired in 1975 having served thirty-six and a half years, longer than any Justice in American history; and died in 1980 after a long illness.[1]

The story is worthy of Horatio Alger: The crippled son of an itinerant minister works day and night to graduate second in his class in law school, becomes a reformer who strikes terror in the hearts of the greedy moguls of Wall Street, then becomes an internationally renowned jurist who spends the rest of his life championing the cause of the underdog. This account also conceals much—a man who was always deeply troubled, never at peace with himself or his world; a judge who was alternately—and sometimes simultaneously—brilliant and careless, eloquent and unpolished, cynical and idealistic.

DOUGLAS THE MAN

I first—and very briefly—met William O. Douglas in 1958 when I interviewed him about some research I was doing. He was crisp, polite, and reasonably responsive. About a year later, he visited Princeton to give the Walter Edge Lectures, and I was assigned the role of guide dog for an afternoon. We passed the time by meeting with a group of seniors who were writing their theses on the Supreme Court.

These young men were bright, well informed, and determined to find out more than the Justice was—at first—willing to tell them about his constitutional thinking. For two hours they grilled him, politely but mercilessly, reacting to vague replies with comments like, "That won't wash, sir, because in 1949 you said," with a long and exact quote following. Douglas squirmed, then fought back, and at times the exchange became heated as he argued with the students and they with him. Sometimes they scored points, sometimes he did. Neither asked nor gave quarter.

It was dark and cold when we left the library to return to the President's house, and I was glad the distance was short, for I was certain that the great man would be angered by the students' effrontery. As we walked out of the building I could see that Douglas was agitated. Then he grabbed my arm, and I was afraid I was about to be struck by a Justice of the Supreme Court. But all he had was a question: "What do you do to excite students like that? I haven't had so much fun since I was in law school!"

I thought it best not to mention that Alpheus Thomas Mason and William M. Beaney had been responsible for the students' excitement. And out of his mistake and my admiration for a famous judge who would take on students as equals and admit error when they bested him, a friendship was born, although it took me a decade to realize that we were friends. We worked together for several years on his papers with only slight indications that he knew or cared more about me than my name and telephone number. My assumption turned out to be false, but Douglas was not the most demonstrative, or sensitive, of men; and his ego was as enormous as his need for success.

He seemed to be a bundle of contradictions. What appeared to be coldness was usually evidence of his shyness. I say "usually" because he would sometimes cover anger with a glacier of disregard. He could and often did freeze people out of his life, practicing as a fine art the ghetto curse of "Forget you." Yet, despite his introversion, he loved to lecture and basked in the hero worship that students, especially in his later years, heaped on him.

When he took the rostrum he could be as dull as the worst of professors. He could also be as quick-witted as a stand-up comedian. After one of his lectures at Princeton in the spring of 1973, just as the Senate's

Watergate hearings were getting under way and H. R. Haldeman and John Ehrlichman were invoking executive privilege as grounds for not testifying, a student asked the Justice what he thought of that as a constitutional defense. Douglas affected a puzzled look and replied disingenuously: "I don't think they're invoking executive privilege at all; I think they're invoking the Fifth Amendment." The audience roared in appreciation.

In his personal relations, he could exasperate even close friends. I remember receiving a call from him one day asking me to come down to Washington immediately. I explained I could not because I was teaching that day, but would be there the next morning. He grunted something and hung up. The next morning I took a 6:30 train, arrived in Washington three hours later, and walked over to the Court to be greeted with a surprised look from the Justice's secretary. She buzzed him on the intercom and, after about ten minutes, he came storming out. "What do you want?" I explained that I didn't want anything: He had called me. He shrugged his shoulders and said he was too busy to talk, turned his back, and strode into his office, slamming the door behind him. It was another three-hour ride back to Princeton.

Some of his law clerks worshipped him; others hated him for engaging them in a master-slave relationship. The latter saw only his coldness without understanding his shyness, his obsession that the Court's work be done rapidly. Some of them realized he whipped himself even harder than he drove them, but they never saw the other side of the man. And he bears much responsibility here, for his moods—and his manners—could swing widely. He could grapple friends to his heart, a short time later shut them out of his consciousness, and then be genuinely hurt when they made their resentment known.

Yet there was, in fact, another warm, loving side to the man. He could be charming and droll in conversation, and would pay people whom he respected the same compliment he had given the students in 1958, that of arguing with them as equals, caring what they thought, and changing his mind on those very rare occasions when he believed they were right.

The clerks who loved him saw that side pop through his shy aloofness. Some of them realized he had a sense of humor and could occasionally be teased into laughing at himself. That humor had a boyish aspect. He delighted in playing pranks on friends, such as putting an inebriated colleague on a plane to Chicago instead of Boston and doubling over in laughter when a confused voice came over the telephone: "Bill, what am I doing in Chicago?" Furthermore, he could do a good deed behind one's back—an unsolicited and praising telephone call to Princeton's president when I was a struggling young assistant professor and an offer, also unsolicited but gratefully accepted, to use his office and the Court's library during the summer months when I was working on a new book.

If in private life Douglas was a bundle of paradoxes, he was even more so in public affairs. As a citizen he was as avid an anti-communist as J. Edgar Hoover, although much more concerned about foreign than domestic communism. On one occasion he took army equipment with him on hikes through the Soviet Union so he could test it under "real" conditions. On other occasions, he reported to the CIA or even directly to the White House with information he had gathered during his travels abroad.

On the other hand, as a judge he was the great defender of communists' civil rights. Unlike Hoover, Richard Nixon, Joseph McCarthy, and their ilk, Douglas never lost sight of why communists' ideas were "abhorrent": because they did not—could not, consistently with the notion of the "dictatorship of the proletariat"—respect the basic rights of mankind. Thus, unlike many of his contemporaries, he was not willing to "get" communists at the price of twisting the Constitution and squashing those cherished rights. To sacrifice freedom of speech, "the glory of our government," was too much to ask for whatever gain there might be in ridding the country of a few "miserable merchants of unwanted ideas."[2] Concerned that anyone could rank an abstract value like liberty ahead of putting suspected communists behind bars, Douglas's old friend J. Edgar Hoover put him under surveillance.

The war in Vietnam created a special crisis for Douglas. It was difficult for him to speak out when Americans were dying on battlefields; nevertheless, he openly opposed the war. And he did so as a patriot, as a man who genuinely loved his country and hated communism. As a judge, he viewed the whole affair as an unconstitutional exercise of executive and to some extent even legislative power; it was a bloody war that Congress had never declared. As a citizen, he was appalled at the war's brutality and senselessness. He was convinced that we would not only lose Vietnam but also cause Asians to look on the United States as an imperialist oppressor rather than as the great defender of individual liberty.

Here, as in most aspects of his life, it is difficult to separate Douglas the judge from Douglas the democratic citizen—and either from Douglas the very private human being. These were tasks he himself never accomplished. He slid from one role to the other with an ease that angered enemies and sometimes bothered friends. Douglas's view of the judicial role could be as austere as that which Felix Frankfurter proclaimed; but Douglas could get involved in public controversy and even, although not as often, as deeply, nor perhaps as astutely as Frankfurter, in the operations of the executive department.

As a judge, Douglas was extraordinarily complex, although his opinions generally masked the subtlety and intricacy of his thought. Usually, he wrote for intelligent lay people, never, except on highly technical matters such as the Securities Exchange Act, for professors of law, and seldom for his fellow judges.

Moreover, when he had taught at the Columbia and Yale law schools, he had been a leading member of the so-called Legal Realists, men who looked with scorn on the law's claim to objectivity. The Realists had followed Oliver Wendell Holmes's advice to "wash the law in cynical acid." It was something that Professor, later Commissioner, and even Justice Douglas could do with skill, indeed relish. Almost at the same instant, however, he could look on law as an idealist would, as embodying society's noblest aspirations. For him, the Constitution of the United States had a status that was almost sacred, representing an American vision of the good society.

His background as a Realist and his training in the step-by-step, take-one-problem-at-a-time tradition of the common law gave him an atheoretical, even an anti-theoretical, approach to law. Still, displaying another of the contradictions he could never resolve, he could try theoretical approaches and search for grand generalizations beyond the confines of the American legal system.

His early friendship on the Court with Hugo Black led him, for a time, to embrace the crude legal positivism that Black typically preached but did not always follow. But after a decade, Douglas drifted away from Black's jurisprudence, perhaps because he saw that version of positivism committing a strange form of suicide as it contradicted the plain words of the constitutional document itself. Perhaps the break came because Douglas finally realized that such mechanical reasoning was based on a view of the state and society that ran counter to his own notions of the nature of man and his relation to his Creator.

As a private person and as a judge, Douglas could speak glowingly of duties as well as rights. But, just as he tended to leave his family and friends alone to fend for themselves—"I have only one soul to save," he was fond of saying, "my own"—so he seldom tried to persuade his brothers on the Court of the rightness of his position. He would state his views tartly and tersely. The bargaining, the give-and-take of compromise among the Justices that is typically an integral part of the Court's work, was something that he never enjoyed and in which he engaged only when absolutely necessary. "I would argue with Bill about anything except his vote," one colleague is reported to have said.

Douglas could operate with grand indifference to normal rules of consistency. He could, for instance, join Hugo Black's concurring opinion in *New York Times v. Sullivan* (1964), arguing that citizens should have complete immunity from libel and slander suits for criticizing public officials, then later seriously consider filing a libel suit against one of his own critics.

Many of these paradoxes were more apparent than real. If he hated communism, he loved the Bill of Rights more. If he opposed the war in Vietnam, it was because he saw it as violating the Constitution, corroding American ideals, and destroying the nation's rightful image in the world. If he made sorties into the political processes, it was because he thought he had such a right as a citizen. And circumspection was not a word in his vocabulary—which is not to say that he was completely naive about politics. He had come to the federal government in 1934 and was familiar with the Washingtonese behind which public officials shrouded their thoughts. He preferred to be blunt and candid in his speech, well aware that, as Holmes once put it, candor is one of the cleverest forms of deception.

Douglas's agreement with Black's absolutist position on the First Amendment was always more tentative than one might think from his joining Black's separate opinions. I can remember Douglas's conceding, after a long argument one night, that he did not fully agree with Black, but he thought Black's reasoning better than any he or others had yet discovered.

But at least some of these paradoxes were quite real. Most obviously, Douglas's personality fit no stereotypes, or perhaps it fit too many. He was, as Sidney Davis, his closest friend, put it, "an introverted and private man who led an active and public life, a peaceful man who lived with conflict, and a quiet man who would not hold his silence."[3] Douglas was the dour Scot as well as the witty Celt; a workaholic on the Court, a relaxed, luxuriating hiker and fisherman at play; a meticulous craftsman writing on the law of securities or monopolies, a careless composer of judicial opinions for public consumption; a shrewd participant in domestic politics, a simplistic, moralistic commentator on international relations.

The key to understanding the Justice, Mercedes, his second wife, once told me, was his Calvinist heritage.[4] His father had been a Presbyterian minister; and, although he had died when young Bill was scarcely more than an infant, Douglas had become almost a parody of Max Weber's Protestant ethic. He needed frequent reassurances that he was among the elect, reassurances that could only come through continued successes and recognition of those successes. He was, Mercedes believed, beset by the Calvinist's sense of personal unworthiness, frightened, perhaps even convinced, that he was a failure—with all the dire and eternal consequences failure carried.

This hypothesis does explain much about the man. One can reasonably claim that his basic need for reassurance drove him to work feverishly, as year after year he wrote more opinions than any of his brethren, while lecturing around the country—indeed, the world—and writing spates of volumes ranging from his autobiographical *Of Men and Mountains* to travel books like *West of the Indus* to popular tracts like *Points of Rebellion* to serious and erudite studies of comparative constitutional law like *We, the Judges* and eloquent pleas to protect the environment like *My Wilderness* and *The Three Hundred Year War*. One might see his need for constant success impelling him to finish projects quickly rather than carefully, sketching, outlining rather than finely detailing. Only with his autobiography did he take the time to work and rework again and again what he wanted to say. But by then it was too late. The final revisions came after his mind had been ravaged by a debilitating stroke, which fused memory and imagination.

At first glance, it might seem that even a neurotic would have difficulty not recognizing Douglas's life—at least before his stroke in 1974—as a string of resounding successes. He was typically the brightest and the youngest in any company he kept, whether at Whitman, Columbia, Yale, the Securities and Exchange Commission, FDR's poker parties, or the Supreme Court. But he also suffered a fair share of misery and defeat. His father's death had left the family so poor that his mother had to take in washing to feed her children. And, stricken with an attack of polio that left his legs withered, Douglas became the object of other children's ridicule. He was poor and sickly in a culture that worshipped wealth and health as signs of God's favor.

Fortunately, his mother had read about Sister Kenny and refused to accept the "medical fact" that her son would be permanently crippled; she treated him at home, eventually bringing life back into his limbs. She also managed to implant in her son some of her spirit; and, when he was able, he began taking longer and longer hikes, often alone, into the mountains to build up his legs. In time, he completely recovered from the physical effects of polio, but the deeper wounds from its psychological savaging never healed.

On those hikes, which soon turned into camping trips, Douglas sometimes met mountain men, rugged individualists who faced life alone, without concern for material benefits. Later he met cowboys and hoboes. The loneliness of their lives, their independence, their affinity with nature, struck a responsive cord in his soul. One of the songs he had asked to be sung at his funeral he associated with an old cowboy.

Money, or rather its scarcity, was a constant problem in Douglas's life. He went to Whitman College on a full-tuition scholarship but still had to work part-time. To travel from Yakima to Columbia he had taken a job on a freight train to Minnesota and rode the rails to Chicago. Outside that city, he was almost killed when he could not produce enough money to bribe a railroad crewman and had to jump off the moving train.

When he arrived in New York he had less than $10 and could not register at Columbia Law School, but he immediately persuaded a lawyer who was running a correspondence school to give him an advance for drafting a business-law course—before he had yet attended a single class. To stay at Columbia he held a series of jobs, mostly tutoring and writing term papers for others.

Out of all these youthful experiences, William O. Douglas took shape. As judge, administrator, professor, husband, and father, he was always leery of most other people, afraid to express his own emotions, convinced that, like the mountain man, cowboy, or hobo, all of us have to face—and conquer—life alone. And he was determined to do so by dint of his willpower. He was grateful for friendship once he saw it was truly offered, yet he usually remained fearful that it would be withdrawn. As a father, he seemed cold and aloof and became estranged from his children. His record as a husband fell short of the ideal. Three of his four marriages, the last two to women one-third his age, ended in divorce.

On the Securities and Exchange Commission, he was bright and brash, delighting in exposing the myriad sins of the rich and famous barons of Wall Street. His quick intelligence and willingness to work 12-, 14-, 16-, and occasionally 24-hour days allowed him to master the operations of the stock exchange and to expose the scandalous ways in which Wall Street's old-boy network had bilked billions from a trusting public.

One can see all of this life shaping Douglas's work on the Court: a Realist's cynicism for orthodox legal doctrines, a poor boy's disdain for the "establishment," an outsider's suspicions about the way authorities treated those marginal persons likely to be accused of crime, and a libertarian's constant refrain that the Bill of Rights was meant to get government off the backs of the people. One can also see those influences in his concern for the underdog and his idealistic view of the Constitution. Douglas's youth echoes in his opinion for the Court striking down a local ordinance that made vagrancy a crime:

> Walkers and strollers and wanderers may be going to or coming from a burglary. Loafers or loiterers may be "casing" a place for a holdup....
>
> The difficulty is that these activities are historically part of the amenities of life as we have known them. They are not mentioned in the Constitution or the Bill of Rights. These unwritten amenities have been in part responsible for giving our people the feeling of independence and self-confidence, the feeling of creativity. These amenities have dignified the right of dissent and have honored the right to defy submissiveness. They have encouraged lives of high spirits rather than hushed, suffocating silence.
>
> They are embedded in Walt Whitman's writings, especially in his "Song of the Open Road." They are reflected, too, in the spirit of Vachel Lindsay's "I Want to Go Wandering," and by Henry D. Thoreau.[5]

In each of his roles, whether as father, husband, administrator, or judge, Douglas was a loner. He saw himself as an outsider, an alien, at times even a pariah. It was a self-image that was heightened by the orchestrated hostility of minions whom Felix Frankfurter had helped place on the faculties of law schools and by four serious efforts in Congress to impeach him. But Douglas had enough pluck and puck to act that part with glee.

CONSTITUTIONAL JURISPRUDENCE[6]

General Patterns

For the Supreme Court, Roosevelt carefully chose men who agreed with him on the constitutional issues that he considered critical; and most critical during the 1930s was the question of the constitutionality of governmental, federal as well as state, regulation of the economy. He had, after all, just fought and narrowly won a war with the Supreme Court over that matter. In Douglas, FDR found his man. The former chairman of the Securities and Exchange Commission, the youthful *bête noir* of Wall Street, was not apt to be sympathetic to big businesses' claims to immunity from governmental control.

If Douglas's position on government and the economy had been predictable, his views on civil rights were completely unknown, even to himself. These were issues about which FDR had cared little and thought less and to which Douglas himself had paid no attention. It was in this area, however, that he would make his principal substantive contribution to constitutional law. Soon he allied himself with Hugo L. Black and later with Frank Murphy and Wiley Rutledge to form the libertarian wing of the Court. In Douglas, poor people, blacks, defendants in criminal cases, insular religious minorities, and political dissidents found an eloquent advocate.

He wanted to make all the Bill of Rights applicable to the states, and he tried to give each of these clauses a generous interpretation. Equal protection of the law was holy to Douglas. He helped erode, and then erase, the old doctrine of "separate but equal," and he pled for the Court to treat classifications based on race, ancestry, or wealth as "suspect" and thus not entitled to the presumption of constitutionality the Court usually accords challenged legislation.

The great blot on his constitutional honor was *Korematsu v. United States* (1944).[7] During World War II, the army had locked up in concentration camps more than a hundred thousand American citizens of Japanese ancestry, and it had done so without formal charges or trials. As the general in command of the operation said, "A Jap is a Jap." Relying on the war power rather than the racism that underpinned the policy, the Court, by a 6 to 3 vote, sustained the imprisonment. Initially, Douglas had circulated a dissent, but Black talked him out of publishing it. In return, Black made a number of changes in the opinion he was writing for the Court and joined in Douglas's opinion in another case, holding that—as a matter of statutory, not constitutional, interpretation—the government had to release Nisei from the camps as soon as it had established their loyalty to the United States.[8]

I can remember talking to him about *Korematsu* several times. Each conversation was strained. I "folded up," he replied when I asked him why he had not published his dissent.[9] Later, when I pushed him to explain how he felt about his vote, he said angrily: "I am ashamed." It was clear that this part of our conversation had abruptly ended. When he wrote his memoirs, he was only a bit kinder to himself. He referred to the whole program as one of "grave injustices." "Fine American citizens had been robbed of their properties by racists—crimes that might not have happened if the Court had not followed the Pentagon so literally. The evacuation case . . . was ever on my conscience."[10]

Korematsu was an aberration in Douglas's life. He had put aside his own views for those of "the establishment," in this instance the military. It was a mistake he would remember during the war in Vietnam and would not repeat, then or ever.

Integral to his overall sympathy for civil liberty was a concern for the instrumental, political rights to speak, publish, associate, assemble, and vote. He was a true believer in democracy, with profound faith both in the right of the people to hear all the evidence and arguments before they voted and their capacity to make proper choices without government's intervention, even its well-intentioned intervention.

But Douglas was a constitutionalist as well as—probably even more than—a democrat. He distrusted all government, even popular government, and believed that the American political system reflected a similar distrust in its many restrictions on majority rule. Most salient for his career would be the functions the Supreme Court was supposed to play in that system. His early foil was Felix Frankfurter, although later Douglas and Black also developed intense differences here. Frankfurter constantly preached, although he less regularly practiced, a gospel of judicial humility and deference to elected officials. Adapting James Bradley Thayer's doctrine of "the clear mistake," Frankfurter urged the Court to sustain legislation unless it was patently unreasonable.

Douglas, however, would have no part of judicially imposed constitutional amendments allowing legislatures to violate rights as long as they did so "reasonably." As he protested against one of Frankfurter's opinions:

> The philosophy of the opinion that sustains this statute is foreign to our constitutional system. It gives supremacy to the Legislature in a way that is incompatible with the scheme of a written constitution. A decision such as this could be expected in England where there is no written constitution, and where the

House of Commons has the final say. But with all deference, this philosophy has no place here. By proclaiming it we forsake much of our constitutional heritage and move closer to the British scheme. That may be better than ours or it may be worse. Certainly it is not ours.[11]

A few years later he took out after one of Frankfurter's concurring opinions:

Reference is made to British law and British practice. But they have little relevance to our problem, since we live under a written Constitution. What is entrusted to the keeping of the legislature in England is protected from legislative interference or regulation here.[12]

Because of his militant protection of civil liberties in cases involving states' claims to authority, Douglas was widely believed to have little regard for what Americans refer to as "states' rights." This view, however, was false. Where the Bill of Rights or equal protection was not at issue, Douglas was staunch defender of the authority of the states, repeating Brandeis's claim that, as "laboratories" for the larger polity, states deserved broad constitutional latitude in experimenting with socioeconomic regulations.

Private Property and Governmental Regulation

Douglas found no constitutional problems in either federal or state regulation of the economy, but he saw corporations as more than mere extensions of private property. They were a form of governmental benefit, and for that benefit government could exact a price. Moreover, manufacturing and most other forms of commerce were much more complicated than older, simpler forms of commercial enterprise and the notions of property they entailed. It was a grave mistake, he thought, to equate the framers' conceptions of private property with the operations of giant corporations, employing thousands of people in a dozen states and perhaps as many foreign countries, and whose ownership was typically separate from management. A good Lockean would argue, he believed, that if the title to goods came from mixing one's sweat with raw material, then the ownership of property at the end of a production line presented a very tangled question, and one that capitalists might not wish to unsnarl.

Where property that was truly owned by private citizens was at stake, Douglas's attitude was quite different. "Man's liberty," he wrote in 1968, "is, of course, often related to his property rights."

The home and its privacy are property interests. Ownership of a press is essential to the freedom granted [sic] newspapers, magazines, pamphlets, and books.

> Ownership of a church or cathedral is basic to the free exercise of religion by those whose faith brings them together in congregations. These cannot be taken away without impairing the right.[13]

Nine years later, he joined in Justice Potter Stewart's opinion for the Court, saying that "the dichotomy between personal liberties and property rights is a false one. Property does not have rights. People have rights. . . . [A] fundamental interdependence exists between the personal right to liberty and the personal right in property. Neither could have meaning without the other."[14]

Furthermore, Douglas understood that "property" consisted of more than mere tangible goods. And, true to his Lockean philosophy, he saw man's own labor as a critical element in both liberty and property. "The right to work, I had assumed," he wrote in dissent,

> is the most precious liberty that man possesses. Man has indeed as much right to work as he has to live, to be free, to own property. . . . To work means to eat. It also means to live. . . . The great values of freedom are in the opportunities afforded man to press to new horizons, to pit his strength against the forces of nature, to match skills with his fellow man.[15]

Approaches to Constitutional Interpretation

Douglas typically addressed constitutional problems in a pragmatic, even ad hoc fashion. "No feature of Douglas' career," G. Edward White claimed, "caused more commentary from both critics and admirers than his apparent unwillingness to buttress results he reached in cases by resort to the common analytical techniques employed by twentieth-century Justices as justificatory devices."[16] I think it more accurate to say that Douglas used whatever accepted interpretative "approach," "mode," or "technique"[17] would yield the result he thought best fit the problem a particular case presented; and, if no approach fit, he invented his own. With personal liberty as his lodestar, the result that the problem demanded was usually crystal clear in his mind.

As already noted, Douglas's early career as a Realist left a thick crust of distrust of and distaste for grand theorizing about law. Still, he held such a theory, or perhaps several of them, even if he never explained his legal philosophy with any meaningful degree of completeness.

This failure was fueled not only by his Realism but also by his huge intelligence, impatience, and need for instant results to confirm his status among God's chosen. Articulating a general theory requires concerted work across many years; and his craving for constant reassurance did not allow him to wait. His capacity to cut rapidly to the core of even the most complex problems and his restlessness also contributed to his atheoretical bent.

In addition, both characteristics contributed to his preference for short opinions like those Holmes had written over the longer, scholarly, even pedantic essays that some of his brethren wrote. And, while overburdened students may welcome terse opinions, Douglas's, like Holmes's, often left unexplained to lesser mortals what to either man was obvious. When someone would point out to Douglas that, in Holmes's phrase, he was proceeding from "inarticulate major premises," he would respond that anyone with any intelligence would grasp what that premise was. "Do I need to spell everything out?" would be his annoyed reply. The answer, of course, was yes; but he could never quite believe it.

THE RIGHT TO PRIVACY

A close examination of one issue can demonstrate the interworkings of Douglas's passion for liberty, his willingness as a judge to play a creative role to defend individual rights, his ability to begin to articulate a theory of constitutional interpretation, his rapid tiring with careful theoretical argument, and the frustrations he could inflict on those who expected a learned and brilliant jurist to explain and defend a coherent jurisprudence. Perhaps that process is best illustrated by his part in developing a general constitutional right to privacy.

One would suspect that a shy man, a loner who felt his alienation from much of the larger society, would treasure such a right. Douglas's off-the-bench writings, extolling independence and the joys of being free from many of the artificial restrictions that living in a mass, industrialized society necessarily imposed, provided additional, strong hints.

There were other indications as well. First, he was a great admirer of Louis D. Brandeis, whose place he had taken on the Court and whose opposition to "bigness," whether in business or government, Douglas had shared as a political and economic reformer. And Brandeis had been heavily responsible for the growth of a notion of a general right to privacy. In 1890 he had coauthored a seminal article;[18] and in 1928 he had written, in dissent, a powerful and eloquent constitutional creed built around "the right to be let alone":

> The makers of our Constitution undertook to secure conditions favorable to the pursuit of happiness. They recognized the significance of man's spiritual nature, of his feelings and of his intellect.... They conferred against the Government, the right to be let alone—the most comprehensive of rights and the right most valued by civilized men. To protect that right, every unjustifiable intrusion by the Government upon the privacy of the individual, whatever the means employed, must be deemed a violation of the Fourth Amendment.[19]

Second, although during his early service on the Court Douglas tended to vote with Black, the two often disagreed in cases involving questions about what constituted an "unreasonable" search or seizure under the Fourth Amendment. Black was much less suspicious than Douglas of police intrusions into personal liberty or privacy.[20]

On the other hand, the constitutional document made no mention of any general right to privacy, explicitly protecting certain specific aspects. And, early on, Douglas seemed quite content with Black's literalistic approach to constitutional interpretation. A dozen years older than Douglas, Black had been a populist senator from the red clay country of Alabama. He had grown up and begun his political career during the decades when the Supreme Court found the concept of "freedom of contract" in the due process clauses of the Fifth and Fourteenth amendments and used that notion to strike down much economic legislation.

Black came to the Court in 1937 determined not to repeat—and to do all he could to prevent his colleagues from repeating—what he looked on as the cardinal judicial sin of finding unwritten rights in the Constitution. His belief in liberty persuaded him that *all* of the first eight amendments in the Bill of Rights, not merely some, as many other Justices argued, should be included in due process; but his fear of judicial discretion led him to exclude from due process any unlisted right. Thus, he fell back on a crude kind of legal positivism, one that was not completely consistent, for he could never tolerate the Ninth Amendment, one of only two constitutional provisions that instruct how the Constitution must be (or must not be) interpreted: "The enumeration in the Constitution, of certain rights, shall not be construed to deny or disparage others retained by the people."[21]

As late as January 1952, Douglas endorsed a black-letter reading of the constitutional document, joining in Black's dissenting opinion and writing one of his own.[22] Both Justices repeated their view that due process included the first eight amendments, but nothing more.

Douglas had been brooding about such matters, however; and, less than six months later, he wrote a somewhat different view into another dissent:

> Liberty in the constitutional sense must mean more than freedom from unlawful governmental restraint; it must include privacy as well, if it is to be a repository of freedom. The right to be let alone is indeed the beginning of all freedom.

Not yet willing to move outside of the four corners of the constitutional document, Douglas found "the right to be let alone" partly grounded in the Fourth Amendment, partly in the First:

> But even in his activities outside the house, he [the citizen] has immunity from controls bearing on privacy. He may not be compelled against his will to attend a religious service; he may not be forced to make an affirmation or observe a

ritual that violates his scruples; he may not be made to accept one religious, political, or philosophical creed as against another. Freedom of religion and freedom of speech guaranteed by the First Amendment give more than the privilege to worship, to write, to speak as one chooses; they give freedom not to do nor to act as the government chooses. The First Amendment in its respect for the conscience of the individual honors the sanctity of thought and belief. To think as one chooses, to believe what one wishes are important aspects of the constitutional right to be let alone.[23]

We see here the germ of what would come to be called "textual structuralism,"[24] examining the constitutional document as a whole, rather than merely dissecting a particular clause or set of clauses, to determine whether a right or power is implicit in the overall plan. Indeed, in 1949 Douglas had suggested that interpreters should look to the Constitution's "architectural scheme,"[25] a phrase that captures the essence of structural analysis, but he had not yet systematically pursued that idea.

Some forms of structural analysis need not be incompatible with legal positivism. But Douglas was also abandoning the cornerstone of Black's constitutional jurisprudence: the idea that the Constitution was a complete code of law. In 1956 Douglas wrote that the Constitution is "a compendium, not a code; a declaration of articles of faith, not a compilation of laws."[26] Furthermore, he rejected Black's second principle, that limiting judicial power to close interpretation of the actual words of the text and, more specifically, restricting "due process" to include *only* the first eight amendments. "Though I believe," Douglas wrote in 1961, "that 'due process' as used in the Fourteenth Amendment included all of the first eight amendments, I do not think it is restricted and confined to them. . . . 'Liberty' is a conception that sometimes gains content from the emanations of other specific guarantees or from experience with the requirements of a free society."[27]

Positivism might well accommodate the notion that liberty gained meaning from various clauses in the constitutional document. After all, structuralism would probably demand such acceptance. But the terms "emanations" and "experience with the requirements of a free society," insofar as they implied a creative function for judges, ran directly counter to Black's goal of reining in judicial choice.

Moreover, Douglas was at the same time moving toward accepting the sort of theory of natural rights[28] that Jefferson had expressed in the Declaration of Independence, a theory that Black endorsed for legislators but thought taboo for judges. "In our scheme of things," Douglas said in 1954, "the rights of men are inalienable. They come from the Creator, not from a president, a legislator, or a court."[29] "Man," he reiterated in 1958, "is a child of God, entitled to dignified treatment."[30] In 1963, he spoke even more emphatically: "Men do not acquire rights from the government. One man does not give another rights. Man gets his rights from the Creator. They come to him because of the divine spark in every human being."[31]

In 1965, *Griswold v. Connecticut* presented Douglas with a chance to present a fully developed constitutional theory of privacy. Connecticut forbade using, aiding, abetting, or counseling use of contraceptives. In *Poe v. Ullman* (1961),[32] over Douglas's dissent, the Court had dismissed a suit challenging the statute's constitutionality because five of the Justices believed that Connecticut had a policy against enforcing the law. After *Poe*, however, Connecticut cooperated with the opponents of its ban on birth control by prosecuting a physician and the director of the state's Planned Parenthood League for disseminating the forbidden information. Thus, the underlying issues that the Court had been able to avoid in *Poe* were now fully justiciable, and the Justices voted 7 to 2 to invalidate the statute. Chief Justice Warren assigned Douglas the task of writing the opinion of the Court.

Despite his dissent in *Poe* and other pronouncements about a general right to privacy, his initial draft stressed the importance of marriage. Indeed, in stating the facts of the case, Douglas italicized that the accused had been charged with instructing "*married persons*." The draft went on to hold the statute invalid because it violated the First Amendment, the right to discuss ideas, and the right to associate in marriage. "The right to learn, the right to read, the right to know have overtones in freedom of speech and of the press. Without those peripheral rights, the specific rights would be less secure." He continued:

> The family is an instruction unit as much as the school; and husband and wife are both teachers and pupils. And the family, together with its physician, is an instruction unit as much as a school is. To narrow, as does the Connecticut statute, discussion and advice on a problem as important as population and procreation is to introduce a dangerous state influence over the First Amendment right to disseminate knowledge.[33]

Apparently, Douglas sent this early version only to Justice William J. Brennan, Jr., who was not impressed with its argument and knew that several other Justices would also be bothered by its reasoning. At the conference, Black had commented sarcastically that the "right of husband and wife to assemble in bed is a new right of assembly to me." Brennan thus suggested to Douglas that he revise his opinion along the lines of his dissent in *Poe*.

Douglas accepted this advice, but only in part. The gist of his revised version did follow and expand on his dissent in *Poe* and provided a remarkable example of structural analysis, but one that was combined with a notion of freedom of association suffused with ideas about the sanctity of marriage. Douglas began by arguing that, although the Court did not sit as a superlegislature, the Constitution protected more than listed rights, and judges had to defend those rights. Freedom of association, he pointed out, was not a listed right, yet the Court had protected it as well as other rights not in the document, such as those of parents to educate their children; of the public to inquire into, distribute, receive, and read information; of freedom of thought; of academic freedom; of association, whether for political, social, or economic purposes; and of "privacy in one's associations." "Without those peripheral rights the specific rights [to speech, press, and assembly in the First Amendment] would be less secure."

This interpretive history, Douglas wrote, suggested "that specific guarantees in the Bill of Rights have penumbras, formed by emanations from those guarantees that help give them life and substance. Various guarantees create zones of privacy," such as the right to association, the Third Amendment's prohibition against quartering troops in civilian homes in time of peace, and the Fourth's explicit affirmation of "the right of the people to be secure in their persons, houses, papers, and effects, against unreasonable searches and seizures." Furthermore, the Fifth Amendment's protection against self-incrimination "enables the citizen to create a zone of privacy which government may not force him to surrender to his detriment." Then came the trump card in any argument for unlisted rights, the plain words of the Ninth Amendment commanding interpreters not to restrict rights to those mentioned in the document.

So far, the revised version had argued for a general right to privacy by elaborating a classical form of textual structuralism: Douglas had examined the document as a whole rather than isolating any single clause. But, then, as the opinion closed, he returned to his earlier draft to append a panegyric to marriage and a specific right to privacy in marriage:

> We deal with a right of privacy older than the Bill of Rights—older than our political parties, older than our school system. Marriage is a coming together for better or for worse, hopefully enduring, and intimate to the degree of being sacred. It is an association that promotes a way of life, not causes; a harmony in living, not political faiths; a bilateral loyalty, not commercial or social projects. Yet it is an association for as noble a purpose as any involved in our prior decisions.[34]

Black, of course, was furious at this reincarnation of the beast of judicial discretion. He immediately threw up a positivistic defense, repudiating structuralism along with unwritten rights: "I get nowhere in this case by talk about a constitutional 'right of privacy' as an emanation from one or more constitutional provisions. I like my privacy as well as the next one, but I am nevertheless compelled to admit that government has a right to invade it unless prohibited by some specific constitutional provision." The argument from the Ninth Amendment Black dismissed as a "recent discovery that . . . can be used to strike down all state legislation which this Court thinks violates 'fundamental principles of liberty or justice,' or is contrary to the 'traditions and [collective] conscience of our people.' "

Seven years later, Douglas added to the confusion in *Eisenstadt v. Baird*, a case from Massachusetts. The facts were quite similar to those in *Griswold*, except that the speaker had given a packet of contraceptive foam to an *unmarried* woman. Six of the seven participating Justices agreed the state law was invalid. For the majority, Brennan wrote:

> If the right of privacy means anything, it is the right of the *individual*, married or single, to be free of governmental intrusion into matters so fundamentally affecting a person as the decision whether to bear or beget a child.[35]

Douglas joined the opinion of the Court but added a set of concurring views that returned to his initial draft in *Griswold*—although, of course, without the paean to marriage. He saw the case as presenting "simple" issues of the First Amendment, which "protects the opportunity to persuade to action whether that action be unwise or immoral, or whether the speech incites to action."[36]

DOUGLAS'S JUDICIAL AND CONSTITUTIONAL LEGACIES

A decade after his death, William O. Douglas remains an enigmatic and frustrating figure. And one senses that he, no less than his analysts, deeply felt that frustration. A loner, a crippled, poor boy who rose to the highest ranks in the fiercely competitive worlds of academia, politics, and law—and did so largely because of intellectual brilliance linked to fierce determination and iron will—he was still painfully in need of constant reassurance that he had not been a failure. A devoted patriot, he was often depicted as a man who loved America less because he loved its ideals more than Lyndon Johnson's or Richard Nixon's foreign policy. A man who extolled the sanctity of marriage[37] and the centrality of family, he was not only three times divorced but also estranged from his own children. A judge who worked obsessively, a legal scholar whose learning was almost as immense as his curiosity, he was often hasty in the opinions he wrote and was unable to articulate—which is not to say unable to formulate in his own mind—and follow a comprehensive theory of constitutional interpretation or to order the Constitution's values to explain and justify his devotion to the Court or his passion for liberty.

But as much as the academic wishes Douglas had been more careful, more systematic, or even simply more consistent in his work, one cannot escape the broader unity in his constitutional interpretation. He became, even more than Hugo Black ever was, a Jeffersonian, perhaps even a follower of Thomas Paine, a fervent believer in "the rights of man." Moreover, Douglas was more of a constitutionalist than Black, who, although he typically construed rights broadly and governmental authority narrowly, firmly believed that Americans had only the rights listed in the constitutional document. Douglas, too, construed rights broadly and power narrowly, but he came to believe that Americans retained all rights they had not specifically surrendered. For Black, the citizen had to find a documentary peg for a right; for Douglas, the government had to meet that burden. His presumption was in favor of individual liberty.

After Douglas's death, Chief Justice Warren Earl Burger said that the brethren sorely missed Douglas's capacity—willingness, indeed, eagerness—to force the Court to face up to the difficult issues cases presented. The sometime professor of law understood legal technicalities, and he recognized their importance to a system of law. But he also knew that most such rules had been made by judges and most could be changed by judges, that most rules were the instruments of the law, not its masters. The Court should never allow them to blind itself to reality.

Douglas remained both a Realist and an idealist: a Realist in that he cared not for the appearance of what the Court was doing but for its actual effect on litigants, the political system, and on the Constitution; an idealist in his vision of the United States as a city on a hill, of the Constitution as the polity's sacred scripture, and the Court as guardian of both the image and reality of America. He thought liberty and justice were important concepts, not vacuous slogans. He was prophetic in the true double sense of convicting his world of sin in foreign and domestic affairs and showing the path to salvation. There was more of the Presbyterian preacher's genes in his personal constitution than Douglas would have liked to admit. And the promised land to which he would have led his people was summarized in the Constitution's Preamble: a more perfect union, the common defense, domestic tranquillity, justice, and the blessings of liberty. He pursued that vision as a citizen, professor, federal administrator, and judge. And in his continuous, if seldom systematic, efforts to make the United States true to its ideals lies his great legacy.

NOTES

I am obliged to Mark Brandon, Esq., of Princeton University for a careful and critical reading of the manuscript for this chapter. I am also indebted to the late Sidney M. Davis, Esq., who was a dear friend and attorney to both Douglas and to me, for long conversations that helped form and clarify my thoughts. The Center of International Studies of Princeton University supported the research for this chapter.

1. James F. Simon published a book-length biography of Douglas, but without having had access to the Justice's voluminous papers: *Independent Journey: The Life of William O. Douglas* (1980). James C. Duram's smaller work, *Justice William O. Douglas* (1981), suffers from the same limitation. Stephen L. Wasby has edited a series of papers on Douglas: *"He Shall Not Pass This Way Again": The Legacy of Justice William O. Douglas* (1990). The Justice wrote a two-volume autobiography: *Go East, Young Man* (1974), and *The Court Years: 1939–1975* (1980). In some ways more revealing of the man himself than either of these two was his *Of Men and Mountains* (1950). During the early 1960s, I worked for several years with Douglas, going through his papers with him and taping his responses to assorted questions about his life and work. Most of these tapes have survived their long hibernation in storage and are available, along with a typescript, "Transcriptions of Conversations between William O. Douglas and Walter F. Murphy," in the Mudd Manuscript Library of Princeton University. The Justice's papers are in the Manuscript Division of the Library of Congress.

2. *Dennis v. United States*, 341 U.S. 494, 589 (1951) (dissenting opinion).

3. Eulogy at the funeral of William O. Douglas.

4. The Justice and I had been scheduled to go to lunch that day and then spend a few hours working on his papers for his autobiography; but he had had a barium series that morning and had come to the Court pale and nauseated and asked if I would take his wife to the Explorers' Club at the Zoo. The main course was zebu. In Southeast Asia, there is a curse laid on those who eat this animal's flesh. Such a deterrence is quite functional in societies that depend on zebu as the principal beast of burden; but Mrs. Douglas and I could testify that the curse also operates in other cultures, for within a few weeks she was badly hurt in an automobile accident and I injured my back playing squash.

5. *Papachristou v. Jacksonville*, 405 U.S. 156, 164 (1972). Douglas had long been waiting for a case like this one. In 1960 he had delivered a lecture at the University of New Mexico Law School explaining in detail why vagrancy laws were unconstitutional, published as "Vagrancy and Arrest on Suspicion," 70 *Yale Law Journal* 1 (1960). Earlier, he and Black had dissented in *Edelman v. California*, 344 U.S. 357 (1953), against the Court's dismissing a challenge to the constitutionality of another vagrancy law because the petitioner had not properly raised the question in the state courts.

6. In general, see V. Countryman, ed., *The Douglas Opinions* (1977), and K. Karst, "The Return of the Natural-Law–Due-Process Formula," 16 *UCLA Law Review* 716 (1969); for more specialized studies, see L. Poe, "Evolution to Absolutism: Justice Douglas and the First Amendment," 74 *Columbia Law Review* 371 (1974); B. Wolfman et al., *Dissent without Opinion* (1975); S. Ulmer, "Parabolic Support of Civil Liberty Claims: The Case of William O. Douglas," 41 *Journal of Politics* 634 (1979); and G. White, "The Anti-Judge: William O. Douglas and the Ambiguities of Individuality," 74 *Virginia Law Review* 17 (1988).

7. 323 U.S. 214 (1944).

8. *Ex parte Endo*, 323 U.S. 283 (1944).

9. "Transcriptions of Conversations," p. 165.

10. W. Douglas, *The Court Years*, p. 280.

11. *Perez v. Brownell*, 356 U.S. 44, dis. op., 79 (1958).

12. *Kingsley Corp. v. Regents*, 360 U.S. 684, concur. op., 698 (1959).

13. William O. Douglas, *The Anatomy of Liberty* (1963), p. 87.

14. *Lynch v. Household Finance Corp.*, 405 U.S. 538, 552 (1972).

15. *Barsky v. Board of Regents*, 347 U.S. 442, dis. op., 472 (1954).

16. White, "The Anti-Judge," p. 65.

17. For definitions and discussions of these three terms, see W. Murphy, J. Fleming, and W. Harris, II, *American Constitutional Interpretation* (1986), ch. 8.

18. S. Warren and L. Brandeis, "The Right to Privacy," 4 *Harvard Law Review* 193 (1890).

19. *Olmstead v. United States*, 277 U.S. 438, dis. op., 478 (1928).

20. For an early study, see C. H. Pritchett, *The Roosevelt Court: A Study in Judicial Politics and Values, 1937–1947* (1948), pp. 153–55.

21. Nor could Black cope with that part of the Tenth referring to "powers" reserved to the people. The other clause instructing interpreters is contained in the Eleventh Amendment.

22. *Rochin v. California*, 342 U.S. 165 (1952). See also Douglas's joining Black's dissent in *Adamson v. California*, 332 U.S. 46 (1947), probably Black's most elaborate statement of his positivistic view of constitutional interpretation.

23. *Public Utilities Commission v. Pollak*, 343 U.S. 451, dis. op. 467–68 (1952). *Rochin* had been argued on October 16, 1951, and the Court announced its decision on January 2, 1952; *Pollak* was argued on March 3, 1952, and the Court announced its ruling on May 26, 1952.

24. This mode of analysis has a long history in American constitutional interpretation, although only recently has it taken on its current title. For the most famous, and perhaps most important, use of structuralism, see Chief Justice John Marshall's opinion for the Court in *McCulloch v. Maryland*, 17 U.S. (4 Wheat.) 316 (1819). For fuller discussions of the concept, see Murphy, Fleming, and Harris, *American Constitutional Interpretation*, chs. 8–10, espec. pp. 292–94; and W. Harris, II, "Bonding Word and Polity: The Logic of American Constitutionalism," 76 *American Political Science Review* 34 (1982).

25. "Stare Decisis," 4 *Record of the Association of the Bar of the City of New York* 152, 157 (1949).

26. W. Douglas, *We, the Judges* (1956), p. 429.

27. *Poe v. Ullman*, 367 U.S. 497, dis. op. 516–17 (1961).

28. See Karst, "The Return of the Natural-Law–Due-Process Formula."

29. W. Douglas, *An Almanac of Liberty* (1954), p. 5.

30. W. Douglas, *The Right of the People* (1958), p. 145. The book contains the 1957 North Lecture at Franklin and Marshall College.

31. W. Douglas, *Anatomy of Liberty*, p. 2.

32. *Poe v. Ullman*, 367 U.S. 497, 516 (1961).

33. The text of the draft is reprinted in B. Schwartz, ed., *The Unpublished Opinions of the Warren Court* (1985), pp. 227–39.

34. *Griswold v. Connecticut*, 381 U.S. 479, 486 (1965).

35. 405 U.S. 438, 453 (1972).

36. *Id.*, p. 459.

37. See also his opinion for the Court in *Cleveland v. United States*, 329 U.S. 14 (1946), sustaining the conviction, under the Mann Act, of a member of a Mormon sect that advocated polygamy for bringing several of his wives across a state line.

7

John Marshall Harlan: A Modern Conservative Justice

William M. Beaney

The Supreme Court of the immediate post–World War II era was essentially conservative in outlook and deed. The Vinson Court (1946–53) was graced by five Roosevelt era holdovers—Hugo Black, William Douglas, Stanley Reed, Felix Frankfurter, and Robert Jackson—but the latter three were in varying degrees located in the conservative camp. President Truman's appointments of Fred Vinson, Sherman Minton, Tom Clark, and Harold Burton embodied Truman's fondness for old and trusted friends and associates. Ideologically, the Truman appointees were traditional conservatives.[1] President Eisenhower, a man of conciliatory and conservative leanings, although not "political" in the usual sense, was expected to maintain the conservative character of the Court through appointment opportunities that were certain to arise. However, two of Eisenhower's five appointments during his two terms turned out to be activist liberals. Earl Warren, appointed Chief Justice to pay off a heavy political debt arising out of the President's successful party nomination, quickly became a leader of the Court in the famous case of *Brown v. Board of Education* in 1954.[2] With some exceptions, Warren was to play an activist, liberal role until his retirement in 1969. Eisenhower's third appointment in 1956 of William Brennan, a New Jersey Democrat, produced a valiant proponent of civil liberties and civil rights whose influence on the Court remained substantial until his retirement in 1990.

Eisenhower's second appointment of John Marshall Harlan in 1955 was of a character quite different from his first and third. Harlan, grandson of an earlier Supreme Court Justice with an identical name, proved to be an ideal conservative appointee. Along with the President's subsequent appointment of Charles Whittaker (who served for less than five years) and Potter Stewart, a substantial middle-of-the-road jurist, Harlan represented the mainstream ideology that was so congenial to Eisenhower.[3]

In appearance and demeanor Harlan is often described as "patrician":

> Tall and erect, with sparse white hair, and conservatively dressed in his London-tailored suits, with his grandfather's gold watch chain, Harlan exuded the dignity associated with high judicial office. Yet underneath this dignified surface was a warm nature that enabled him to be close friends with those with whom he disagreed intellectually....
>
> The term most frequently used to describe Harlan by those who knew him is *gentleman.* To the other Justices, Harlan was the quintessential patrician, with his privileged upbringing and Wall Street background.[4]

Harlan's credentials were impeccable,[5] even if his legal education, after graduation from Princeton in 1920, was unorthodox. After three years at Oxford as a Rhodes Scholar, Harlan returned to the United States and obtained a position in the prominent New York law firm of Root, Clark, Buckner & Howland.[6] He completed his legal education in the United States by taking several evening courses at New York Law School. Harlan became an expert litigator, specializing in corporate matters, and he was an active member of the Association of the Bar of the City of New York. Stationed in England during World War II, Colonel Harlan served in the U.S. Eighth Air Force as officer in charge of the Operational Analysis Section. He returned to practice at the end of the war and was therefore engaged in numerous public service activities; one of these involved the role of investigator and prosecutor of corrupt New York public officials.

Early in the Eisenhower administration, Harlan was appointed to the federal Court of Appeals for the second circuit. The death of Justice Robert H. Jackson in 1954 produced a vacancy on the Supreme Court, which Eisenhower, on advice of his Attorney General and others, filled by elevating Harlan, whose qualifications were described in glowing terms by the President. Confirmation by the Senate was easy: The few negative votes arose from Harlan's supposed "internationalist" leanings (he had, after all, attended Oxford for three years). There was also a rather dubious accusation that he would likely favor a civil rights philosophy similar to that of his grandfather, the lone dissenter in *Plessy v. Ferguson* who had insisted that the Constitution was "color blind."[7] To certain southern senators this suggested that Harlan would support with enthusiasm the application of *Brown v. Board of Education*[8] to southern school districts. It should be noted that Harlan did not at that time have a recorded philosophy, as reflected in speeches or a substantial volume of Court decisions. What neither the President, Congress, nor the new nominee realized was that an era of liberal, activist judicial lawmaking was in the offing, with Harlan's role to be that of effective spokesman for a more conservative tradition that emphasized the powers of the political branches and the enduring values of federalism.

During the course of his seventeen-year tenure on the Court, Harlan wrote 168 opinions for the Court, 296 dissenting opinions, and 149 concurring opinions. This is an impressive output testifying to the unwillingness of Harlan to simply "go along." These numbers also emphasize that the ideological direction of the Supreme Court during the Warren era (1953–69) was contrary to Harlan's fundamentally conservative approach.

The following paragraphs contain a brief summary of the discrete elements of Justice Harlan's judicial philosophy as expressed in his Court opinions. However, a caution is in order. A judicial philosophy as rich as Harlan's is not necessarily well served by piecemeal sketches of isolated elements. The problems that appear before the Court typically defy simple categorization into "federalism cases" or "separation of powers cases." Instead, each case probably presents a set of issues that involve many of the basic ideological elements that make up a Justice's judicial philosophy. Oftentimes the issues involve elements that directly clash, and here logic and principle are strained to their utmost. It is nonetheless useful to try to view the pure elements in as much isolation as is possible, for it is only with the thorough understanding of the foundation principles that the complex interactions between them can be appreciated.

Constitutional history shows that the Supreme Court has been continually engaged in refereeing the constant struggle between nationalist and state-local political tendencies.[9] This complex clash of interests was central in the very creation of the Constitution, and even today there is no reason why the nation should lack disputes about the proper allocation of power between state and nation. If the general, long-term trend has produced a significant growth of national power, that growth has not been evident or equal in all fields. Many conservatives equate federal power with unwanted regulatory policies and higher taxes. But there is no, or at least very little, evidence that Harlan emphasized states' rights for these reasons.

Harlan's passion for federalism was a reflection of his deep concern for maintaining free government. He feared a concentration of political and economic power in Washington;[10] and, like Justice Louis Brandeis, he had great faith in the ability of the states to serve as laboratories in which instructive social and political experiments might take place.[11]

With respect to the political branches of the federal government and their powers, Harlan expressed great tolerance. In rare instances he would allow invocation of an individual right to justify invalidating an act of Congress. A good example is Harlan's position on the troublesome issue of whether civilian dependents of U.S. military personnel stationed overseas could be tried in military courts. In *Reid v. Covert*[12] he concurred with the majority in denying Congress's power to use courts-martial for this purpose, at least in capital cases, but he dissented when the Court refused to allow overseas military trials of civilians for non-capital offenses.[13] Ever the great respecter of tradition, Harlan chose to retain an age-old distinction between capital and non-capital criminal cases.

Where the powers of the President were under challenge, Harlan reflected a similar respect for the essential attributes of that office. A good example is Harlan's dissent in the Pentagon Papers Case.[14] Decrying the haste with which the case had been pushed up to the Supreme Court, he insisted that the obsession of the majority with the issue of "prior restraint," admittedly an important value, had obscured another important basic consideration:

> It is plain to me that the scope of the judicial function in passing upon the activities of the Executive Branch of the Government in the field of foreign affairs is very narrowly restricted. This view is, I think, dictated by the concept of separation of powers upon which our constitutional system rests.[15]

He cited a statement of Chief Justice Marshall, then a member of the House of Representatives, that [t]he President is the sole organ of the nation in external relations. . . . "[16] He concluded that the final determination of the degree of harm to national security caused by disclosures of classified documents must be an executive decision. Harlan would have retained the restraint on publication of the papers until the courts could respond responsibly to the issues.[17]

Harlan's approach to individual rights reflects his attitude toward the issues of separation of powers and federalism. Like Madison and Hamilton, he thought that the very structure of our governmental system was designed to protect free government.[18] While recognizing that the Bill of Rights provided additional security for various liberties, he did not believe that every claim deserved judicial protection. He strongly opposed the Supreme Court's nationalization of the Bill of Rights through an "incorporation" role for the Fourteenth Amendment. For Harlan, the "due process" limitation was distinct from the specific guarantees of the Bill of Rights and should be treated as an independent basis for determining whether a state law should be held invalid. He therefore refused to accept either piecemeal or total incorporation and favored the looser, less restrictive limitation of due process.[19]

This did not mean that there were no due process limits on state actions affecting substantive rights. Concurring in *Griswold v. Connecticut*,[20] Harlan found the state law restricting use of contraceptives a violation of due process because the enactment violated basic values "implicit in the concept of ordered liberty," citing *Palko v. Connecticut.*[21] He rejected both historical and policy grounds for resting the Court's decision on the incorporation theory.

During the Warren Court years, where the Supreme Court incorporated most of the procedural as well as substantive guarantees, Harlan reminded his colleagues, usually in dissent, that "a state criminal conviction comes to us as the complete product of a sovereign judicial system."[22] He had no quarrel with the longtime use of the exclusionary rule in federal trials, but he believed that principles of federalism should allow the states to adopt a different rule.

His consistent passion for principles of federalism meant that only when due process limits were exceeded would Harlan invalidate a state rule of criminal procedure. A statement from *Jackson v. Denno*[23] captures this outlook: "Limitations on the states' exercise of their responsibility to prevent criminal conduct should be imposed only where it is demonstrable that their own adjustment of the competing interests infringes rights fundamental to a decent society."[24]

In the same vein, he dissented from the landmark holding of the Court in *Miranda v. Arizona.*[25] In an extreme example of judicial activism, the majority directed law enforcement officers to give suspects in custody a full set of warnings. Confessions or inculpatory statements obtained in circumstances where the warnings as to the right to remain silent, to counsel, and other warnings were not given or given improperly were declared inadmissible. Harlan's dissent saw this massive imposition by the Supreme Court as destructive of the balance between states and nation.

He was equally disturbed by the Court's conclusion in *Duncan v. Louisiana*[26] that the Sixth Amendment's right to jury trial was applicable to the states. He thought a charge of simple battery could be tried without use of a jury as provided in the state constitution. In juvenile proceedings, he thought that only those rights essential to a fair trial were necessary. Others, which the majority thought necessary, did not meet Harlan's due process requirement.[27] He concurred in the case of *Gideon v. Wainwright*,[28] holding that indigents must be afforded counsel in all felony cases, principally because the old rule of *Betts v. Brady*[29] (requiring state-appointed counsel only where certain factors were present) had become so riddled with exceptions as to be meaningless. He also concurred in *Pointer v. Texas*,[30] holding that testimony produced against an unrepresented defendant at a preliminary hearing could not be used at his trial where the witness was unavailable to testify. He also agreed that a defendant's objections sufficed to bar television cameras from a Texas trial.[31] In short, Harlan did more than invoke due process as a formality—for him it had real bite, based on history, tradition, and fundamental fairness.

Labeling Harlan a conservative fails to capture the richness of the Justice's approach to the Constitution. The great document, in his view, provided guidance, but it was not a straitjacket. The people's representatives had the main burden of governance, but the Court's role was not insignificant. He respected the various guarantees of liberty in the Constitution, but he felt that the Bill of Rights limited only the national government. The due process clause in the Fourteenth Amendment was the only limitation on state governmental action. Above all else, he treasured our system of federalism. In an age dominated by centralizing tendencies in governments throughout the world, he fought hard to retain the virtues of government close to the people.

This brief summary of the constituent elements of Justice Harlan's judicial philosophy gives some idea of the bricks and mortar making up the strong foundation that supports his ideological system. However, many architects may construct a building that is sturdy, but only the most skillful and artistic can erect upon the foundation a building that provides both optimum utility and flexibility for those who have to live or work in it—and of such beauty that it is a pleasure for all who may pass by. Justice Harlan, as an architect of opinions, was of this superior type.

In his foreword to a collection of Justice Harlan's writings, Professor Paul Freund comments:

> Like the true artist, however, the great judge—and especially a Justice of the Supreme Court, called on to draw the frontiers of legal doctrine—is not content with reproduction or recapitulation; bound by fidelity to his subject, he also succeeds in enhancing it by bringing to bear on it his experience, insights, and judgment, by persuading and even moving us to see that the ultimate composition is right.
>
> Justice Harlan's special quality is precisely this gift of cojoining the particular with the general, or rather of finding the general implanted within the particular. Thus one reads his opinions with the secure feeling that they will convey an understanding of the exact controversy to be resolved and will disclose the philosophical wellsprings of the Justice's position.[32]

It was of great importance to Harlan, as it is to any craftsman, that the product of his labors be of maximum utility and longevity.[33] The clearest example of this awareness is his comments in a line of obscenity decisions by the Court. Harlan commented that anyone who took the trouble to read the Court's own decisions "would find himself in utter bewilderment."[34] He noted that the Court was demanding more precise language from the state legislatures in defining obscenity offenses than the Court itself had been able to achieve.

A few examples may help, however inadequately, to illustrate Harlan's judicial craftsmanship. *Yates v. United States*[35] provides an excellent example of how Justice Harlan enlisted the precise analysis of statutory wording to the service of the First Amendment. The defendants in *Yates* had been convicted under the Smith Act, which punished anyone who "organizes . . . any group . . . [which] . . . advocate[s] . . . the overthrow or destruction of any [government of the United States]."[36] The heart of Harlan's opinion was based on the definition of "advocate" as used in the statute. The government drew a meaningless line between the "advocacy" of the overthrow of the U.S. government, irrespective of its inciting qualities, and "the mere discussion or exposition of violent overthrow as an abstract theory."[37] Thus, under the government's theory, the boundary lines of the Smith Act were to be drawn with reference to the subjective intent of the speaker. Justice Harlan rejected this reading as an "unconstitutional application of the Smith Act."[38] Instead, he found that the distinction between advocacy that was protected by the First Amendment and advocacy that fell afoul of the Smith Act was that "those of whom the advocacy is addressed must be urged to *do* something, now or in the future, rather than merely to *believe* in something."[39] Note what is accomplished by this reading: First, the statute is not rendered unconstitutional and is interpreted in accordance with prior interpretations. Second, the boundary line between legal and illegal advocacy is now susceptible of objective proof instead of subjective intent. Finally, because the boundary line has been made clear, the advocacy of unpopular ideas is given the full measure of First Amendment protection.

Justice Harlan authored another First Amendment majority opinion a number of years later in *Cohen v. California*.[40] The defendant in *Cohen* was convicted under a California statute that made it a criminal offense to disturb any person by offensive conduct. The conduct complained of in this case was the wearing of a jacket boldly carrying the words "Fuck the Draft" in the Los Angeles County Courthouse. In his analysis, Harlan held the statute up to each of the recognized First Amendment exceptions that allowed reasonable time and manner restrictions on a citizen's First Amendment rights. Finding that California's action fitted none of the exceptions, Justice Harlan concluded that the state was acting as a guardian of public morality in trying to "remove this offensive word from the public vocabulary."[41] That some speech is offensive and perhaps without merit is a "necessary side effect . . . of the broader enduring values which the process of open debate permits us to achieve. That the air may at times seem filled with verbal cacophony is, in this sense not a sign of weakness but of strength."[42] Noting that the principle argued by the state is "inherently boundless," Harlan wrote:

> Surely the State has no right to cleanse public debate to the point where it is grammatically palatable to the most squeamish among us. Yet no readily ascertainable general principle exists for stopping short of that result were we to affirm the judgment below. For while the particular four-letter word being litigated here is perhaps more distasteful than others of its genre, it is nevertheless often true that one man's vulgarity is another's lyric. Indeed, we think it is largely because governmental officials cannot make principled distinctions in this area that the Constitution leaves matters of taste and style so largely to the individual.[43]

As has been noted, opinions for the majority represented the smallest portion of Justice Harlan's writing for the Court. Harlan would not abide by a loosely reasoned opinion. Frequently, although joining with the majority, he would write a concurrence that would "square off the corners" of the majority's opinion.

Katz v. United States[44] involved the actions of FBI agents in attaching a listening and recording device to the outside of a public telephone booth. The evidence obtained was admitted, over the defendant's objection, by the federal district court. Justice Stewart, for the Court, held that the Fourth Amendment protected people, not places, and he refused to follow a line of precedents stressing trespass doctrines. In concurring, Justice Harlan sought to refine Stewart's analysis by pointing out that there were two elements that must coexist in order for the Fourth Amendment protection to apply:

> My understanding of the rule that has emerged from prior decisions is that there is a twofold requirement, first that a person have exhibited an actual (subjective) expectation of privacy and, second, that the expectation be one that society is prepared to recognize as 'reasonable'.[45]

Thus, in reasoning that influences Fourth Amendment jurisprudence more than two decades later, a public phone booth can become a private place if the user closes the door and speaks softly, while a loud, careless user of the booth would not be protected.

A second example is *Terry v. Ohio*,[46] where Chief Justice Warren was spokesman for the Court. Here the issue was whether a plainclothes detective had acted within the law in stopping and frisking for weapons three men whose observed actions suggested that they were about to commit a criminal act. Warren's somewhat rambling opinion correctly noted that there had been a serious gray area in the law with respect to police investigative practices.[47] Short of an arrest, it was unclear whether officers were legally justified in stopping persons on grounds less than probable cause and subjecting them to a pat-down for weapons. Warren concluded that an appropriate search for weapons was a permissible part of the stopping and interrogation of subjects.

Harlan's concurring opinion[48] focused more clearly on the first step—the stopping of a suspect. He argued that "the right to frisk in this case depends on the reasonableness of a forcible stop to investigate a suspected crime." He added a realistic note, not found in the majority opinion, that where the articulable suspicion concerns a crime of violence, the right to frisk "must be immediate and automatic." Warren's opinion seemed to require an independent judgment as to whether each particular suspect was armed.

This tendency to lay out all the elements necessary to the resolution of the case at hand was characteristic. Generations of law students and teachers have recognized that one's appreciation of a case is greatly strengthened by Harlan's opinions, whether for the Court, concurring, or in dissent. Perhaps his long career as a skilled litigator, where he established a reputation for thoroughness in preparation and careful organization of analysis, prepared him to play a significant role as a conservative Justice of the highest caliber.

NOTES

The author wishes to thank Todd Linn for his research assistance in preparing the original lecture for publication.

1. See H. Abraham, *Justices and Presidents* (2d ed., 1985). See also V. Blasi, *The Burger Court* (1983); R. Sayler, B. Boyer, and R. Goodling, Jr., eds., *The Warren Court* (1969); A. Mason, *Harlan Fiske Stone* (1956); C. Pritchett, *The Roosevelt Court* (1948); F. Rudko, *Truman's Court* (1988).

2. 347 U.S. 483 (1954).

3. See N. Dorsen, "John Marshall Harlan," in 4 *The Justices of the United States Supreme Court, 1789–1969* (L. Friedman and F. Israel, eds., 1969), p. 2803. While this excellent survey of Harlan's contributions was written before the end of his judicial career, it is a warm appreciation by a writer with a liberal, activist philosophy. For an in-depth survey of Harlan's judicial philosophy, I am in debt to J. Bourguigon, "The Second Mr. Justice Harlan: His Principles of Judicial Decision Making," 1979 *Supreme Court Review* 251. A short collection of Harlan's opinions is found in D. Shapiro, ed., *The Evolution of a Judicial Philosophy: Selected Opinions and Papers of Justice John Marshall Harlan* (1969).

4. B. Schwartz, *The Ascent of Pragmatism: The Burger Court in Action* (1990), p. 17 (emphasis in original).

5. See sketch in V. Blasi, *The Burger Court*, p. 246.

6. Before dropping his name from the letterhead when Harlan left for the Court of Appeals in 1954, the firm was named Root, Ballantine, Harlan, Bushby and Palmer.

7. 163 U.S. 537, 559 (1896) (dissenting opinion).

8. 347 U.S. 483 (1954).

9. See generally A. Mason, *The States Rights Debate: Antifederalism and the Constitution* (1972); W. Murphy, *Elements of Judicial Strategy*, (1964), chs. 4–6.

10. [I]t was upon the *structure* of government that the founders primarily focused in

writing the Constitution. Out of bitter experience they were suspicious of every form of all-powerful central authority and they sought to assure that such a government would never exist in this country by structuring the federal establishment so as to diffuse power between the executive, legislative, and judicial branches. The diffusion of power between federal and state authority serves the same ends and takes on added significance as the size of the federal bureaucracy continues to crow.

J. Harlan, "Thoughts at a Dedication: Keeping the Judicial Function in Balance," 49 *American Bar Association Journal* 943–44 (1963) (emphasis added).

11. "It has often been said that one of the great strengths of our federal system is that we have, in the forty-eight states, forty-eight experimental social laboratories." *Roth v. United States*, 354 U.S. 476, 505 (1957) (concurring and dissenting).

12. 354 U.S. 1 (1957).

13. *Kinsella v. Singleton*, 361 U.S. 234 (1960).

14. *New York Times Co. v. United States*, 403 U.S. 713 (1971).

15. *Id.*, p. 756.

16. *Id.*

17. *Id.*

18. See J. Harlan, "Thoughts at a Dedication," p. 943.

19. See *Roth v. United States*, 354 U.S. 476, 505 (1957) (concurring and dissenting) (federal censorship was abhorrent; the states should have a wider discretion in restricting publications).

20. 381 U.S. 479 (1965).

21. 302 U.S. 319 (1937).

22. *Mapp v. Ohio*, 367 U.S. 643, 682 (1961).

23. 378 U.S. 368 (1964).

24. *Id.*, p. 439.

25. 384 U.S. 436, 504 (1966).

26. 391 U.S. 145 (1968).

27. See *In re Gault*, 387 U.S. 1 (1967).

28. 372 U.S. 335 (1963).

29. 316 U.S. 455 (1942).

30. 380 U.S. 400 (1965).

31. See *Estes v. Texas*, 381 U.S. 532 (1965). This holding was severely modified, if not overruled, by *Chandler v. Florida*, 449 U.S. 560 (1981).

32. D. Shapiro, ed., *The Evolution of a Judicial Philosophy*, p. xiii.

33. "[Justice Harlan] is not an anthologist's judge but a lawyer's and a judge's judge." *Id.*

34. *Interstate Circuit v. Dallas*, 390 U.S. 676, 707 (1968).

35. 354 U.S. 298 (1957).

36. *Id.*

37. *Id.*, p. 313.

38. *Id.*

39. *Id.*, pp. 324–25 (emphasis in original).

40. 403 U.S. 15 (1971).

41. *Id.*, p. 23.

42. *Id.*, p. 25.

43. *Id.*

44. 389 U.S. 347 (1967).

45. *Id.*, p. 360.

46. 392 U.S. 1 (1968).

47. Professor Yale Kamisar maintains that Justice Brennan was the principal author of the majority opinion in *Terry*, which bears Warren's name. Remarks at the BNA Constitutional Law Conference, Washington, D.C., September 14, 1990.

48. 392 U. S., p. 31.

8

Affirmative Action and the Supreme Court

Jesse H. Choper

The extent to which the Constitution's guarantee of equal protection of the laws permits government to use racial classifications to remedy prior discrimination, or to implement an affirmative action program, has been one of the most significant and controversial issues of our time. It has been addressed by Justices of the Supreme Court in at least ten decisions, all within the past two decades. But there is still no authoritative opinion on many critical aspects of the matter, and continued claims of majority judicial support from partisans on both sides of the issue indicate that an enormous degree of uncertainty persists.

The purpose of this chapter is not to analyze how the constitutional questions should be resolved, for in this respect the chapter has nothing new to contribute. Rather, the chapter discusses cases that have prompted at least one member of the Court to speak to the issue of constitutionality, and then explores the question of where the matter presently stands.

In 1971, the Court decided *Swann v. Charlotte Mecklenburg Board of Education.*[1] It unanimously held that a federal court may use race-based mathematical ratios as a starting point to remedy deliberate racial segregation in public schools. Indeed, in two companion cases, the Court ruled that often race must be used to remedy this problem.[2] But since the Court has tended to view the school desegregation issue as unique, its approach in these cases has had limited predictive value on the broader question of the permissibility of remedial racial classifications.

The earliest "conventional" affirmative action case to be reviewed by the Court came three years later in *DeFunis v. Odegaard*,[3] involving the University of Washington Law School's preferential admissions program for members of designated racial and ethnic minorities. Unlike *Swann*, the challenged government action in *DeFunis* had not been adopted to remedy prior deliberate discrimination by the state or its law school, but rather as an effort to increase the number of students in the law school from minority groups who would otherwise be seriously underrepresented. The Court avoided deciding the case on the technical ground of mootness. However, one member—Justice William O. Douglas, who left the Court shortly thereafter—found that a law school's use of an explicit racial classification violated equal protection.

In 1977, in *United Jewish Organizations v. Carey*,[4] all but one of the Justices—and that was then–Chief Justice Warren Burger—voted to uphold a New York districting plan that overtly used racial criteria in order to create a larger number of state legislative districts containing nonwhite majorities. As in *DeFunis*—and in contrast to *Swann*—there had been no finding that the State of New York had ever engaged in deliberate discrimination against racial minorities in respect to voting. There was, however, an important factor in *UJO* not present in *DeFunis*. New York had been required by the Attorney General to undertake the challenged action because certain counties were subject to the Voting Rights Act passed by Congress in 1965: They had used a literacy test for voting during the 1968 presidential election and less than half of their eligible residents had gone to the polls. Under these circumstances, it may be said that the state legislation was based on a congressional presumption that the counties had engaged in deliberate racial discrimination. In any event, prior to the Court's well-known decision in *Regents of the University of California v. Bakke*[5] the following year, there had been only two dissenting votes from the constitutional permissibility of the use of remedial racial classifications.

Bakke, decided in 1978, involved an affirmative action program adopted by the faculty of the Medical School of the University of California at Davis, reserving sixteen places in each entering class of 100 for qualified minority applicants. It was undisputed that there had been no history of deliberate discrimination by the Davis Medical School. By a vote of 5 to 4, the Court held that the set-aside or quota was invalid. But, in what was then, and probably continues to be, the most important part of the decision for affirmative action programs in higher education, a majority of the Justices were willing to hold that race could be used as a "plus" in the admissions process in order to achieve diversity in the student body.

This seemingly contradictory outcome was possible because of the Court's voting alignment. Chief Justice Burger and Justices Potter Stewart, John P. Stevens, and William H. Rehnquist stated that the Davis quota violated Title VI of the Civil Rights Act of 1964. Justice Lewis Powell concluded that the quota contravened the Fourteenth Amendment. This grouping meant that there were five votes against the quota. At the same time, Justices Byron White, Thurgood Marshall, William J. Brennan, and Harry A. Blackmun found no constitutional violation. Because Justice Powell believed that race could be "considered" without violating the Constitution, there were five votes to support the use of race in the admissions process.

The second major affirmative action ruling was *Fullilove v. Klutznick*,[6] decided in 1980. It involved the Public Works Employment Act of 1977, in which Congress appropriated $4 billion to state and local governments for construction projects. Specifically at issue was the "minority business enterprise"—or MBE—provision, which stipulated that ordinarily at least 10 percent of the funds be expended for minority businesses (defined as those at least half owned by minority group members). There is a substantial ambiguity in *Fullilove* as to whether the MBE provision was enacted by Congress to remedy prior deliberate discrimination on the part of government—that is, discrimination that is itself unconstitutional—or whether it was simply an effort by Congress to remedy societal discrimination that had existed against minority group members. Six members of the Court voted to uphold the MBE provision.

Minnick v. California Department of Corrections,[7] a case raising several important issues that are still unresolved, reached the Court in 1981. It involved an affirmative action program voluntarily undertaken in the California prison system, not responding to any prior history of deliberate discrimination, which set hiring goals for prison employees of 38 percent women and 36 percent minorities. The Court granted review but, as has often been true with affirmative action cases, managed to avoid reaching the merits. Of the present members of the Court, now–Chief Justice Rehnquist felt that California's hiring goals violated equal protection.

In the late 1980s, there were four major cases in which the Court again discussed the constitutionality of remedial racial classification. The first case, *Wygant v. Jackson Board of Education*,[8] involved a collective bargaining agreement between the Board of Education and the teachers' union. It had the usual seniority procedure for layoffs—last hired, first fired—but provided that no layoffs could result in a smaller percentage of minority teachers than were employed at the time. Since most minority teachers had been hired quite recently, were it not for this provision a much larger proportion would have been dismissed when cutbacks occurred. As a consequence, although there had been no finding of prior racial discrimination by the school district, non-minority teachers with greater seniority were laid off.

The Court—by a 5 to 4 vote, with no majority opinion—held that this arrangement violated equal protection. The five who found it unconstitutional were Justice Powell and Chief Justice Burger—both now gone from the Court—Justice Rehnquist, Justice O'Connor (the first time she had expressed her views on affirmative action), and Justice White (the first time he had ever voted to hold an affirmative action program invalid). On the other side were Justices Brennan, Marshall, and Blackmun—who have been very consistent on this issue—and Justice Stevens (the first time he had ever approved an affirmative action program).

The second major decision, also in 1986, was *Sheet Metal Workers v. Equal Employment Opportunity Commission.*[9] It involved a union with a long record of deliberate discrimination against non-whites in violation of Title VII of the Civil Rights Act of 1964. In 1983 a federal district judge, after several unsuccessful attempts to remedy this situation, set a goal for the union of 29.23 percent non-white members by 1987, based on the racial makeup of the relevant labor pool. It is important to understand that this goal did not simply seek to make the victims whole. Rather, it aimed for proper representation in the union of the racial and ethnic groups that had been discriminated against. By a 5 to 4 vote, again with no majority opinion, the Court upheld the order. The swing vote was cast by Justice Powell.

The aspect of the case that received the most media attention was its rejection of the position by the Solicitor General that, under both the Civil Rights Act and the equal protection clause, only the actual victims of discrimination may benefit from a race-based remedy. But the fact that a majority of the Court refused to accept the Reagan administration's argument was wholly predictable. In *Bakke*, five members of the Court ruled that race-conscious action need not benefit the actual victims of discrimination, even when there had been no prior deliberate discrimination. In *Fullilove*, six Justices approved the congressional program that set aside 10 percent of federal public works funds for minority businesses that were plainly not themselves victims of prior discrimination. If they had been, it was purely coincidental. And, in a nonconstitutional context, *United Steelworkers v. Weber*[10] validated a collective bargaining agreement between a private company and a union that established an affirmative action program for job training that did not benefit the actual victims of prior discrimination.

The next decision was *United States v. Paradise.*[11] In 1972, a federal district judge found that the Alabama state trooper corps had deliberately discriminated against blacks—not a surprising conclusion since the force had had no black state troopers at all in the full thirty-seven years of its existence. In 1979, seven years later, the Alabama state troopers still had no blacks above the rank of private. In 1983, following eleven years of recalcitrance during which the state trooper corps never produced an acceptable promotion procedure despite the fact that it had been ordered to do so, the federal district judge constructed his own remedy—for every white promoted to the rank of corporal and above, a black must also be promoted as long as qualified black applicants were available and until the state trooper corps produced an acceptable nondiscriminatory promotion procedure.

The Court upheld the order—by a 5 to 4 vote, and once again with no majority opinion. The prevailing opinion was extraordinarily narrow. It emphasized that this one-for-one quota was only imposed after eleven years of obstinacy by the Alabama state trooper corps in failing to remedy deliberate and persistent racial discrimination.

One of the most recent decisions is *Richmond v. J. A. Croson Co.*[12] In 1983, the city council of Richmond, Virginia, adopted a "Minority Business Utilization Plan," patterned after the minority business enterprise provision enacted by Congress and upheld in *Fullilove v. Klutznick.* The Richmond plan required prime contractors to whom the city awarded construction contracts to subcontract at least 30 percent to "minority business enterprises," defined exactly the same way as in *Fullilove.* Justice O'Connor delivered the principal opinion, significant parts of which were joined by at least four other Justices, thus constituting an official "opinion of the Court"—a rare occurrence in respect to this subject. By a vote of 6 to 3, the Richmond plan was held violative of equal protection.

From this summary, it is clear, then, that in judging the validity of remedial racial classifications in this line of cases, different members of the Court have placed varying emphasis on a series of factors—to which this chapter now turns.

As the emphasis in the case descriptions has already suggested, no factor has been more important than whether the challenged race-based remedy is in response to a prior illegality (a violation of either the Constitution or an antidiscrimination law) or whether it seeks simply to remedy what has been labelled the "effects of societal discrimination" (a situation in which minorities are underrepresented not because the government unit involved has deliberately discriminated against them, but rather when a racially neutral policy—say, in hiring or college admissions—produces a racial imbalance that is probably attributable, at least in part, to society's long history of discrimination against minorities).

All Justices agree that a race-based remedy may be used to make the actual victims of prior illegal discrimination whole. For example, when a member of a racial minority has been denied employment, promotion, or seniority in violation of the Civil Rights Act, several decisions of the Supreme Court have approved of a federal judge ordering those who have been discriminated against to be hired or to be awarded retroactive seniority. Indeed, since this does no more than specifically rectify the misconduct, it is really not "race-based" relief at all.

Moving a step further, in *Wygant*, even the Court's most conservative Justices said that race-based remedial plans for prior discrimination by the government unit involved were constitutional even though the programs went beyond making the identified victims whole. Indeed, their opinion made clear that it would have been permissible for the Jackson Board of Education voluntarily to have undertaken its race-based plan if there had been a determination that it had engaged in prior discrimination against the minority groups whose members were now being benefited.

Finally, in *Croson*, at least six Justices ruled that a race-based remedy need not be restricted to curing prior discrimination by the governmental unit involved, but that it might extend to dismantling a system of private discrimination as well. They stated that if Richmond could show that it had essentially become a "passive participant" in a system of racial exclusion practiced by elements of the local construction industry, the city could take steps to remedy it.

Whether a government agency may, on its own initiative, set numerical goals to remedy the effects of past societal discrimination falls at the opposite end of the spectrum. In *Swann*, the Court stated that, even in the absence of past discrimination, a school board may conclude, as a matter of educational policy, "that in order to prepare students to live in a pluralistic society each school should have a prescribed ratio of Negro to white students reflecting the proportion for the district as a whole."[13]

It should be emphasized first that this was dicta—language that was unnecessary to the Court's actual decision. The issue in *Swann* was the validity of a judicial order to remedy a conceded violation of the Fourteenth Amendment. Second, unless busing to desegregate is perceived as imposing little (or no) harm, or unless remedies for deliberate school segregation are wholly unique, the *Swann* dicta are of doubtful validity today. As will be discussed, this is because of the aversion by a majority of the Justices (indeed, the seeming discomfort by all of them) to any fixed ratios, irrespective of the context.

The strongest support for numerical goals to remedy the effects of societal discrimination may be found in the *Bakke* opinion of Justices Brennan, White, Marshall, and Blackmun—all of whom, except Brennan, are still on the Court—approving a set-aside of sixteen places in the entering class of 100 of the Davis Medial School. (Justice Brennan retired in July 1990.) On the other hand, four other Justices stated flatly in *Wygant* that remedying societal discrimination will not justify any racial classification. And I believe, accounting for changes in the Court's membership since them (the arrivals of Justices Scalia and Kennedy), that there were four unambiguous votes for that position as of the time of the *Croson* decision in 1989.

The member of the Court unaccounted for in this issue is Justice Stevens. His view has become clear that as long as adequate procedures are followed, a numerical racial quota may be valid even though not used to remedy a prior illegality. This would seem to produce a 5 to 4 division on the issue, but it seems that Justice White's apparent movement since *Bakke* now places him against the use of numerical goals to remedy the effects of societal discrimination that have produced racial imbalance. Thus, as of the spring of 1990, a majority of the Justices would hold them invalid.

Given this situation, what it takes to find that a race-based program was adopted to remedy a prior illegality assumes great significance. A reading of the cases leads to two basic points.

First, a government employer (and assumedly a state university as well) that voluntarily undertakes a race-based affirmative action program need not make a contemporary finding that it was doing so to remedy its own prior illegality. (Justice O'Connor has underlined this point, noting that an opposite rule would severely undermine the incentive of public employers to voluntarily meet their civil rights obligations.)

Second, if a non-minority employee challenges the plan's constitutionality in court, the government agency cannot successfully defend simply by conceding that it had been previously guilty of illegal discrimination. Rather, the trial court must make a factual determination that the employer had a strong basis for its conclusion that remedial action was necessary—in other words, that it is remedying its prior unlawful conduct.

A series of crucial questions remains unanswered. May a challenger prevail by proving that, despite the government agency's strong belief that remedial action was necessary, it had never in fact engaged in any illegal discrimination? Or must a challenger go further and show not only that there had been no prior illegality, but also that the government agency has no strong basis for believing that there had been? The key vote here is Justice O'Connor's—and she answers the last question affirmatively. Thus, until Justice Brennan retired at least, a majority held the view that there need be no prior unlawful conduct in fact to justify a remedial racial classification.

If one assumes that all there is required is that the government unit must have a "strong" basis for believing that remedial action was necessary, what exactly does this standard mean? Must there be a strong basis for its conclusion that it had engaged in a constitutional violation, or does only a statutory violation suffice? There is a vast difference between these. The settled rule is that there cannot be a constitutional violation without an intent to discriminate.[14] But under Title VII of the Civil Rights Act of 1964, there can be a statutory violation even though there is no intent to discriminate; all that a plaintiff need show is that an employment practice has produced a statistical disparity between the employer's work force and the relevant labor pool that cannot be explained on the basis of hiring criteria that are job related.[15] Again, Justice O'Connor may hold the key, and she strongly implies that a violation of Title VII is enough.

If one assumes that a statutory violation is adequate, the question again arises of whether a challenger can prevail by showing that even though the government employer had a strong basis for concluding that it had violated the Civil Rights Act, there was in fact no statutory violation—that is, although there was a statistical disparity, the agency's hiring criteria were job related. Or can the challenger win only by proving that there was no statistical disparity and therefore the government employer did not even have a prima facie case? If it is the latter, challenges will never succeed because there are statistical disparities in virtually all situations where affirmative action programs are undertaken, whether in the context of employment or admission to public schools, colleges, or professional schools.

The recent opinion by Justice O'Connor in *Croson* said that all that the government employer need have is a firm basis for believing that there is a statistical disparity between those minorities actually employed and those who are *qualified* in the work force. This plainly leaves some room for a challenge to succeed. Nonetheless, an informed guess—if one reads Justice O'Connor correctly—is that very few affirmative action plans that simply use race as a factor (rather than employing a quota) will fail to pass constitutional muster.

This chapter has already indicated that through June 1990, all members of the Court accepted the principle that a government unit may use some form of race-based relief to remedy its prior unlawful discrimination once its existence is properly determined. Moreover, virtually every Justice has acknowledged that the remedy may extend to persons beyond the actual victims of the discrimination, and it may disadvantage persons who were not responsible for the misconduct that took place. But there is substantial disagreement about how great a burden innocent persons may be called upon to bear—that is, non-minorities who do not get jobs, or who are fired, because of a racially preferential hiring system or a reverse seniority plan, or who are refused university admission because of an affirmative action program.

While Justice Souter's views will have to become known, it seems fairly clear that a majority of the Court would probably uphold hiring goals—either to remedy a prior constitutional violation or even to cure under-representation of minorities in positions where qualified persons are available. The Court has declared that the burden to be borne by innocent individuals from hiring goals is diffused to a considerable extent among society generally. Similarly, before Justice Brennan's retirement a majority observed that school admission is akin to hiring, pointing to the fact in the famous *DeFunis* case that even though Marco DeFunis was not admitted to the University of Washington Law School, he was accepted by several other law schools in the geographic area. And, on the basis of a nonconstitutional gender-based ruling in *Johnson v. Santa Clara Transportation Agency*,[16] one should expect that a majority of the Justices will uphold an affirmative action program affording preferential promotions.

Layoffs, on the other hand, present a different question. It seems fairly clear that a majority of the Justices oppose layoffs in order to remedy the effects of societal discrimination. Less clear is the question of whether innocent persons may be laid off in order to remedy a prior violation of the Constitution or an antidiscrimination statute. Minus Brennan, three Justices—Marshall, Blackmun, and Stevens—would plainly approve; four others would apparently disapprove. Once again, Justices O'Connor and Souter appear to hold the key to resolving this problem.

Another very influential factor in determining the validity of a race-based remedy is whether it imposes a strict quota or merely sets a flexible goal. Even those justices—such as Marshall, Blackmun, and Stevens—who are most ready to uphold affirmative action programs sometimes appear hesitant to approve inflexible quotas. Thus, in *Sheet Metal Workers*, these Justices (plus Brennan) strained to find that the goal of 29.23 percent union membership to be reached by 1987 was not an "inflexible racial quota," reasoning that the district judge had in the past changed prior numerical goals of this sort "to accommodate legitimate reasons" put forward by the union.

Although the position of the remaining Justices now on the Supreme Court is less than crystal clear, one may fairly conclude that Chief Justice Rehnquist and Justices White, O'Connor, and Scalia are strongly opposed to any kind of quota, even to remedy prior deliberate discrimination. The vote of Justice Powell—who cast the fifth vote necessary to sustain the 29.23 percent goal in *Sheet Metal Workers* and the one-for-one quota in *Paradise*—had been critical, and his replacement, Justice Kennedy, holds one of the keys to the future of goals or quotas of any kind, even those employed to remedy deliberate or egregious prior discrimination. The indication to be gleaned from his separate opinion in *Croson* is that Justice Kennedy will ally himself close to the latter group of Justices. And any prediction must take account of the fact that Justice Souter has replaced Justice Brennan.

The chapter now turns to a final concern: Where did each Justice stand as of the spring of 1990?

At least since *Bakke*, Justices Brennan, Marshall, and Blackmun stood together in upholding all remedial programs. As has already been indicated, their opinions periodically highlighted certain qualifications of the plans that they have voted to sustain. They often emphasized the relatively modest nature of the burdens imposed on innocent persons, and they stressed that the challenged remedies had a limited duration and that the numerical goals were both flexible and reasonable. Nonetheless, the evidence was that these three could generally be counted on to approve any program that realistically might come to the Court.

After the decisions of the past several years, Justice Stevens can also now be generally counted on to approve affirmative action programs, at least if proper decision-making procedures are followed, although both *Fullilove* and *Croson* reveal that he is opposed to public contract set-asides. Justice Stevens dissented in *Bakke* on the ground that the program violated the Civil Rights Act, but one suspects that if he were now to reach the constitutional question—an issue the Stevens group of four Justices side-stepped in *Bakke*—he would uphold the set-aside of sixteen places in the class.

If one moves to the opposite end of the spectrum, it appears that Chief Justice Rehnquist is inclined to approve race-based remedies in only one situation: a judicial finding of deliberate discrimination and relief fashioned to make the victims whole. Even though he joined opinions in *Wygant* and *Croson*—the reasoning (but not the result) of which go further—all other indications suggest that Chief Justice Rehnquist would subsequently disclaim that broader language that may be found in those cases.

The *Croson* decision gave Justices Scalia and Kennedy the opportunity to explicate their views. Justice Scalia would forbid all race-based classifications with two exceptions. First, he would permit such a remedy to fulfill the promise of *Brown v. Board of Education* in dismantling a dual school system. Second, he indicated that he would adhere to *Fullilove* on the ground that Section 5 of the Fourteenth Amendment affords Congress special legislative power to use race-based remedies to enforce the Constitution's guarantee of equal protection. In contrast, Justice Kennedy was less certain than Justice Scalia that most race-based classifications were forbidden, but he was also more hesitant than Justice Scalia in confirming any unique authority in Congress to enact them.

Two members of the Court whose positions are somewhat more complicated, and thus less predictable, remain to be considered. Justice O'Connor would find a compelling interest for a race-based classification when it is used to remedy a prior illegality. Whether there is prior discrimination, therefore, would appear to be critical. But the seeming ease with which Justice O'Connor would permit a finding of prior illegality goes a long way in diminishing the significance of this factor. As for other racial classifications, Justice O'Connor is willing sometimes to uphold an affirmative action plan when she finds that the government interest is compelling. She has strongly suggested approval of Justice Powell's position in *Bakke* that diversity in college and graduate admissions may sustain a racial classification, and she said that there may be other compelling justifications as well. But this does not mean that she will uphold them readily. She rejected a relatively strong reason in *Wygant*: the school board's desire to have a racial and ethnic distribution among its faculty to serve as role models for its students.

Probably more important, Justice O'Connor employs a balancing process even when remedying a prior legal violation, particularly in regard to the weight of the burden imposed on innocent individuals. Moreover, she seems especially adverse to fixed goals or quotas even in connection with remedying an egregious and persistent constitutional violation.

Last, one comes to the source of greatest uncertainty. When Justice White, in *Bakke*, approved an inflexible goal even though there was no prior deliberate discrimination by the Davis Medical School, advocates of affirmative action justifiably felt that they had a solid vote. But less than a decade later, in *Sheet Metal Workers*—a case involving a remedy for egregious and persistent deliberate discrimination—Justice White found a fixed goal invalid. It is unclear whether his objection was based on his conclusion that the relief involved a "strict racial quota," or on his judgment that the context of the remedy would require some nonminority workers to be expelled from the union, thus amounting to a firing. But his subsequent objection to a fixed remedial quota in *Paradise* and his strong distaste for layoffs may mean that he has shifted his place on the spectrum to the right of Justice O'Connor, and perhaps even to the area occupied by Chief Justice Rehnquist (and Justices Scalia and Kennedy).

In conclusion, the purpose of this chapter has not been to reveal the Court's undisclosed answers to most of the important constitutional questions concerning the validity of affirmative action programs or other remedial racial classifications. Those who presently claim that there is clarity in this area (and some do) are either deluded or deluding. Rather, the effort has been to identify better the important pieces of the puzzle. Now, with Justice Souter aboard, only the Court has the authority ultimately to fit them together.

NOTES

1. 402 U.S. 1 (1971).
2. *McDaniel v. Barresi*, 402 U.S. 39 (1971); *North Carolina State Board of Education v. Swann*, 402 U.S. 43 (1971).
3. 416 U.S. 312 (1974).
4. 430 U.S. 144 (1977).

5. 438 U.S. 265 (1978).
6. 448 U.S. 448 (1980).
7. 452 U.S. 105 (1981).
8. 476 U.S. 267 (1986).
9. 478 U.S. 421 (1986).
10. 443 U.S. 193 (1979).
11. 480 U.S. 149 (1987).
12. 57 U.S.L.W. 4132 (1989). In *Metro Broadcasting v. F.C.C.*, 58 U.S.L.W. 5053 (1990), however, the three *Croson* dissenters were joined by Justices Stevens and White in upholding two minority preference policies adopted by the Federal Communications Commission. This was Justice Brennan's last majority opinion before he announced his retirement in July 1990. The F.C.C.'s policies in question were adopted primarily to promote programming diversity, rather than to remedy past discrimination. Congress had approved the policies in a 1988 appropriations act.
13. 402 U.S., p. 16.
14. *Washington v. Davis*, 426 U.S. 229 (1976).
15. *Albemarle Paper Co. v. Moody*, 422 U.S. 405 (1975).
16. 480 U.S. 616 (1987).

9

Chief Justice Rehnquist and the Future of the Supreme Court

Martin Shapiro

In 1932 the United States experienced what political scientists call a realigning election. The Democratic party won the presidency by a landslide and gained overwhelming majorities in Congress. Moreover, a permanent shift in voter allegiance occurred that has left the Democratic party the majority party in terms of voter registration even until this day. Everyone knows the story of how the Supreme Court, still in Republican hands, held out against the realignment until 1937 and then fell into New Deal hands, first through a retreat on the part of a few members of the old Court and then through a flood of Democratic appointments.

The voting realignment of 1932 led to a realignment of constitutional law that was completed by 1942. The Republican Court had served Republican clients, providing some degree of protection from government action impinging on property interests, largely by employing the Fourteenth Amendment's prohibition on taking property without due process of law and the commerce clause's prohibition on congressional regulation of local commerce. The new Democratic Court was united in its determination to end this service to Republicans. It completely read out of the Constitution any commerce clause limitations on congressional regulatory power. It read the word "property" out of the Fourteenth Amendment by creating a presumption that all legislative regulation of property was constitutional and by holding that such regulations need only pass a constitutional test of minimum rationality, a test that no regulatory legislation ever flunked.

As this dismantling of Republican constitutional law was going on, a family quarrel broke out among the New Deal Justices about what to do next. Following capture of the judicial fortress that had been shooting at Democrats for forty years, one option was to level it so it could never shoot at Democrats again. This was the choice of the school of judicial self-restraint led by Justice Felix Frankfurter, who argued that the Court should cease to engage in judicial review because such review was inherently undemocratic (ostensibly with a small d, but really with a capital D). Others argued that once such a powerful weapon had been captured, it was stupid to destroy it. Instead, constitutional law should be turned from a weapon of Republicans to a weapon of Democrats. This was the choice of the preferred position school led by Justice Hugo Black, who argued that the Court should cease to engage in judicial review in economic regulation cases where property rights were threatened by government—but that it should actively intervene to protect civil rights and liberties. The Court was to protect the rights of minorities and to enforce the specific prohibitions of the Bill of Rights such as the First Amendment. After 1932, of course, minorities had become a significant element of the Democratic voting coalition.

The fondness of Justice Black and company for freedom of speech and religion might, at first glance, appear to have nothing to do with political parties. In fact, however, this fondness was announced at a time during which historically the principal speakers who had invoked the First Amendment to protect themselves from government interference were left-wing intellectuals and labor union organizers. Such intellectuals and the unions were, like minorities, major participants in the New Deal coalition. As to freedom of religion, the principal assaults on freedom of religion had been made by the Protestant majority on Catholic and Jewish minorities, and after 1932 Catholic ethnics and Jews were other important elements of the Democratic coalition. The poor in general were, of course, the most important element of that coalition. They were not explicitly promised anything by the preferred position doctrine, but presumably they would be the beneficiaries of all the economic regulation that the preferred position doctrine promised would now be free of any restraints imposed by the Constitution. Indeed, the only significant element in the New Deal Democratic coalition that the preferred position did not serve was conservative southern whites. But nobody in the New Deal was really fond of them anyway. Indeed, President Roosevelt was attempting to purge them from the party at the very time the preferred position doctrine was being announced.

At first, Democratic judicial self-restrainers had their day. Preferred position attained no more than four Justices' votes in the 1940s. In the

1950s, New Deal Democrats dominated not only the Court but the whole academic world of constitutional law. Even after the great desegregation decision, *Brown v. Board*,[1] in 1954, judicial self-restraint so dominated places like the Harvard Law School that to suggest that judicial activism was a good thing simply labeled one as unprofessional in such precincts.

One introduces the Harvard Law School here because it is important to understand that there is a constitutional law industry that manufactures constitutional law and announces what the people are permitted to think about the Constitution, what lawyers are permitted to argue to courts about the Constitution, and what judges are permitted to say that the Constitution is. The Justices are important producers in that industry. But it is the academic teachers of constitutional law in the law schools who teach whole generations of lawyers the "true" meaning of the Constitution. They also produce most of the arguments that those generations will transmit to courts. And the opinions of courts are heavily shaped by what the lawyers say to them. From the early 1940s until well into the 1970s, nearly all of the teaching and writing about constitutional law and all of the casebooks and textbooks from which law students learned constitutional law were produced by academic lawyers identified with the New Deal. The absolutely central fact of their lives, the governing myth of their belief system, was the opposition of the nine old men to the New Deal and the triumph of the New Deal in 1937. Even to this day, nearly every word put on paper by an academic lawyer is tested by asking, "Would writing this word in 1936 have put me on the side of Roosevelt or on the side of the bad, old Court?" If the answer is "on the side of the bad, old Court," the word is erased and another one chosen.

Brown v. Board was not a product of the New Deal judicial self-restraint constitutional law industry. It was a product of a deviant offshoot of the New Deal lawyers, the black faculty and alumni of the Howard Law School who did not want to level the fortress but to turn it to their own crusade for racial justice. For the new generation of academic lawyers under age fifty, a new founding myth has been added to the New Deal triumph. It is the civil rights triumph of *Brown* and its successor cases. Judicial self-restraint was progressively replaced by its New Deal rival, preferred position, as civil rights became a central agenda item of the Democratic Party and of Democratic lawyers including nearly all of the academic lawyers who teach constitutional law. Today, the constitutional law industry has manufactured a complete line of preferred position products that absolutely dominates all the shelves of the constitutional marketplace. Preferred position is, of course, ideal for Democrats because it combines withholding all constitutional protections for Republican property interests while providing maximum Supreme Court service to such Democratic clients as racial and linguistic minorities, women, and the poor. (The vast and relatively recent constitutional law of rights of accused persons is, of course, constitutional service to the poor, because most defendants are poor and the new law is particularly solicitous of poor defendants.)

In the 1960s, 1970s and 1980s, the United States did not experience a realigning election comparable to that of 1932, but it has experienced a new political alignment. The Congress is dominated by incumbents from the Democratic party who are almost never defeated in reelection contests. The Republicans have been winning the presidency about two-thirds of the time, culminating now in the at least twelve-year-long continuous reign of Presidents Reagan and Bush. This realignment produces a situation in which the Republicans can now think of defeating the Democratic Supreme Court in the way Roosevelt defeated the Republican Supreme Court, by appointing a majority of new Justices on their side. The situation is not exactly the same, however. With an overwhelming majority in the Senate, Roosevelt could appoint nearly anyone he wanted to the Court. As President Reagan learned with the nomination of Robert Bork in 1987, the Republicans must deal with a Democratic Senate.

In this situation the Republicans are now replaying the old Democratic family feud between judicial self-restraint and judicial activism. Faced with a Democratic Supreme Court that had been actively serving Democrats, it was natural for Republicans to trumpet self-restraint as the prime judicial virtue. Get enough self-restrainers on the Court and they could stop the Court from further extending services to Democratic clients and even cut those services back a bit.

A number of aspects of Republican judicial self-restraint render it relatively unsatisfactory, even from a Republican perspective. The Democratic judicial self-restraint of the 1930s was essentially radical. It argued that the long-established doctrine of judicial review had been a major historical mistake and should now be abandoned. Forty or more years of Supreme Court precedents should now be rejected wholesale by taking the Court entirely out of the judicial review business, which had created those precedents. Thus, judicial self-restraint, Democratic style, offered Democrats a quick, thorough destruction of the whole regime of Republican constitutional law.

Not unnaturally, Republican judicial self-restraint is conservative, not radical. It does not argue for an end to judicial review, but for the essentially conservative position that judges not readily break new constitutional ground but stick to the old ways. The paradox that almost totally emasculates such Republican self-restraint for the purpose of achieving Republican goals is, of course, that the old ways are now the ways the Democrats have been manufacturing for the last fifty years. Respect for precedent, much talked of by Republicans, translates into respect for Democratic precedents. For the Democrats used self-restraint to wipe out all the Republican precedents and preferred position to create all the Democratic constitutional law that is now the sole body of precedent.

Moreover, even a Republican self-restraint that was less reverential to precedent would serve only to roll back Democratic client services incrementally, not to reinstate Republican client services. A Court dominated by Republican self-restraint *cum* respect for precedent would whittle away at the Democratic constitutional law, as the Court is currently doing in cases involving rights of the accused, but it would only whittle slowly and it would do nothing positive for Republicans. Only a doctrinal position that as firmly rejects precedent as the New Deal self-restrainers did—and as firmly shifts the Court's services from one party to the other as the New Deal preferred position doctrine did—would turn the Republican realignment in presidential politics into a Republican revolution in constitutional law comparable to the Democratic revolution in constitutional law achieved by the New Deal. Moreover, unlike the New Deal, Republicans do not have the services of the constitutional law industry. That industry remains overwhelmingly in the hands of the New Deal and post–New Deal civil rights Democrats. It is as unprofessional around the Harvard Law School now to oppose civil rights Democratic judicial activism as it was in the 1950s to oppose Democratic judicial self-restraint. The line-up of distinguished constitutional law teachers who in 1987 successfully denounced Judge Robert Bork as out of the mainstream of constitutional law—because he argued for the same judicial self-restraint that Democrats had espoused three decades earlier—shows how complete is the monopoly achieved by the preferred position industry.

Democrats, however, have not quite achieved their complete constitutional agenda. One major item remains. Beginning with the Social Security Act, Americans have built up a welfare state apparatus step by step. Though not yet completely, the government has become responsible for providing minimums of food, clothing, housing, medical care, and education for everyone. Many of these minimums are legislatively enacted in the form of "entitlements" that make the benefits semipermanent in the sense that they are freed of the annual presidential budget and congressional appropriation cycle. Unless the legislation that establishes them is repealed, all the money necessary to support them must be provided.

There remains the risk of repeal or subsequent new statutes that alter the level of benefits. And there remain major gaps that Congress has not legislated to fill. If the welfare state could be constitutionalized—that is, if the Supreme Court would hold that there were constitutional rights to adequate subsistence, housing, health care, and education—

then benefits would be protected from the vagaries of the congressional process. Congress could not repeal them or reduce them, and it would be commanded by the Court to fill in the gaps. The left has made the constitutionalizing of the welfare state a major element in its constitutional agenda ever since the middle years of the Warren Court. It had begun to win a few preliminary victories by the end of the Warren Court,[2] was quickly stymied at the beginning of the Burger Court,[3] and has won an occasional skirmish since. Post–New Deal academics continue to manufacture the theoretical constitutional rights to welfare that they hope the Court will eventually declare.

The right also has an agenda. It seeks to destroy the negative part of the preferred position doctrine and return the Court to the defense of property interests. A whole array of constitutional interpretations and legal theories are employed by a small but vocal number of Republican academics. They include (1) a theory of legislation and statutory interpretation that renders most regulatory laws unreasonable, putting teeth back into the reasonableness requirement of the due process clause by weakening the judicial presumption that all economic legislation is constitutional, (2) an adaption of the equal protection clause to do the work that the due process clause used to do for property, (3) a revival of the commerce and/or contract clauses, (4) an expansion of the takings clause, and (5) an invigoration of the Tenth Amendment. Also central to the effort of the right to deconstruct New Deal constitutional law is an attempt to reconstruct some kind of constitutional federalism that would impose some real boundaries on the powers of the central government. Before 1937, one of the principal constitutional guarantees of federalism was the commerce clause, which gave control of local economic matters to the states and gave Congress control only of interstate commerce. So one would expect Republicans to attempt to revive the commerce clause or something like it.

It has been noted that both Republicans and New Deal preferred-position activists have been hampered by their own judicial self-restraint proponents. Republicans are also hampered by a considerable diversion of energies into attempting to erode the non-property constitutional rights that have been created by the preferred positioners. Republican judges have been paying a great deal of attention to taking constitutional rights away from Democrats and consequently less to recreating property rights for Republicans.

In their attempts to whittle away at assorted civil liberties, Republican judges are reflecting a major unresolved tension within the Republican party. Is that party to be conservative in the sense of protecting autonomy from the ever-increasing incursions of ever-growing big government? Or is it to be conservative in the sense of seeking to preserve and foster traditional values, life-styles and social structures? Republican conservatism of the first kind would not be anxious to attack post–1937 Democratic extensions of civil liberties to Democrats, but only to remedy post–1937 Democratic deprivations of civil liberties to Republicans. Such a conservatism would be anxious to restore property rights but not to erode other rights against government intrusion. Republican conservatism of the second kind would be as anxious to erode those rights that protect the libertine as they would to restore those that protect the sober, respectable, propertied.

It may appear that this chapter has spent a great deal of time talking about everything but its subject, which is Chief Justice Rehnquist and the future of the Supreme Court. It is certainly true that if the purpose of the chapter were to evaluate fully the Chief Justice as a jurisprudent, lawgiver, moral teacher, and intellectual, one would have focused on him sooner and said more about him and less about the general contours of American constitutional politics. However, if the concern is largely with the Chief's impact on the present and future Court, then the matters discussed so far are the real forest, and Rehnquist's positions in particular cases and his specific arguments on various doctrinal questions are the trees. The central issue is how well Chief Justice Rehnquist understands the dynamics of the constitutional campaigns that have been unfolding since 1932 and the degree to which he is able to influence their outcomes. A brief look at some of the cases in four recent terms of the Court will allow us to begin to assess how well the Chief Justice has been doing at capturing the forest for his side.

Chief Justice Rehnquist has played his most active leadership role in the segment of the Republican campaign that aims at the reconstruction of federalism. Between 1937 and 1942, the New Deal Court so expanded the constitutional clause empowering Congress to regulate commerce among the several states that every aspect of life came to fall within congressional authority. Nothing, no matter how purely local, was reserved solely to state authority. In the process the Court declared merely a "truism" the Tenth Amendment, which reserves to the states and the people all authority not conveyed to the federal government by enumeration in specific clauses of the Constitution. In the recent terms examined here, only one major case, *South Carolina v. Baker*,[4] raises these issues directly. Rehnquist files a brief concurring opinion that avoids the issues. Why he does so illustrates his leadership role in this field.

In *National League of Cities v. Usery*[5] in 1976, then Justice Rehnquist wrote an opinion for four Justices in which, for the first time since 1937, the Court struck down a congressional statute as a violation of the commerce clause. The statute extended federal wages and hours regulations to state employees. The opinion stresses repeatedly that the Constitution does not permit the federal government to expand its powers so far that the integral functions of state government fall under the control of the central government. Rehnquist apparently despaired of actually cutting back the congressional commerce power itself from the unlimited condition with which the New Dealers had endowed it by 1942. Instead, he adopted the now frequent Republican ploy of seizing upon some long unused constitutional provision and using it as a foundation on which to establish a new Republican constitutional law.

The preferred position doctrine of the Democrats said that Congress could do whatever it pleased to economic rights but that the Court would actively enforce the civil rights and liberties of the Bill of Rights. Thus, even though Congress could regulate any economic matter it wanted to without fear that the Court would impose commerce clause limitations, its economic regulations would still be constitutionally limited by the Bill of Rights. For instance, suppose Congress used its commerce powers to shut down a small, local newspaper that was printed in and sold all its 200 copies a week in a little Vermont town. After 1937 the Court would not say, "You can't do that because the Congress can only regulate interstate commerce, and nothing this paper does is interstate. It is purely local and so subject only to state regulation." But New Dealers believed in the Bill of Rights, and the First Amendment says that "Congress shall make no law abridging freedom of . . . the press." So the post–1937 Court would presumably declare the congressional statute unconstitutional because it violated not the commerce clause, but the First Amendment. In *Usery*, Justice Rehnquist seeks to revive the Tenth Amendment, which the New Dealers had called a truism and ignored. After all, inconvenient as it may be to the New Dealers, the Tenth Amendment is in the Bill of Rights, too. Rehnquist's opinion treats the Tenth as New Dealers would the First. He says that no matter how much commerce Congress may regulate, its commerce regulations are unconstitutional if they violate the freedom of the state, which he finds embodied in the Tenth Amendment.

Nine years later in the *Garcia*[6] case, the Republicans suffered their most resounding defeat and New Deal constitutional law one of its most resounding reconfirmations of recent times. Justice Harry Blackmun went over to the other side, and the dissenters in *Usery* got to reverse it. In doing so they read federalism right out of the Constitution, or at least that part of the Constitution the Supreme Court chooses to enforce. They said that the Supreme Court should never again declare any Congressional statute unconstitutional because it invaded the authority of the states. Justice Rehnquist was, of course, among the dissenters.

Those dissenters (with some subtractions caused by retirements, and addition of Justices Antonin Scalia and Anthony Kennedy, appointed since) have been laboring ever since to overrule *Garcia* and return to *Usery*, or somehow to read *Garcia* to mean the opposite of what it says. So far, however, they have at most four votes on the Court. *South Carolina v. Baker* is one of those cases in which they are still losing. Chief Justice Rehnquist provides a highly equivocal concurrence rather than a dissent in that case, probably because he feels that every closely divided repeat of *Garcia* ever further spotlights the constitutional status of that case. He would prefer to render these subsequent defeats as inconspicuous as possible until he can pick up the one or two more votes he needs to return to *Usery*. (Newly appointed Justice Kennedy did not vote in this case. Even if he is assumed to be anti-*Garcia*, Rehnquist has only four votes. If the Chief Justice had voted in dissent in this case, the vote would have been 5 to 3 against him.)

Chief Justice Rehnquist's behavior in criminal justice cases, including death penalty cases, can be interpreted in one of two ways. Conservatives in general and the Republican party have been "tough on crime" as part of that tendency in conservatism that fosters government repression of bad guys rather than freedom of individuals from repressive government. Rehnquist's very consistent stance in favor of government and against those accused (and, by the time he sees them, convicted) of crime may be viewed as part of this repressive conservatism. His opinion in *United States v. Salerno*,[7] upholding the preventive detention provisions of the Federal Bail Statute can be offered as evidence of this train of conservatism.

The Chief Justice's general pattern of criminal justice opinions may, however, be viewed in another light as part of the conservative reconstruction of the federalism that was destroyed by the New Deal. The New Deal expansion of the commerce and spending clauses left the states almost totally at the mercy of Washington. One of the few arenas of undivided state authority left after 1942 was the prosecution of at least those crimes that Congress did not choose to federalize. Confusion often arises over the Warren Court because its Chief Justice was nominally a Republican. That Court, however, was a thoroughly preferred-position New Deal Court. Indeed, it advanced numbers of aspects of Democratic constitutional law much further than the Roosevelt Courts had, and during its time the Democratic constitutional law became the absolutely unchallengeable orthodoxy of the legal academy in the United States. (It ought not to be forgotten that the New Deal Court itself was presided over by a nominal Republican, Harlan Fiske Stone, who had been promoted to Chief Justice by President Franklin D. Roosevelt.) The Warren Court, quite on its own and without congressional action, federalized all of criminal procedure. In a series of landmark decisions such as *Gideon*[8] and *Miranda*[9] and then a host of follow-up cases, the Warren Court created a detailed, uniform national code of police conduct binding on every state and local police officer and supreme over the rules enacted by the governments that those police officers serve. From a Republican point of view, what little was left of federalism after the economic decisions of 1937 to 1942 was destroyed by the criminal justice decisions of 1963 to 1969.

Chief Justice Burger was appointed to change all this. Then Justice Rehnquist was his loyal supporter. But they never had the votes. Now Chief Justice Rehnquist still does not. As a result, Rehnquist seeks—by an endless and widely assorted series of tactics often focused on some special factual or procedural peculiarity of a given case—to give the states as much breathing space as he can, given his inability to overthrow the basic uniform, national rule approach of the Warren Court.[10] A whole series of relatively minor cases in the four terms we are examining—such as *Witt*,[11] *Ake*,[12] *Connelly*,[13] *Van Arsdall*,[14] and *Ford*[15]—exhibit this pattern. Rehnquist and company have succeeded in blocking some of the furthest extensions of the rule against self-incrimination proposed by the liberal Justices. They have succeeded in creating a "good faith" exception to the unreasonable search and seizure rule, which liberals say threatens to swallow up the rule itself.[16] But that greatly exaggerates the extent of their victory.

The revival of federalism may be one foundation of the conservative constitutional law agenda, but its keystone is renewed constitutional protection of private property rights. The New Deal Court read the word "property" right out of the Fifth and Fourteenth Amendment requirements that no person be deprived of life, liberty, or property without due process of law. The preferred position doctrine says that government regulation of property shall be presumed constitutional by the Court unless no legitimate reason at all for the regulation can be imagined, the so-called minimum rationality test. And of course unless legislatures and lawyers are completely stupid and incompetent, they can always come up with some reason if the statute is challenged in court.

So one Republican tactic would be to try to put the word "property" back into the due process clause by ending the almost unrebuttable presumption that all economic regulation passes the due process clause test. A small step in that direction may have been taken in the *Cleburne* case[17]—or may not have been taken, depending on how one reads the case. Conservatives see it one way and liberals another. In *Cleburne*, a property interest was given due process clause protection because for the first time in many years an economic regulation flunked the minimum rationality test. The case is complex, however, and then-Justice Rehnquist did not write an opinion in it, limiting himself to voting silently with the conservatives. So analysis of it as a reflection of Rehnquist's thinking awaits another day.

As already noted, an alternative to direct attack on long-standing New Deal constitutional interpretation is to find other constitutional clauses than commerce and due process (or its equal protection equivalent) on which to hang conservative positions. It is pretty hard to read the word "property" out of the last clause of the Fifth Amendment, which reads, "nor shall private property be taken for public use, without just compensation."

The takings clause, however, is severely limited as a property protection. It does not forbid taking. It only requires that government pay compensation. If the process of getting compensation is extremely complex, time consuming, costly, and risky for the property owner, the clause can be defeated in practice. Moreover, if government does not literally take your land and buildings away from you and run a highway over them, but instead just passes regulations that forbid persons the use of their property, is that a taking? It has not been taken away. The owners still have it. The property simply is not worth anything any longer. This is the problem of so-called "regulatory takings," in which government does not take possession of the property but regulates it in such a way that it cannot be used profitably.

Many government regulations such as zoning laws and environmental protection laws inevitably limit the uses to which an owner can devote property and, therefore, the value of that property. If a person owns a gravel pit that makes a lot of dust and noise, and a law is passed limiting dust and noise, the gravel company may have to process less gravel and therefore make less money. So the business is worth less. But this situation does not seem to be a literal taking of the property. On the other hand, if the regulations are stringent enough, the company may not be able to run its gravel operation at all because there is always some noise and dust. And if the company cannot run the gravel pit as a gravel pit, the firm may be left only with a hole in the ground that is of no use at all. Can the government then say, "Well, you've still got your hole in the ground. We haven't taken it away from you, so no compensation"? The Supreme Court has long recognized that at some point a regulation becomes a taking.

In two major takings cases in 1987, the conservative Justices seemed to be breaking new ground in turning the takings clause into a constitutional limitation on government regulation of property, although the extent to which these cases actually alter takings law is unclear. Viewed as first steps, they are portentious, but nearly everything depends on what, if any, later steps occur. In one of these cases, *Nollan v. California Coastal Commission*,[18] Chief Justice Rehnquist silently joined Justice Scalia's majority opinion. In the other, *First Lutheran*,[19] he wrote the opinion.

The First Lutheran Church owned a recreation area complete with buildings along a stream. There was a forest fire on the nationally owned watershed lands above the stream. As a result, during the next rainy season, there was a flood and the buildings were washed away. Then a local government unit passed a regulation forbidding any building along the stream because of the flood danger. First Lutheran could not rebuild its camp buildings and said its property was, therefore, useless for the only purpose for which it could be used.

The California Supreme Court ruled as a matter of state constitutional and statutory law that First Lutheran could not go into a state court and ask for compensation for a taking. Instead, it first had to go to the local government and try to persuade it that the regulation was illegal. If it failed, it then had to go to a state court and ask the state court to find the regulation illegal. If the state court did so, then the regulation would be invalid and First Lutheran would be free to build buildings—and so there would have been no taking and, consequently, no compensation would be required. Of course, during the five or more years it might take to go through all these legal procedures, First Lutheran would have been unable to use its land, but such a temporary loss of land use did not constitute a taking in the eyes of the California Supreme Court—a court that for many years had been notably unsympathetic to property claims.

Because of the peculiar procedural stance of this particular case, the Chief Justice could assume that the land had been rendered completely useless by the regulation; therefore, he did not have to address the question of just how much reduction in the value of property a regulation had to cause before it became a taking. His decision instead dealt with the problem of delay of compensation. He ruled that the rendering valueless of a property for the period between the passage of a regulation and its final declaration of unlawfulness by a court constituted a temporary taking for which the owner could seek compensation.

The concept of a temporary taking is important. Many zoning and land use authorities have used the tactic of making a regulation of doubtful legality that stayed in force during the period in which the property owner fought it in court. Even if the owner won, the regulator could then make another very similar regulation. The owner would have to go to court again; while he did, the land would be controlled by the second regulation. And so on indefinitely. The Supreme Court's recognition of temporary takings puts some restraint on this tactic because it requires government to compensate the owner for each period in which his land is rendered useless. (The practical impact of the decision standing alone will be relatively small because most land regulations reduce rather than totally destroy the value of land; therefore, the owner's loss is temporary but is usually not a taking.)

We have seen that the constitutionalizing of the welfare state was stymied early in the Burger Court. Liberals won one new victory in *Plyler v. Doe*,[20] which moved the Court toward the position that there was a constitutional right to public school education. The conservatives managed to whittle *Plyler* back slightly in *Kadrmas v. Dickinson Public Schools*,[21] in an opinion by Justice O'Connor in which the Chief Justice silently joined.

Of course, welfare state protectors want not only to turn statutory entitlements into constitutional rights, but to assure full constitutional procedural protections for those seeking their entitlements. Recent Republican administrations have been putting pressure on entitlements by treating claimants to them as ungenerously as possible. Given Democratic majorities in Congress, the legislation granting the entitlements cannot be much amended to reduce them, so the Republican executive branch, which controls handing out the entitlement benefits, tries to give as little benefit to as few claimants as it can. The procedures for granting these benefits thus become the liberal-conservative battleground. There is a statutory fee cap of $10 per claim on lawyers representing veterans in agency proceedings seeking to gain disability benefits from the Veterans Administration. The result is that veterans do not get legal assistance with their claims. In 1970, the liberals of the Warren Court had sought to extend constitutional rights like the right to counsel from criminal procedure into welfare procedure in *Goldberg v. Kelly*.[22] This move had been cut back somewhat four years later by conservatives in *Mathews v. Eldridge*.[23] In that same year in *Arnett v. Kennedy*,[24] Justice Rehnquist wrote a major opinion, but only for a plurality, which sought to block the move entirely. In *Walters v. Radiation Survivors*,[25] the Chief Justice follows the *Mathews* line and upholds the statutory limit on fees.

Thus, Chief Justice Rehnquist has been carefully tending the conservative economic agenda and attending to the liberal one—although he has had to content himself with relatively limited victories.

New Deal dedication to freedom of speech clearly had something to do with the fact that it was left-wing speakers who had sought the protection of the First Amendment in the 1920s and 1930s. Liberal support for freedom of speech recently has become less than monolithic. Feminists have discovered the evils of pornography. Peace proponents see the evils of violence on television. And it is Nazis, Klansmen, and anti-abortion militants (besides flag-burners) who now wrap themselves in the First Amendment.

Conservatives basically concerned with individual autonomy against big government should, of course, very strongly favor freedom of speech. Alas, however, most Americans, liberal and conservative alike, have tended to be far more in favor of freedom of speech for the good guys than the bad guys.[26] So it would not be surprising to find conservatives not quite so strongly solicitous of liberal as of conservative speech. Moreover, the other strain of conservatism that supports the traditional virtues rather than individual freedom per se will encounter many enemy speakers. For speech is a major way in which traditional values are challenged.

Chief Justice Rehnquist has adopted a generally constricted view of free speech protection, but one that is not notably more favorable to Republican than Democratic speakers. Most notably in the *Pacific Gas & Electric* case,[27] he has restated his earlier position that corporations are not entitled to as broad speech protections as are individuals, and he does so in a context in which conservative speakers are seeking First Amendment protection against left-wing speakers. Another two of his recent free speech opinions involve clashes between traditional morality and speech, and in both the Chief Justice favors morality over speech.[28]

In only one recent case does Chief Justice Rehnquist take a position resoundingly in favor of free speech: *Federal Elections Commission v. National Conservative Political Action Committee*.[29] The issue was whether the independent campaign expenditures of political action committees (PACs) could be limited. The Court has held that the Constitution forbids limitations on individual expenditures (as distinguished from individual contributions to candidates). Limitations on corporate expenditures, on the other hand, have been upheld. The Chief Justice characterizes PACs as associations of individuals and, therefore, as enjoying the individual's constitutional protection against government limitation of campaign expenditures. It is possible to characterize PACs simply as masks for corporate campaign spending and, thus, to characterize Chief Justice Rehnquist's decision as essentially one for Republican corporate speech.

This interpretation, however, would be difficult to reconcile with his anti–corporate speech stance in *Pacific Gas and Electric*. The original campaign financing case, *Buckley v. Valleo*,[30] was decided by the Court in part on a leveling-down, egalitarian version of free speech. Limiting campaign spending would mean that rich speakers would not get to speak more than poor speakers. If one is not seized by egalitarian visions, one must see congressional statutes limiting campaign spending as limiting the political freedom of those who can afford to make them. Chief Justice Rehnquist is not seized by egalitarian visions, and consequently his decision in this case must have appeared to him a rather routine defense of standard First Amendment values. This may be why Rehnquist joined Justice Marshall's opinion for the Court in *Austin v. Michigan Chamber of Commerce*,[31] where the majority upheld state restrictions on independent campaign expenditures by a nonprofit corporation.

Besides speech, the First Amendment deals with religion. One would expect the traditional values strain of conservatism to come most clearly to the fore in this area. Moreover, most religion cases involve varying state policies on religion, which the Supreme Court is asked to limit by creating and applying a uniform national rule. So, conservative attitudes on federalism are bound to come to the fore as well. On the other hand, no issue more dramatically involves the invasion by government of matters of individual concern than do state laws prescribing or proscribing religious belief and practice. Thus, we would expect conservatives to be particularly concerned about state laws that enter the sphere of religion. In many instances the goals of fostering religious values, preserving the authority of state government, and protecting individual religious conscience will come into conflict. We would expect the conservative constitutional position to be a confused and even self-contradictory one.

In the area of religion the Chief Justice takes his most openly radical stance against the constitutional law that has been manufactured by the post–New Deal constitutional rights industry. In three decisions of the 1984 Term, Rehnquist spells out his rejection of current Supreme Court doctrine on the clause of the First Amendment banning an establishment of religion. He agrees with the standard doctrines that the establishment clause forbids the establishment of an official state religion and the favoring by government of any religion over another. In doing so, of course, he protects the religious conscience of individuals, and he limits state governments relatively little—because no state government seeks to have an official church, and few would care to discriminate openly in favor of some religions and against others. The Chief Justice, however, goes on very firmly and completely to reject the third aspect of modern establishment clause jurisprudence, that the state may not favor religion over non-religion, that there must be a wall of separation between the state and any religious activity. Relying on the historical intent of the framers and pointing to the massive inconsistencies in the Court's previous decisions, Chief Justice Rehnquist calls for new constitutional doctrine that would permit the states to act positively to support religious values as long as they did so in a way that did not favor some religions over others.[32]

In Rehnquist's one other significant opinion of recent years on religion, he upheld the Army in its insistence on enforcing uniform regulations on an orthodox Jew who believed himself to be under a religious obligation to wear a yarmulke.[33] This decision may be dismissed as merely pro-government/anti-individual or as showing excessive deference to the military. On the other hand, if one concedes at all that there is a value to having military uniforms that are uniform, a dilemma necessarily arises. Ours is a nation of many religions and one in which new ones are created and imported. And each is, of course, as entitled as any other to announce religious observations—including the wearing or not wearing of certain kinds of clothes or beards or hair styles. Moreover, although the nation does not have a draft army at the moment, it often does. Many draftees would prefer to be elsewhere or at least to signify that they serve under protest. In this situation the decision on yarmulkes (which, if decided in favor of the wearer, would surely be the forerunner to other cases about all sorts of religious accoutrements) may have been simply a commonsense outcome to an irreconcilable conflict between military service and religious freedom.[34]

It may seem perverse in dealing with the Chief Justice and the future of the Supreme Court to leave abortion and affirmative action to the end. As the Bork and Souter nominations showed, many people see them as the crucial issues for the future Court. Justice Rehnquist dissented in *Roe v. Wade*[35] and has consistently voted with the anti-*Roe* block of Justices ever since. At the time of *Roe*, many states had been changing their abortion laws. Some had not. The *Roe* majority substituted a detailed, uniform national rule for the varied and changing state practice. The argument could not even be made that the states were so hopelessly bogged down in an obsolete status quo that only federal intervention could liberate policy from the dead hand of the past. The Rehnquist federalism response in this situation is surely unremarkable. Advocates of judicial self-restraint have attacked *Roe* because it judicially creates a major public policy without democratic support and without any specific warrant in the actual words of the Constitution or the intentions of the framers. Chief Justice Rehnquist has often used judicial self-restraint and framers' intent language, but they are hardly needed to account for his votes in *Roe* and subsequent cases.

Today, the voting alignment on the abortion issue depends on Justice Souter. Depending on whether he accepts or rejects the Court's current constitutional doctrine, the degree of shift in the Court's stance may come to depend on Justice O'Connor, who has been building up a highly articulated doctrinal position for which Rehnquist may supply one of the supporting votes. That position would abolish the trimester system of *Roe* and acknowledge a constitutional right to freedom of choice, but would balance that right against the state's interest in preserving the potential life of the fetus.

Initially, abortion was one of those phenomena of "single-issue politics" that cut across party lines and was essentially a matter of individual conscience rather than left-right ideology. Over time, opposition to abortion became a Republican campaign position, but one to which many Republican leaders were only slowly, reluctantly, and partially converted under pressure from the Christian fundamentalists who have become an element in Republican strategy. The Democrats tried desperately to avoid a firm, official position because they recognized the issue as more likely to divide Democrats than unite them. The Democratic party became more pro-choice as Republicans became, for a time at least, more anti-abortion.

It is not at all clear why conservatives in general or Republicans in particular should have any united stance on abortion. Legal prohibition of abortion involves grave government interference with individual and family autonomy, even if for some conservatives it seems to support traditional morality. And individual views on whether a fetus is a person do not depend on party identification or dedication to any particular theory of the economy and government's role in it. While to some degree abortion is today a political issue and has become even more so since the Court has seriously modified *Roe*,[36] it remains an issue that cuts across long-term Republican-Democratic, left-right constitutional agendas.

Chief Justice Rehnquist's position on affirmative action issues is somewhat similar. He silently joined the block of four Justices in *Bakke*,[37] which held that Title VI of the Civil Rights Act forbade discrimination against whites as well as racial minorities. In the key *Weber* case,[38] he wrote a bitter dissent against the majority view that in spite of its explicit wording and legislative history, Title VII did allow employment discrimination against whites. In recent years he has silently joined other dissenting and occasionally majority opinions that hold that Title VII prohibits various affirmative action schemes. In the recent *Johnson* case,[39] Justice Scalia, joined by Rehnquist, strongly restates Rehnquist's views in *Weber*. Because all these opinions hold that a statute bars the affirmative action, they do not commit themselves on what the equal protection clause itself requires or allows.

In *Wygant v. Jackson Board of Education*[40] and *City of Richmond v. Croson*,[41] the Court held by plurality or bare majority vote that the equal protection clause required the Court to engage in strict scrutiny of affirmative action programs that discriminated against whites. "Strict scrutiny" has almost always been a preliminary to judicial rejection, so these cases may presage a very tough stance toward affirmative action in the future. Here again, however, Justice Souter and Justice O'Connor may sit in the swing seats. Justice O'Connor tends toward moderate, intermediate, balancing positions that uphold affirmative action where it is clearly aimed at correcting past discrimination and where current discrimination against while males is mitigated as much as possible. In these cases the Chief Justice is not a significant spokesman, but he does provide one of the generally anti–affirmative action votes that allow balancing exponents like O'Connor to prevail.

This review of the work of the Chief Justice in recent years reveals that he is aware of and acting in support of the conservative or Republican constitutional agenda. In the key locus of commerce clause/federalism/property rights, he has been exceptionally active and vocal in attempting to deconstruct the negative portion of the New Deal preferred position doctrine. This is the portion that commands the Court to stay away from everything except the civil rights and liberties of the constituent parts of the Democratic party. In the criminal justice area, he has been active in attempting to trim back the positive side of preferred position, the side that urges the Supreme Court to make uniform national rules defending those rights that Democrats prefer. He has played a supporting role in blocking left-wing attempts to constitutionalize welfare state benefits and a very active role in holding back on constitutionalizing the procedures involved in the distribution of such benefits.

A number of the most important areas of constitutional law do not so directly implicate left-right agendas and the deconstruction of New Deal and post–New Deal constitutional law. Free speech for leftist speakers was a major item in the New Deal's agency, but one that was never fully consolidated in First Amendment doctrine. Today's Court is an inheritor of a large amount of very mixed free speech doctrine and a growing hesitancy from the left about granting complete free speech to everyone. At the same time, the right is torn between a commitment to individual autonomy from big government that ought to make it favor free speech and the knowledge that many speakers use that freedom to attack traditional values. The Chief Justice reflects these conditions in a mixed position on freedom of speech that particularly favors government over "bad" speakers, that even sometimes favors government over such "good" speakers as corporations, but that does acknowledge the value of the First Amendment as a protection for individuals. In his religion cases, Chief Justice Rehnquist has announced a clean-cut and quite radical position that he believes would protect individual conscience while allowing government to place itself firmly on the side of religion.

In the areas of abortion and affirmative action, the Chief Justice has not been a leading spokesman in recent years and is likely to lend his vote to the new, intermediate position that appears to be emerging in both areas.

It is often said of Chief Justice Rehnquist that he is inclined toward quibbling over the details of particular cases, failing to provide rigorous and analytically complete arguments, and avoiding fully articulated doctrinal stances. It would take a very long and detailed analysis of the hundreds of opinions he has written to evaluate these charges fully. Even if they are true, however, a number of factors must be borne in mind in assessing their seriousness. Common lawyers love precedent. The Supreme Court is supposed to follow precedent. Between 1937 and 1942, the New Dealers joyously overturned the earlier Republican precedents and replaced them with new Democratic precedents. And then the Warren Court added flocks of new liberal precedents. If the Burger Court and the Rehnquist Court had had the votes that the New Dealers had, they could have done just what the New Dealers did—joyously overthrown the precedents of the other side and announced their own. The new Courts have not had the votes and consequently have had to live with the last generation of precedents created by their opponents. Thus, their attempts to deconstruct preferred position and reconstruct constitutional law along conservative lines have necessarily been, from the common lawyer's point of view, piecemeal, poorly argued, internally contradictory, and lacking in craftsmanship—as an article by David Shapiro on Justice Rehnquist argued.[42]

As the existence of Shapiro's article suggests, the Republican Justices faced another handicap, a handicap that had a kind of multiplier effect on their problem of reconstructing constitutional law without a Court majority. The New Dealers and post–New Dealers not only had five to seven votes, but they had a constitutional law industry in the law schools that was itself overwhelmingly New Deal Democratic. The Court was sometimes chided by the self-restraint wing of this industry for doing too much, but never for doing the wrong thing. Particularly after 1954, the liberals on the Court have had the active and constant support of at least 90 percent of those who write about constitutional law. The liberal Justices have the home team advantage in every game. Occasionally they get a story that says their play was sloppy, but it is still clear which is the better team. When the conservative team gets written up in the law reviews, readers are told not only that they played badly but that they are heading for the wrong goal line. If the Chief Justice were heading toward the proper goal line, we would hear fewer complaints about his resorting to the end run and the lateral rather than heading straight up the middle. Most of Rehnquist's problem about heading up the middle does not result from his inability to run straight but from his knowledge that if he does he will be stopped for no gain.

In the final analysis, great judicial craftsmanship comes from winners or judges who are willing to lose in glorious dissents. If one is trying to win without the votes, judicial life is harder. Chief Justice Rehnquist is in pursuit of the conservative agenda, but for most of his tenure, he has not been, and may never be, playing on the winning team.

NOTES

1. 347 U.S. 483 (1954).
2. *Shapiro v. Thompson*, 394 U.S. 618 (1969).
3. *Dandridge v. Williams*, 397 U.S. 471 (1970); *Wyman v. James*, 400 U.S. 309 (1971).
4. 485 U.S. 505 (1988).
5. *National League of Cities v. Usery*, 426 U.S. 833 (1976).
6. *Garcia v. San Antonio Metropolitan Transit Authority*, 469 U.S. 528 (1985).
7. 481 U.S. 739 (1987).
8. *Gideon v. Wainwright*, 372 U.S. 335 (1963).
9. *Miranda v. Arizona*, 384 U.S. 436 (1966).
10. For example, see *Butler v. McKellar*, where the Court cut back on the use of federal habeas corpus, 58 U.S.L.W. 4924 (1990). See also "Rehnquist Takes Aim at Death Penalty Delays," *National Law Journal*, May 28, 1990, p. 31.

11. *Wainwright v. Witt*, 469 U.S. 412 (1985).
12. *Ake v. Oklahoma*, 470 U.S. 68 (1985).
13. *Colorado v. Connelly*, 479 U.S. 157 (1986).
14. *Delaware v. Van Arsdall*, 475 U.S. 673 (1986).
15. *Ford v. Wainwright*, 477 U.S. 673 (1986).
16. *United States v. Leon*, 468 U.S. 897 (1984).
17. *Texas v. Cleburne Living Center*, 473 U.S. 432 (1985). The case involved a home for the mentally retarded, and there were no dissents. The Court liberals, however, did not join Chief Justice Burger's majority opinion.
18. 483 U.S. 825 (1987).
19. *First English Evangelical Lutheran Church of Glendale v. Los Angeles County*, 482 U.S. 304 (1987).
20. 457 U.S. 202 (1982).
21. 487 U.S. 450 (1988).
22. 397 U.S. 254 (1970).
23. 424 U.S. 319 (1976).
24. 416 U.S. 134 (1974).
25. 473 U.S. 305 (1985).
26. Lee Bollinger, *The Tolerant Society* (1986), pp. 73–196.
27. *Pacific Gas & Electric Co. v. Public Utilities Commission*, 475 U.S. 1 (1986).
28. *Posadas de Puerto Rico v. Tourism Co. of Puerto Rico*, 478 U.S. 328 (1986); *City of Renton v. Playtime Theatres*, 475 U.S. 41 (1986).
29. 470 U.S. 480 (1985).
30. 424 U.S. 1 (1976).
31. 58 U.S.L.W. 4371 (1990).
32. *Wallace v. Jaffree*, 472 U.S. 38 (1985).
33. *Goldman v. Weinberger*, 475 U.S. 503 (1985).
34. But Rehnquist joined Justice Scalia's opinion in *Oregon Department of Human Resources v. Smith*, 58 U.S.L.W. 4433 (1990), which denied a free exercise claim for the use of peyote in the Native American Church.
35. 410 U.S. 113 (1973).
36. *Webster v. Reproductive Health Services*, 57 U.S.L.W. 5023 (1989).
37. *Regents of the University of California v. Bakke*, 438 U.S. 265 (1978).
38. *United Steelworkers v. Weber*, 443 U.S. 193 (1979).
39. *Johnson v. Santa Clara County Transportation Agency*, 480 U.S. 616 (1987).
40. 476 U.S. 267 (1986).
41. 57 U.S.L.W. 4132 (1989).
42. D. Shapiro, "Mr. Justice Rehnquist: A Preliminary View," 90 *Harvard Law Review* 293 (1976).

Selected Bibliography

Abraham, Henry J. "A 'Bench Happily Filled': Some Historical Reflections on the Supreme Court Appointment Process." 66 *Judicature* 282 (1983).

———. *Freedom and the Court.* 5th ed. New York: Oxford University Press, 1988.

———. *The Judicial Process: An Introductory Analysis of the Courts of the United States, England, and France.* 5th ed. New York: Oxford University Press, 1985.

———. *The Judiciary.* 7th ed. Boston: Allyn & Bacon, 1987.

———. *Justices and Presidents: A Political History of Appointments to the Supreme Court.* 2d ed. New York: Oxford University Press, 1985.

Aichele, Gary J. *Oliver Wendell Holmes, Jr.: Soldier, Scholar, Judge.* Boston: Twayne, 1989.

Altfeld, Michael F., and Harold J. Spaeth. "Measuring Influence on the United States Supreme Court." 24 *Jurimetrics Journal* 238 (1984).

Basset, John Spencer. *The Federalist System 1789–1801.* New York: Harper and Brothers, 1906.

Beaney, William M. "The Constitutional Right to Privacy in the Supreme Court." 1962 *Supreme Court Review* 212.

———. "The Griswold Case and the Expanded Right to Privacy." 1966 *Wisconsin Law Review* 979 (1966).

———. *The Right to Counsel in American Courts.* Ann Arbor: University of Michigan Press, 1955.

Becker, Theodore L., and Malcolm M. Feeley, eds. *The Impact of Supreme Court Decisions.* 2d ed. New York: Oxford University Press, 1973.

Berger, Raoul. *Government by Judiciary: The Transformation of the Fourteenth Amendment.* Cambridge, Mass.: Harvard University Press, 1977.

Beveridge, Albert J. *The Life of John Marshall.* 4 vols. Boston: Houghton Mifflin, 1916.

Bickel, Alexander M. *The Supreme Court and the Idea of Progress.* New York: Harper & Row, 1970.

Black, Hugo, Jr. *My Father: A Remembrance.* New York: Random House, 1975.

Blasi, Vincent. *The Burger Court: The Counter-Revolution That Wasn't.* New Haven, Conn.: Yale University Press, 1983.

Boles, Donald E. *Mr. Justice Rehnquist, Judicial Activist: The Early Years.* Ames, Iowa: Iowa State University Press, 1987.

Bollinger, Lee. *The Tolerant Society.* New York: Oxford University Press, 1986.

Bork, Robert H. *The Tempting of America.* New York: Free Press, 1990.

Bourguigon, J. G. "The Second Mr. Justice Harlan." 1979 *Supreme Court Review* 251.

Caplan, Lincoln. *The Tenth Justice: The Solicitor General and the Rule of Law.* New York: Knopf, 1987.

Cardozo, Benjamin. *The Nature of the Judicial Process.* New Haven, Conn.: Yale University Press, 1921.

Carter, Leif. *Reason in Law.* 3d ed. Boston: Little, Brown, 1988.

Choper, Jesse H. *Judicial Review and the National Political Process: A Functional Reconsideration.* Chicago: University of Chicago Press, 1980.

Clayton, James E. *The Making of Justice: The Supreme Court in Action.* New York: E. P. Dutton, 1964.

Cook, Beverly B. "Women as Supreme Court Candidates: From Florence Allen to Sandra Day O'Connor." 65 *Judicature* 314 (1981–82).

Cordray, Richard A., and James T. Vradelis. "The Emerging Jurisprudence of Justice O'Connor." 52 *University of Chicago Law Review* 389 (1985).

Corwin, Edward S. *John Marshall and the Constitution.* New Haven, Conn.: Yale University Press, 1919.

Countryman, Vern, ed. *The Douglas Opinions.* New York: Random House, 1977.

Cummings, Homer, and Carl McFarland. *Federal Justice: Chapters in the History of Justice and the Federal Executive.* New York: Macmillan, 1937.

Cuomo, Mario. "The Constitution, the Courts, and Judicial Competence." 116 *USA Today* 34 (July 1987).

Currie, David P. *The Constitution in the Supreme Court: The First Hundred Years, 1789–1888.* Chicago: University of Chicago Press, 1985.

Danelski, David J., and Joseph F. Tulchin, eds. *The Autobiographical Notes of Charles Evans Hughes.* Cambridge, Mass.: Harvard University Press, 1973.

Davis, Sue. *Justice Rehnquist and the Constitution.* Princeton, N.J.: Princeton University Press, 1989.

Douglas, William O. *An Almanac of Liberty.* Garden City, N.Y.: Doubleday, 1954.

———. *The Anatomy of Liberty.* New York: Trident Press, 1963.

———. *The Court Years: 1939–1975.* New York: Random House, 1980.

———. *Go East, Young Man.* New York: Random House, 1974.

———. *Of Men and Mountains.* New York: Harper & Row, 1950.

———. *The Right of the People.* Garden City, N.Y.: Doubleday, 1958.

———. "Stare Decisis." 4 *Record of the Association of the Bar of the City of New York* 152 (1949).

———. "Vagrancy and Arrest on Suspicion." 70 *Yale Law Journal* 1 (1960).

———. *We, the Judges*. Garden City, N.Y.: Doubleday, 1956.

Duncan, Richard F. "Justice O'Connor, the Constitution, and the Trimester Approach to Abortion: A Liberty on a Collision Course with Itself." 29 *Catholic Lawyer* 275 (1984).

Dunne, Gerald T. *Hugo Black and the Judicial Revolution*. New York: Simon and Schuster, 1977.

———. *Justice Joseph Story and the Rise of the Supreme Court*. New York: Simon and Schuster, 1970.

Duram, James C. *Justice William O. Douglas*. Boston: Twayne, 1981.

Easby-Smith, James S. *The Department of Justice: Its History and Functions*. Washington, D.C.: W. H. Lowdermilk, 1904.

———. "Edmund Randolph, Trailblazer," 12 *Journal of the Bar of the District of Columbia* 415 (1945).

Fahy, Charles. "The Office of Solicitor General." 28 *American Bar Association Journal* 20 (1942).

Fairman, Charles. *Mr. Justice Miller and the Supreme Court, 1862–1890*. Cambridge, Mass.: Harvard University Press, 1939.

Fausto-Sterling, Anne. *Myths of Gender*. New York: Basic Books, 1986.

Fine, Sidney. *Frank Murphy*. 3 vols. Ann Arbor: University of Michigan Press, 1975 and 1984, for vols. 1 and 3; Chicago: University of Chicago Press, 1979, for vol. 2.

Frankfurter, Felix. "Some Observations on the Nature of the Judicial Process of Supreme Court Litigation." 98 *Proceedings of the American Philosophical Society* 233 (1954).

Funston, Richard Y. *Constitutional Counter-Revolution? The Warren Court and the Burger Court*. Cambridge, Mass.: Schenkman, 1977.

Garraty, John, ed. *Quarrels That Have Shaped the Constitution*. Rev. ed. New York: Harper & Row, 1987.

Goldman, Sheldon. "Judicial Selection and the Qualities That Make a 'Good' Judge." 462 *Annals* 112 (1982).

———. "Reaganizing the Judiciary: The First Term Appointments." 68 *Judicature* 313 (1985).

Halpern, Stephen C., and Charles M. Lamb, eds. *Supreme Court Activism and Restraint*. Lexington, Mass.: Lexington Books, 1982.

Harbaugh, William H. *Lawyer's Lawyer: 'The Life of John W. Davis*. New York: Oxford University Press, 1973.

Harlan, John Marshall. "Thoughts at a Dedication: Keeping the Judicial Function in Balance." 49 *American Bar Association Journal* 943 (1963).

Harris, Joseph P. *The Advice and Consent of the Senate*. Berkeley and Los Angeles: University of California Press, 1953.

Harris, William F., II. "Bonding Word and Polity: The Logic of American Constitutionalism." 76 *American Political Science Review* 34 (1982).

Hendel, Samuel. *Charles Evans Hughes and the Supreme Court*. New York: King's Crown Press, 1951.

Highsaw, Robert B. *Edward Douglass White: Defender of the Constitution*. Baton Rouge: Louisiana State University Press, 1981.

Hirsch, H. N. *The Enigma of Felix Frankfurter*. New York: Basic Books, 1981.

Holdsworth, W. S. *A History of English Law*. 7th ed. London: Methuen, 1956.

Holmes, Oliver Wendell. *Collected Legal Papers*. New York: Peter Smith, 1952.

Howard, A.E.D. "Justice Rehnquist—A Key Fighter in Major Battles." *ABA Journal* 49 (June 1986).

Howard, J. Woodford. *Mr. Justice Murphy: A Political Biography*. Princeton, N.J.: Princeton University Press, 1968.

———. "On the Fluidity of Judicial Choice." 62 *American Political Science Review* 43 (1968).

Hughes, Charles Evans. *The Supreme Court of the United States*. New York: Columbia University Press, 1928.

Jackson, Robert H. *The Struggle for Judicial Supremacy*. New York: Knopf, 1941.

———. *The Supreme Court and the American System of Government*. Cambridge, Mass.: Harvard University Press, 1955.

Karst, Kenneth L. "The Return of the Natural-Law–Due-Process Formula." 16 *U.C.L.A. Law Review* 716 (1969).

Kelly, Alfred H., Winfred A. Harbison, and Herman Belz. *The American Constitution: Its Origins and Development*. 6th ed. New York: Norton, 1983.

King, Willard L. *Melville Weston Fuller*. New York: Macmillan, 1950.

Lash, Joseph P., ed. *Diaries of Felix Frankfurter*. New York: Norton, 1975.

Learned, H. B. *The President's Cabinet: Studies in the Origin, Formation, and Structure of an American Institution*. New Haven, Conn.: Yale University Press, 1912.

Lerner, Max. *The Mind and Faith of Mr. Justice Holmes*. Garden City, N.Y.: Halcyon House Reprint, 1948.

Lewis, Anthony. "A Talk with Chief Justice Warren on Crime, the Court, and the Country." *New York Times Magazine*, October 19, 1969, p. 128.

Lodge, Henry Cabot. *Selections from the Correspondence of Theodore Roosevelt and Henry Cabot Lodge, 1884–1918*. New York: Charles Scribner's Sons, 1925.

———, ed. *The Federalist*. New York: G. P. Putnam's Sons, 1888.

Madison, James. *Notes of the Debates in the Federal Convention of 1787*. Athens, Ohio: Ohio University Press, 1966.

Magrath, C. Peter. *Morrison R. Waite*. New York: Macmillan, 1963.

Mason, Alpheus T. *Brandeis: A Free Man's Life*. New York: Viking, 1946.

———. "The Burger Court in Historical Perspective." 89 *Political Science Quarterly* 27 (1974).

———. *Harlan Fiske Stone: Pillar of the Law*. New York: Viking, 1956.

———. *The States Rights Debate: Antifederalism and the Constitution*. 2d ed. New York: Oxford University Press, 1972.

———. *The Supreme Court from Taft to Burger*. Baton Rouge: Louisiana State University Press, 1979.

———. *William Howard Taft: Chief Justice*. New York: Simon and Schuster, 1964.

———, and D. Grier Stephenson, Jr. *American Constitutional Law*. 9th ed. Englewood Cliffs, N.J.: Prentice-Hall, 1990.

McCloskey, Robert G. *The American Supreme Court*. Chicago: University of Chicago Press, 1960.

McElwain, Edwin. "The Business of the Supreme Court as Conducted by Chief Justice Hughes." 63 *Harvard Law Review* 5 (1949).

McFeeley, Neil D. *Appointment of Judges: The Johnson Presidency*. Austin: University of Texas Press, 1987.

Miller, M. "Justice Sandra Day O'Connor: Token or Triumph from a Feminist Perspective?" 15 *Golden Gate University Law Review* 493 (1985).

Miller, Merle. *Plain Speaking: An Oral Biography of Harry S. Truman*. New York: G. P. Putnam's Sons, 1974.

Murphy, Bruce. *Fortas*. New York: William Morrow, 1988.

Murphy, Walter F. *Elements of Judicial Strategy*. Chicago: University of Chicago Press, 1964.

———. "The Right to Privacy and Legitimate Constitutional Change," in Shlomo Slonim, ed., *The Constitutional Bases of Social and Political Change in the United States*. New York: Praeger, 1990.

———, and C. Herman Pritchett. *Courts, Judges, and Politics*. 4th ed. New York: Random House, 1986.

———, and Joseph Tanenhaus. "Publicity, Public Opinion, and the Court." 84 *Northwestern University Law Review* 985 (1990).

———, and Joseph Tanenhaus. *The Study of Public Law*. New York: Random House, 1972.

———, James E. Fleming, and William F. Harris, II. *American Constitutional Interpretation*. Mineola, N.Y.: Foundation Press, 1986.

Novick, Sheldon M. *Honorable Justice: The Life of Oliver Wendell Holmes*. Boston: Little, Brown, 1989.

O'Brien, David M. *Storm Center*. 2d ed. New York: Norton, 1990.

The Oliver Wendell Holmes Devise History of the Supreme Court of the United States. New York: Macmillan, 1971–. Volumes to date include Julius Goebel, *Antecedents and Beginnings to 1801*, Vol. I (1971); George Lee Haskins and Herbert A. Johnson, *Foundations of Power: John Marshall, 1801–15*, Vol. II (1981); G. Edward White, *The Marshall Court and Cultural Change, 1815–35*, Vols. III and IV (1988); Carl B. Swisher, *The Taney Period, 1836–64*, Vol. V (1974); Charles Fairman, *Reconstruction and Reunion 1864–88*, Vols. VI and VII (1971, 1987); Charles Fairman, *Five Justices and the Electoral Commission of 1877*, supplement to Vol. VII (1988); Alexander M. Bickel and Benno C. Schmidt, Jr., *The Judiciary and Responsible Government, 1910–21*, Vol. IX (1984).

Paschal, J. Francis. *Mr. Justice Sutherland*. Princeton, N.J.: Princeton University Press, 1951.

Phillips, Harlan B., ed. *Felix Frankfurter Reminisces*. New York: Reynal, 1960.

Poe, L. A. "Evolution to Absolutism: Justice Douglas and the First Amendment." 74 *Columbia Law Review* 371 (1974).

Pritchett, C. Herman. *The Roosevelt Court: A Study in Judicial Politics and Values, 1937–1947*. New York: Macmillan, 1948.

Pusey, Merlo. *Charles Evans Hughes*. 2 vols. New York: Macmillan, 1951.

Rehnquist, William H. "Chief Justices I Never Knew." 3 *Hastings Constitutional Law Quarterly* 637 (1976).

———. *The Supreme Court: How It Was, How It Is*. New York: William Morrow, 1987.

Richardson, James D., ed. *A Compilation of the Messages and Papers of the Presidents, 1789–1902*. 20 vols. Washington, D.C.: Bureau of National Literature and Art, 1908.

Rohde, David W., and Harold J. Spaeth. *Supreme Court Decision Making*. San Francisco: W. H. Freeman, 1976.

Sayler, Richard H., Barry B. Boyer, and Robert E. Goodling, Jr., eds. *The Warren Court: A Critical Analysis*. New York: Chelsea House, 1969.

Scheb, John M., II, and L. W. Alshie. "Justice Sandra Day O'Connor and the 'Freshman Effect.' " 69 *Judicature* 9 (1985).

Schmidhauser, John R. *Judges and Justices: The Federal Appellate Judiciary*. Boston: Little, Brown, 1979.

———. *The Supreme Court: Its Politics, Personalities, and Procedures*. New York: Holt, Rinehart and Winston, 1964.

Schwartz, Bernard. *The Ascent of Pragmatism: The Burger Court in Action*. Reading, Mass.: Addison-Wesley, 1990.

———. *Super Chief: Earl Warren and His Supreme Court*. New York: New York University Press, 1983.

———, ed. *The Unpublished Opinions of the Warren Court*. New York: Oxford University Press, 1985.

Seddig, Robert G. "John Marshall and the Origins of Supreme Court Leadership." 36 *University of Pittsburgh Law Review* 785 (1975).

Segel, Jeffrey A. "Supreme Court Support for the Solicitor General: The Effect of Presidential Appointments." 43 *Western Political Quarterly* 137 (1990).

Shapiro, David L. "Mr. Justice Rehnquist: A Preliminary View." 96 *Harvard Law Review* 293 (1976).

———, ed. *The Evolution of a Judicial Philosophy: Selected Opinions and Papers of Justice John Marshall Harlan*. Cambridge, Mass.: Harvard University Press, 1969.

Shapiro, Martin. *Law and Politics in the Supreme Court*. New York: Free Press, 1964.

Sherry, Suzanne. "Civic Virtue and the Feminine Voice in Constitutional Adjudication." 72 *Virginia Law Review* 543 (1982).

Sickels, Robert Judd. *John Paul Stevens: The Search for Balance*. University Park, Pa.: Pennsylvania State University Press, 1988.

Simon, James F. *The Antagonists: Hugo Black, Felix Frankfurter, and Civil Liberties in Modern America*. New York: Simon and Schuster, 1989.

———. *Independent Journey: The Life of William O. Douglas*. New York: Harper & Row, 1980.

———. *In His Own Image: The Supreme Court in Richard Nixon's America*. New York: David McKay, 1973.

Spaeth, Harold J. *An Introduction to Supreme Court Decision Making*. San Francisco: Chandler, 1972.

———. *Supreme Court Policy Making*. San Francisco: W. H. Freeman, 1979.

Steamer, Robert J. *Chief Justice: Leadership and the Supreme Court*. Columbia: University of South Carolina Press, 1986.

Stern, Robert L. "The Solicitor General and Administrative Agency Litigation." 46 *American Bar Association Journal* 154 (1960).

———, Eugene Gressman, and Stephen M. Shapiro. *Supreme Court Practice*. 6th ed. Washington, D.C.: Bureau of National Affairs, 1986.

Stevens, John Paul. "Reflections on the Removal of Sitting Judges." 13 *Stetson Law Review* 215 (1984).

Strum, Philippa. *Louis D. Brandeis: Justice for the People*. Cambridge, Mass.: Harvard University Press, 1984.

Swanson, Wayne R. *The Christ Child Goes to Court*. Philadelphia: Temple University Press, 1990.

Swisher, Carl B. *Roger B. Taney*. Washington, D.C.: Brookings, 1935.

———. *Stephen C. Field: Craftsman of the Law*. Washington, D.C.: Brookings, 1930.

Taft, William H. "Criticism of the Federal Judiciary." 29 *American Law Review* 641 (1895).

Uelmen, Gerald F. "The Influence of the Solicitor General upon Supreme Court Disposition of Federal Circuit Court Decisions. . . ." 69 *Judicature* 360 (1986).

Ulmer, S. Sidney. "Parabolic Support of Civil Liberty Claims: The Case of William O. Douglas." 41 *Journal of Politics* 634 (1979).

Warren, Charles. *The Making of the Constitution*. Boston: Little, Brown, 1937.

———. *The Supreme Court in United States History*. Rev. ed., 2 vols. Boston: Little, Brown, 1926.

Warren, Samuel D., and Louis D. Brandeis. "The Right to Privacy." 4 *Harvard Law Review* 193 (1890).

Wasby, Stephen L., ed. *"He Shall Not Pass This Way Again": The Legacy of Justice William O. Douglas*. Pittsburgh, Pa.: University of Pittsburgh Press, 1990.

White, G. Edward. "The Anti-Judge: William O. Douglas and the Ambiguities of Individuality." 74 *Virginia Law Review* 17 (1988).

———. *Earl Warren: A Public Life*. New York: Oxford University Press, 1982.

Witt, Elder. *A Different Justice*. Washington, D.C.: Congressional Quarterly, 1986.

Wolfe, Christopher. *The Rise of Modern Judicial Review*. New York: Basic Books, 1986.

Wolfman, Bernard, Jonathan F. L. Silver, and Marjorie A. Silver. *Dissent without Opinion*. Philadelphia: University of Pennsylvania Press, 1975.

Index

ABOUT THE CONTRIBUTORS

HENRY J. ABRAHAM is James Hart Professor in the Woodrow Wilson Department of Government and Foreign Affairs at the University of Virginia.

WILLIAM M. BEANEY is Delaney Professor of Law at the University of Denver and Acting Dean of the Law School.

JESSE H. CHOPER is Dean of the School of Law (Boalt Hall) at the University of California at Berkeley.

REX E. LEE was Solicitor General of the United States from 1981 until 1985. From 1985 until 1989 he was Professor of Law at Brigham Young University and was associated with the law firm of Sidley & Austin in Washington, D.C. He is now President of Brigham Young University.

WALTER F. MURPHY is McCormick Professor of Jurisprudence in the Department of Politics at Princeton University.

MARTIN SHAPIRO is Coffroth Professor of Law at the University of California at Berkeley.

JAMES F. SIMON is Dean and Professor of Law at New York Law School and a biographer of Justice William O. Douglas.

HAROLD J. SPAETH is Professor of Political Science at Michigan State University and is a member of the Michigan Bar.

D. GRIER STEPHENSON, JR., is Charles A. Dana Professor of Government at Franklin and Marshall College and was coordinator of the John Marshall Lectures on the Constitution, the Supreme Court, and the Justices, from which this book is derived.